WHISPERING

"*Soul Whispering* is a book dearly needed in our times. Star Wolf and Gage combine their stunning wisdom as both professional therapists and deep-diving shamans to recover what has been fractured and lost and bridge us back to wholeness. Their decades of experience in the addiction and mental health fields and their extensive shamanic training seasoned with their heartfelt sense of humor make them heroines in my eyes. May you read this book and discover how you, too, are a Soul Whisperer."

HEATHERASH AMARA, AUTHOR OF *THE WARRIOR GODDESS WAY*

"*Soul Whispering* is a powerful shamanic map of soul remembering, weaving together ancient wisdom with modern psychology. Told with intimacy and compassion, this beautiful elucidation of the shamanic healing arts is a soul song from two visionary women who have walked the path with wide-open hearts. Their stories are brimming with bone-deep life lessons, embodied solutions, and soul flights of cosmic consciousness, which bridge seamlessly between the worlds."

DR. AZRA AND SEREN BERTRAND, AUTHORS OF *WOMB AWAKENING:
INITIATORY WISDOM FROM THE CREATRIX OF ALL LIFE*

"This is an extraordinary book by two extraordinary women. Star Wolf and Gage, highly respected shamanic healers of the first rank, have brought their considerable experience and wisdom to bear in this illuminating 'guide for the perplexed' that will both reward and mesmerize the reader. For those who have given up on conventional, by-the-numbers therapies that got them nowhere, this brilliant introduction to Soul Whispering is a remarkable and much-needed alternative. You won't be disappointed."

M. GUY THOMPSON, PH.D., AUTHOR OF *THE DEATH OF DESIRE:
AN EXISTENTIAL STUDY IN SANITY AND MADNESS*

"*Soul Whispering* makes the intangible realms shamans work with—such as shamanic consciousness, personality, and the soul—concepts that can be easily grasped. This book goes beyond our fixed ideas of shamanism by teaching us from the depths of the deeper soul, adding life-changing personal stories, all honestly conveyed. This work triggers points of wisdom in us at every turn."

E. ARACELY BROWN, SENIOR PROGRAM DIRECTOR
AT THE NEW YORK OPEN CENTER

"Let *Soul Whispering* be your midwife in the journey of awakening your shamanic consciousness. The great challenge and opportunity we face is to be both fully human and divine at the same time. Star Wolf and Gage weave diverse paths of healing and transformation into wholeness so that we may embrace our full potential as soulful human beings."

ANNA CARIAD-BARRETT, DMIN, AUTHOR OF *SHAMANIC WISDOM*
FOR PREGNANCY AND PARENTHOOD, COAUTHOR OF
SACRED MEDICINE OF BEE, BUTTERFLY, EARTHWORM, AND SPIDER,
PSYCHOSPIRITUAL COUNSELOR, AND SHAMANIC MINISTER

"Shamans view 'soul loss,' the wounding of a person's unique energetic essence from trauma, as a leading cause of physical, emotional, and psychological dysfunction. In this fascinating, easy-to-read, and instructive book the authors guide us in the ways shamans and modern psychotherapy heal. A book for anyone who is on the path of personal transformation."

ITZHAK BEERY, AUTHOR OF *THE GIFT OF SHAMANISM,*
SHAMANIC TRANSFORMATIONS, AND *SHAMANIC HEALING,*
AND PUBLISHER OF SHAMANPORTAL.ORG

"Offered up by two authentic shamans, this book is about shifting our story from being the effect of our life (a victim) to being the cause (a conscious being). Read this book to discover real means to strengthen your shamanic powers in this world that is hungry for such soulfulness."

JULIE TALLARD JOHNSON, MSW, AUTHOR OF
THE ZERO POINT AGREEMENT AND *WHEEL OF INITIATION*

Soul
WHISPERING

The **Art** of **Awakening**
Shamanic Consciousness

Linda Star Wolf, Ph.D.,
and **Nita Gage,** DSPS, MA

Bear & Company
Rochester, Vermont • Toronto, Canada

Bear & Company
One Park Street
Rochester, Vermont 05767
www.BearandCompanyBooks.com

Bear & Company is a division of Inner Traditions International

*Note to the reader: This book is intended as an informational guide. The remedies,
approaches, and techniques described herein are meant to supplement, and not to be a
substitute for, professional medical care or treatment. They should not be used to treat
a serious ailment without prior consultation with a qualified health care professional.*

Library of Congress Cataloging-in-Publication Data

Names: Wolf, Linda Star, author.
Title: Soul whispering : the art of awakening Shamanic consciousness /
    Linda Star Wolf, Ph.D., and Nita Gage, DSPS, MA.
Description: Rochester, Vermont : Bear & Company, 2017. |
    Includes bibliographical references and index.
Identifiers: LCCN 2016046318 (print) | LCCN 2017006259 (e-book) |
    ISBN 9781591432258 (pbk.) | ISBN 9781591432265 (e-book)
Subjects: LCSH: Soul—Miscellanea. | Shamanism.
Classification: LCC BF1621 .W653 2017 (print) | LCC BF1621 (e-book) |
    DDC 299/.93—dc23
LC record available at https://lccn.loc.gov/2016046318

Printed and bound in the United States by McNaughton & Gunn, Inc.

10 9 8 7 6 5 4 3 2 1

Text design and layout by Virginia Scott Bowman
This book was typeset in Garamond Premier Pro, Legacy Sans, and Gill Sans with
Minion, Avenir, and Furtura used as display typefaces

To send correspondence to the authors of this book, mail a first-class letter to the
authors c/o Inner Traditions • Bear & Company, One Park Street, Rochester, VT
05767, and we will forward the communication, or contact Star Wolf directly at
http://shamanicbreathwork.org or Nita Gage at **www.hoffmaninstitute.org
/nita-gage**.

For Brad

October 12, 1955–August 2, 2014

who inspired and believed in us.

Contents

∽

Foreword

I am both honored and, I confess, a little intimidated by the task of writing a foreword to this extraordinary book. Both Linda Star Wolf and Nita Gage have such an evident store of worldly wisdom between them, and all I can say is that you, the reader, are in for a rare treat.

Shamanism is humanity's most ancient form of spirituality, stretching back further in time than any other form of intergenerational human communication. Perhaps one of the reasons for its longevity is its deep connection to the Earth and nature. It has always taken real *grit* to become a shaman. You have to get dirty. You have to be in touch with the soil, the seasons, with animals, with creepy-crawlies, with other people's shit, and, above all, with human wounds.

In our modern technological age there has been a great interest and thirst to know more about shamanism and its mysterious and magical roots. This has proved both a blessing and a curse. The curse is that there is now a flood of people in the world claiming to be and calling themselves "shaman." Many of these people have only a surface understanding of what it takes to don such a mantle. It is not something you choose for yourself. It is something that is thrust upon you through having passed through life's great grinder. The shaman must know the depth of suffering down to her very bones. He must have wept and laughed into every single cell and corner of his body. The shaman is one who must have died and been reborn, not once, but over and over again.

The blessing of our modern age is that we now have access to natural wisdom and those who carry it in a way that has never been possible before. And with this blessing comes the test of discerning the authentic shaman from what I call the "voyeur shaman"—one who likes the idea of being a shaman but without really having to know the true nature of suffering and its hidden meaning.

This book is clearly the work of two powerful and authentic shamanic voices. As they unravel their life stories and the wisdom they have earned, we get to see two great role models of what it takes to live a truly authentic life. And out of the trials, the loves, the disappointments, and the ecstasies, we feel the steady emergence of a deep and practical feminine wisdom tradition. But this is a wisdom for male and female alike. It is delivered in a spirit of humility, honesty, and integrity. In this book, strength is derived from vulnerability, and that is a lesson for every one of us—to surrender and see the impulse of love hidden in all circumstances and all things.

The lessons in this book are deadly serious but also deliciously playful. We are invited to ride the paradoxes of life and transcend the habits of a fearful, doubting mind. We are challenged but supported to take leaps in our lives and break out of our victim tendencies. The most refreshing thing I find about this book is its refusal to break out into the "how-to" marketplace of so many New Age books and teachings. Here we learn through example, through listening, and through the authentic stories of other people's breakthroughs. This is an ancient means of conveying wisdom—to sit around the fire and tell tales together.

This is how I recommend that you approach this book—as though you were sitting around the fire and listening to the voice of the great Grandmother. She has so much of value to impart. Her depth, her humor, her mortality, and the obvious love she feels for all beings provide a rare opportunity to learn something precious that will help us for the rest of our days.

RICHARD RUDD

RICHARD RUDD is an international teacher, writer, and award-winning poet. He is the author of *Gene Keys: Unlocking the Higher Purpose Hidden in Your DNA* and founder of the Gene Keys Synthesis, an integral matrix of all human evolutionary potential. Representing a convergence of many lineages and dimensions, Richard's teachings span the chasm between the heights of mysticism and practical everyday life.

Acknowledgments

We wish to offer our deep respect and gratitude for all the support we received from the many staff members at Inner Traditions • Bear & Company, from the beginning rough drafts to the final edits. Thank you for your commitment of more than four decades publishing books that consistently "Soul Whisper" to the public.

Special thanks to Jon Graham for his immediate faith in and support of our manuscript; also to Jeanie Levitan, Ehud Sperling, and John Hays; to Anne Dillon, a true shamanic wordsmith and editor; to Jamaica Burns Griffin for her fine-tuning and moral support; and to Manzanita Carpenter for her skillful expertise with publicity and marketing.

We thank all the contributors to this project, particularly those Soul Whisperers who shared their stories to enrich the book. We acknowledge and honor their courage in following their inner shaman and allowing us to be Soul Whisperers on their shamanic initiatory healing journeys. Through their academic study, shamanic experiences, and personal healing work, they have shape-shifted into Soul Whisperers capable of facilitating others who've also heard the call to embody their shamanic souls.

In addition, Star Wolf would like to thank:

My beloved late husband and soul mate, Brad Collins, for being my best shamanic cheerleader and co-creator during your time upon this Earth and for now being my beautiful spirit guide and ancestor spirit on the other side of the veils.

Mom and Dad, for sixty-four years of love and support for your rebellious, mystical, shamanic daughter.

Big Wolf howls of love and appreciation to my shamanic teammates at Venus Rising, especially Ruby Falconer, Kathy Morrison, Sarah Jane Fridy, and all the VR shamanic students and graduates over twenty-one years.

Casey Piscitelli for his initial editing on early drafts.

Nikólaus Wolf, for answering the call and for your endless support on all levels, through the tears and the laughter with the dissolution of my old self and the hope of a new vision for my soul's purpose.

Michael DeMaria, for allowing us to use your beautiful songs to enhance the audio of the "Creature Teacher Medicine Journey."

Nita, beloved shamanic sister and soul friend . . . a simple heartfelt thank-you for showing up in my hour of greatest need and for committing to coauthor the book we were always meant to write and in so doing honoring Brad's final request.

Devon Prevost, for your loving support on many levels, and especially animal whispering with my precious four-legged companions during my times away teaching and writing.

Last but not least, thank you to Richard Rudd, author of *Gene Keys*. Your work is groundbreaking and we are humbled by your stunning affirmation and foreword for our book!

Nita Gage would like to thank:

Mary Lou Masko, for always supporting and believing in me.

Gabriella Kapfer, a.k.a. Songbird, an amazing sound healer and dear friend, who co-created the audio tracks with me.

All my clients and students, who remind me why this work is important.

Star Wolf, for your friendship, mentorship, and unending enthusiasm for changing the world one breath at a time.

What the World Needs Now Is Love Sweet Love

You are the soul and the medicine for what wounds the soul.

RUMI

This book focuses on personal transformation as the higher octave of healing. Healing is the work of becoming conscious of our wounds, releasing the energy of victimization, developing self-love and compassion, and forgiving ourselves and others. Healing leads to a state of peace and improves our life. This is a step along the way, yet it is not the goal of living consciously. Living consciously means shifting our story from being wounded victims to being spiritual beings who are undergoing personal initiation on a path of authenticity. We have the capacity to live in a state of love and expanded consciousness. We have become intoxicated and addicted to security and survival, and in the process, the true meaning of life has slipped from our grasp.

For many, the experience of being human is unfulfilling, imbued as it may be with a sense of meaninglessness and soul loss. This pervasive unease is due to identification with a false persona and an energetic disconnection of the mind/body from the soul and from collective wisdom. The sense of disconnection reaches further to keep us in the illusion of separateness from each other, all living things, the planet, and the universe. At this point, we all have two choices. We can focus on the problem or become part of the solution. The world reflects our inner state of being. As we collectively move into the new eon, we need to open to a much larger vision of our future.

Love is the energy of connection, and without love's gravitational pull to anchor and connect us deeply, we feel a sense of isolation, untethered to our lives—unloved and unlovable. As Glinda told Dorothy in *The Wizard of Oz,* "It's been in you all along." While that is true, Dorothy obviously needed a reflection of that deeper truth from Glinda, or a soul recognition from someone or something to whisper that in her ear. The "it" that has been in her "all along" is her true purpose as a human being, that of embodying her birthright and capacity for love and expanded consciousness to bring her home to her authentic self.

Reconnection and integration of mind/body/spirit and remembering who we really are has been the rallying cry of mystics and healers down through the centuries. Today more than any time in history, fully dissolving the artificial separations between self and soul, self and others, and even self and universe is happening. Western healers, physicians, and psychologists find that the old ways of compartmentalizing and fixing are no longer as effective as we once thought they were.

Shamanism and its practice of utilizing shamanic energy medicine has always addressed the whole person and the entire community by embracing a starting point of "As within, so without; as above, so below." In addition to its recent popular worldwide appeal, shamanism is evolving—from being overly mysterious and available to only a chosen few to a practice that is accessible to all of us.

Following in the shamanic tradition, Soul Whispering is a technique that shamans and others may practice to heighten one's spiritual awareness and connect more profoundly with one's own soul. The practice of Soul Whispering allows you to fully reunite with your soul by learning how to listen to its whispers of guidance. Learning to listen to this inner voice of the heart, which should be distinguished from the voice of the ego or inner critic, allows you to move from lower octaves of consciousness to an evolved level of consciousness. As consciousness evolves, liberation from personal patterns and the restrictive tenets of cultural ideology also transpires.

Although one might seek out a therapist, doctor, minister, counselor, or even a shaman to perform the shamanic practice of Soul Whispering on your behalf, you may also receive guidance from your soul without the assistance of a third-party Soul Whisperer. This guidance can take myriad forms—sacred spiritual insights derived from witnessing a spectacular sunset, hearing the melodic song of a hummingbird, or sensing an unseen spirit guiding your actions from someplace in nature or even from some other dimension. If you're open to messages from spirit in whatever form spirit chooses to appear, you will be in receipt of a gift from a Soul Whisperer.

To help you enhance your own abilities as a Soul Whisperer, this book includes an audio component (see "How to Use the Soul Whispering Audio Tracks" on page 274). Each of the four tracks is a guided meditation to help you pull back the veils of your personality so that you may discover and access the guidance that your soul is wanting to offer up to you.

The world is now entering the era where modern-day shamans and Soul Whisperers are discovering our own shamanic wisdom and the consciousness that is hidden within our DNA. Modern-day shamans and Soul Whisperers come in many forms. Increasing numbers of people are on a path of spiritual seeking, traveling to sacred sites to ingest entheogens in the form of plant medicines under the guidance of a trained shaman, thereby accessing and entering into altered states and trance experiences. Other shamanic energy medicine methods include fasting from food and sleep and going on a personal vision quest, or participating in purification and healing processes such as sweat lodges, working with a variety of stone medicine wheels, chakra balancing, crystal therapies, and studying the Mystery schools that are now coming out of the shadows. We're learning how to apply these practices, which have been hidden, back into our daily lives. All of them embrace a perspective of self-responsibility in healing.

Soul Whispering creates a safe container for powerful intervention with our unconscious, inhibiting beliefs and opens us to our authentic essence as loving spiritual beings. It is a practice that embraces being human as the lived path of spirituality. Our ways of being in the world are primarily unconsciously motivated. This is both the catalyst for and the obstacle to spiritual growth. Reconciliation of this paradox is precisely the medicine that is needed for our times. We are vibrant, resilient beings hardwired for joy and spirit-guided lives full of meaning and purpose. The Soul Whisperer holds space and lovingly supports us to awaken our shaman within and remember our true essence.

This book mirrors life—it is not always linear. Stories, musings, ideas, and concepts unfold as if on a spiral. Concepts and stories are revisited in different contexts and different chapters to inform the reader in a variety of ways. Personal accounts written by Soul Whisperers grace the end of almost every chapter. A glossary in the back of the book further articulates some of the key terms for an improved understanding of the material contained herein.

It is not necessary to read this book in sequence from the beginning to the end. In fact, we encourage you to intuitively use the table of contents, or simply pause and take a deep breath into your heart with the desire to discover what is up for you on your path at this time. Then, spontaneously open the book and see what raises your curiosity and read that chapter or section. Following your curiosity you will find the next bread crumbs on your path through the wilderness—both in this book and in your life. And in so doing, you will find your way out of the woods of the unconsciousness into the fields that await you—replete with manifold potential and possibility.

1

Seeking Wholeness

From Baby Boomers to Shamans

The generation that came of age in the late 1960s and early '70s electrified their culture with an explosion of alternative lifestyles and beliefs. Much of the infusion of ideas from the young people of the time was actually ancient indigenous teachings given a psychedelic coating. In an attempt to heal themselves and the planet of its ills, baby boomers embraced spiritual and healing practices from all over the world, though often without the discipline and ceremony that the practices required. Many ended up burned out and disillusioned. Many, though, continued to follow a practice with increasing knowledge and discipline and have matured from experimenters and thrill seekers to wise elders in the shamanic traditions.

EXPLORING THE SHAMANIC WORLD

Have you ever wondered why there is a rising interest in shamanism, and why the word *shaman* itself has become so popular in the past several years? It seems that this is a hot topic with many forward-thinking people today. Some folks just want to know what shamans and shamanism are all about. Others are interested in talking with a shaman or taking a trip to Peru or some other place to seek a blessing, teaching, or healing from one who practices this ancient healing art.

But who and what are shamans exactly? Shamans may be called by many names in many different cultures, but essentially they're the indigenous healers of any given tribe, village, or culture. They are universally known to be the ones who carry the mystical ability to connect the world of the imaginal and symbolic with that of lived experience. Shamanic energy medicine, which is the medicine that shamans employ, is comprised of an integration of shamanism, shamanic psychospiritual practices, and imaginal psychology.

Indeed, the primary tool of the shaman is the power of the imagination. In the early 1800s, German philosopher Johann Gottfried Von Herder wrote a book called *Outlines of a Philosophy of the History of Man*. In it he discussed his views that imagination is the most powerful human force and that it comes directly from the soul. He admonished people to pay more attention to the imagination given that, to his way of thinking, it is the connection between the body and the mind. He also posited that illness is related to imagination and to the brain.[1]

More than two hundred years after Gottfried's assertion, neuroscience has offered empirical evidence about the power of imagination to impact brain chemistry.* Shamans use this power of the imagination, as well as art, song, and poetry, to enter the ethereal energetic fields and tap in to the collective consciousness to communicate with the soul of an individual, group, or community. In so doing, shamans can bring to consciousness information that is generally stored in the unconscious mind and not otherwise readily accessible. Using the power of imagination, shamans work with the energetic body to facilitate healing in the emotional and physical bodies.

By undertaking shamanic work, one may come to the understanding that the life of the soul is eternal. For indeed, shamanism respects the natural cycles of life, and in this, it embraces both birth and death equally. Shamans know that death is not the end, but rather a rebirth. All major religions teach that the soul/spirit is immortal, and in fact, many people refer to Jesus Christ as a shaman. This is because his teachings were clearly about the mystical powers of being born again or

---

*It's also significant to note the prevalence of guided imagery and energy work being utilized in surgical procedures and in post-op recovery rooms of hospitals all over the world today. This underscores how this understanding of the power of imagination to aid in healing is increasingly gaining traction.

rebirthed from his own death. His spiritual path embraced life whole-heartedly, and when the time came, he embraced death fully, as do many actualized saints and teachers.*

In embracing the duality of life and death, shamanism provides a means for us to embody both life *and* death in everyday life. Embracing the reality of death strengthens and deepens our connection to being present in the moment, and practicing death and rebirth is a symbolic experience of letting go. For death is the ultimate letting go—a surrender of one's body and one's present lifetime. Thus does the practice of shamanism develop one's capacity to let go, particularly of that which one clings to the most.

Shamanic practices are inherently integrative and holistic. And the truth of the matter is that we are all shamanic. Thus everyone can learn to connect to the energetic, holistic/integrative healing capacity that is all around us and within us as well.

CHARACTERISTICS OF A SHAMAN

The following may be considered to be characteristics of a shaman.

- Shamans may be considered to be "wounded healers" who have traversed difficult and painful experiences in life and have been strengthened by the experience.
- They are considered medicine men or women and are often kept apart from the rest of the tribe or community.
- They know that there is an unseen world (dreaming body), which is just as real as the one we inhabit in daily life, and that it influences our health as powerfully as germs and nutrition do.
- They are able to enter altered states of consciousness for the purpose of journeying in the imaginal realms, where they often coax

---

*These actualized beings did not have a natural, innate capacity to embrace life and death completely. Instead, they had guides, teachers, and practices that they worked with regularly to develop this greater capacity to live simultaneously in many different realms at once.

dissociated parts of the person into returning to the psyche for integration and healing.

- In the shamanic tradition of old, the healer (shaman) attempted to restore healing and balance to others by performing sacred rites or ceremonies that typically included prayers, songs, and chants.

In the shamanic model, illness—both psychological and physical—is not an enemy to be eradicated. Rather, symptoms or disturbances of mental and physical health are messages from the soul or otherwise indicate obstacles to *hearing* messages from the soul.

THE DEMOGRAPHICS OF DISCONTENT

Many of the baby boomers who were discontent with the strictures of the times in which they grew up explored various alternative realities as a way of finding meaning in their lives. However, many felt that they had gone too far left of the accepted cultural norms. As a result, some made a decision to turn back further to the cultural norms they had left behind to try to regain some stability and grounding in their lives. Unfortunately, many of the boomers threw out the baby with the bath-water and began to settle back into the mundane, living with their disillusionment instead of continuing to seek a way out of it. Others became stuck in the past, becoming lost in a world that had moved on without them. Still others were catalyzed by the times they had lived through, which served to shape them as people/thinkers/healers and allowed them to acknowledge the validity of their alternative experiences.

Star Wolf's Story
MY INITIATORY PATH TO SHAMANISM

I was one of those overly sensitive children. I had a very loving, supportive, grounded grandmother who intuitively understood and saw me. She encouraged my sensitivity, which included psychic abilities such as clairvoyance, precognition, and the ability to see things differently from others. Yet she also understood that for me to be able to be on this planet, I needed to connect to nature, which included her garden and all of the many creatures that resided in it and on the grounds of her property.

I had a menagerie of dogs, cats, chickens, rabbits, hamsters, goldfish, turtles, and an array of insects such as june bugs, large grasshoppers, and even worms. Daytime was spent outside. Shortly after breakfast we began the day's chores of caring for all the animals, watering the plants, and otherwise taking care of the living things around us to create balance in our lives. My grandmother taught me that everything was alive and that we must tend to the physical world to create beauty and pleasure in our lives. She seemed to enjoy everything we did, and I too learned to look joyfully forward to all the little daily tasks.

After lunch, especially in the heat of the summer, we would frequently take a midafternoon nap and, upon awakening, finish our afternoon chores and perhaps take a walk in the woods to discover new creatures and plants. This is when my grandmother might tell me stories about life or ask me my thoughts about things. She told me to pay attention to my surroundings. She also told me that things around us were constantly communicating with us and sending us messages, which she referred to as signs and omens.

She encouraged walking barefoot upon the earth and sitting on the grass or large cool boulders in the woods by the lake. In midsummer we picked fruit from the trees, vegetables from the garden, grapes from the grapevines, and of course gathered eggs daily from the henhouse. If you have never eaten a freshly laid egg from chickens that have been tended with love, you have not tasted a real egg! (The ones in the stores are "soulless," and if we have had the real thing, our bodies know this.)

Evenings were the most magical time of the day for me, although I thoroughly loved the whole day from sunrise to sunset. The evenings held an etheric quality as dusk arrived and the first stars appeared, twinkling in the night sky. Many months out of the year we would find ourselves swinging in the large swing that was in the screened-in porch attached to the outside of the house, swinging away until late at night.

During this time my grandmother would engage my imagination

in a variety of ways and speak to my spiritual questions and concerns. We would talk about star beings, extraterrestrials, fairies, Jesus, and the supernatural world. Nothing was off-limits. We would sing religious hymns and recite poetry and rhymes. We would make up stories and tell jokes. You could call it our imaginations I suppose, but we saw things in the misty night around us and received messages from the other worlds. As long as my grandmother was by my side I was never afraid and in fact was quite brave. Without her, when I was at school and engaging with the outer world, I frequently felt odd, strange, different, and even defective. But somehow knowing that she was there, I knew I could make it and that I would be okay.

When she died rather unexpectedly shortly after my twelfth birthday I was completely adrift without her presence and love in my life. I sensed her reaching out to me from the spirit world, but it was simply not enough to help me to stay grounded. Although I do not remember wanting to die, I did not know how to live without her and wanted to follow her to the other side.

By the time my thirteenth birthday rolled around, I had discovered sex and drugs and rock 'n' roll. I truly do not believe that I would have survived had I not discovered these things, which allowed me to somehow live in both worlds. And even though these substitutes for love were not sustainable long-term, and in fact almost destroyed me, it's as if they filled the absence that I felt at that time, which could not be filled in any other way.

In the 1960s, I couldn't say no to the creative life-force energies that bubbled forth in the collective psyche of the world. I remember my friend Ruby saying it was like the whole world went from black and white to living color, which described so much of what I experienced as well. I came from a small coal-mining and farming town in western Kentucky where most folks—good salt-of-the-earth-type people—worked hard during the week and went to church on Sunday. There was comfort for them in that kind of living and thinking. They didn't take kindly to having their worlds turned upside down or seeing the fragile security they had created be blown apart with any strange new ideas from outsiders.

I remember when I first saw a hippie on the front of a popular publication, *Look* magazine. Immediately I knew that I wanted to be one despite having no real idea of what it was all about. When I was sixteen, I begged my folks to let me take a field trip on a chartered bus from Kentucky to Chicago with my fellow classmates. As we drove slowly in the evening traffic to our downtown hotel, I saw long-haired teenagers dressed in strange colors and hippie attire playing loud music, dancing wildly, smoking pot, and making out in broad daylight.

As we drove by a park, I opened the window (yes, you could do that in those days!), trying to get a better look and to be a little closer to that amazing scene. A young man turned around suddenly, and we made eye contact. He gave me the secret code: he held up one hand with two fingers pointing skyward. Without a moment's hesitation and without knowing exactly what it fully meant, I gave my first peace sign back to him. I felt elated. Energy started coursing through my veins. Secretly, I felt like I had been initiated into the club—whatever that meant!

Shortly after that, my determination to find my lost tribe became even stronger. Over the next few years, I found them in a variety of places around the country, from Kentucky to California and back again. I found those who seemed to know the *truth*—that which others didn't seem to know or even suspect. This secret society was a burgeoning hippie nation that spanned and infiltrated every state and town across our country. Its members ranged from returning, disillusioned Vietnam veterans and college dropouts to students in the know about what were called "aware" college campuses. We came in many shapes and forms, but the main thing we all had in common was that we knew we were being called by an irresistible force rising up in our midst as a huge vortex—a maelstrom of change. We knew that we needed "to get ourselves back to the garden," in the words of Joni Mitchell's "Woodstock."

What I was to learn on my bus trip to Chicago marked the true beginning of my spiritual awakening. What I was to learn in the days and months ahead was that to transform ourselves, and therefore our worlds, we must come back to the place we know and see it again for the very first time. All of life travels on a spiral path and requires that we move through the cycles of change repeatedly. This is not in a circular fashion, nor is it a linear approach. The spiral leads us to greater and greater perspectives and to endless possibilities. The revisioning it entails is the part of the shamanic path that interweaves the past, present, and future in a simultaneous reality. It allows for a vast panoramic view that will inform us and transform us in amazing ways. We too can inherit our divine birthright to grow up and become real human beings—real *humane* beings. Perhaps this is a better goal for all of humanity.

Nita's Story
MY INITIATORY PATH TO SHAMANISM

Growing up on the Akimel O'odam Reservation in central Arizona, I was privileged to experience Native American teachings on a daily basis. My father worked for the Bureau of Indian Affairs, and his job at the time was in a small office in the tiny town of Sacaton. Integrated in my daily life were medicine walks, ceremony, and ritual, although more often than not these events were not considered sacred or even special. They were the activities of daily living in a culture that, to a degree, had not lost contact with the natural world.

My childhood was one of deep connection to the land, sky, and all of Earth's creatures. Rattlesnakes were revered, feared, and yet respected by my Native American friends' parents. While my Caucasian father would immediately shoot them, I also witnessed the snakes being gently and carefully handled with kindness and serious intent by my Native American friends. Even at a very young age, I felt the rightness of this kindness in my bones. I was traumatized seeing the rattlesnake shot, and mystified when I was told that my father had killed it to protect me. Yet, I couldn't work it out—how was I separate from other creatures? Surely, killing one of them was also killing a part of me.

Any attempts to discuss this with my parents were met primarily with laughter. As I got older and insisted on my worldview of nonduality, my mother would counter with: "You don't really think that.

Only terrible people think they are related to things like rattlesnakes or skunks." If I pushed back, my father would intervene with intensity and say, "Stop this talk! You are killing your mother!"

One day, when I was all of five years old, I had a realization. I said to myself, "Clearly, I will be raising myself as they [my parents] don't know what they're doing." I was standing in the majesty of nature that was my backyard. I was facing the distant desert mountains that I related to as my elders, the ones whom I trusted to hold steady when all else was a moving target. A quiet, hot afternoon was dissolving into a warm evening's dusk, and with the naive wisdom of a five-year-old, I discovered that I was on my own—an emotional orphan. Part of me, recognizing my parental inadequacy, both expanded and dissociated.

The beauty of this early awareness was that it led me to seek guidance outside of my nuclear family. The downside was my sense of being unloved and unlovable, leading to years of emotional distress and physical illness. The upside to illness is that it also may be a drive to seek solutions. Blessed with being raised on a Native American reservation, alternative lifestyles and spiritual practices surrounded me.

Further dissociation took place, and I learned to not believe my experience. This is the fundamental characteristic of *soul loss*.

As years passed, I heard over and over that I was killing my mother whenever I asserted my core beliefs that did not conform with the beliefs of my parents. When I was eleven, my mother had a very serious heart attack and almost died. Though she survived it, I believed it was my fault. I threw myself on the mercy of Jesus, prayed for forgiveness, promised to be good and to never cause my mother any trouble again. Yet, she kept having heart problems, and my father kept reminding me that I was the cause. My conclusion was that I was extra bad, and God was punishing me.

Hitting puberty, I rebelled. Begging for forgiveness and trying to be good without being loved for who I was shifted into a deep hatred of my mother. My heart felt as though it had turned to ice, and I felt myself shape-shift into a storybook villain. My fairy tales were analogous to contemporary prequels that depicted the early life of the evil witch, fairy, or other antagonistic villain. These characters were portrayed as evil characters who had been sensitive, loving, and connected to all things until disastrous events plummeted them into darkness, and they incurred soul loss as a result. Gregory McGuire's *Wicked,* the rewrite of *Maleficent* by Disney, and the TV series *Once* are all examples of stories of true soul loss—a dark night of the soul where dissociation protects the self from destruction.

In 1964, I was being initiated into the mystery school we call adolescence. The world was being turned on its head by the Cultural Revolution. My personal rebellion against my internalized parental admonitions was reflected everywhere in rock and roll, antiwar demonstrations, and an invitation to "turn on, tune in, drop out!" Growing up on a reservation had connected me deeply to the Earth. It did not prepare me for the alienation of a material world. My parents did the best they could, meaning that they raised me as they had been parented, through alienation, punishment, and the crushing of hope. Depression-era childhoods had left them focused on the material world as the only reality. The world of rock and roll and the cultural shift of the '60s gave me, as it did many baby boomers, a taste of living beyond the limitations of the material world—and I wanted more of that.

Star Wolf and Nita Gage would not meet for another twenty years. Their biographical stories were very different though both were in search of methods of working with others in ways that were authentic, healing, and transformative. Their stories continue throughout the book as their odyssey to become Soul Whisperers unfolds.

THE WORLD REIMAGINED BY THE SHAMAN'S PRISM

Hippie spiritual seekers advocated dropping out and tuning in, taking psychedelics, and running off to India with flowers in their hair to seek enlightenment. Many of these baby boomers seem to have come full circle in recent years, once again leading the way and forging new territory by exploring shamanism. However, this time they are seeking not to escape from the Earth but rather to inhabit it in a different way.

Eastern religions and cultures have often taught practices enabling one to let go of attachment to desires and earthly things. They focus on opening to cosmic awareness and to surrendering to the void to become self-aware and find inner peace. Conversely, shamanism invites us to come back in to our bodies and our communities. This focus creates a pathway to higher realms of wisdom. Shamanic consciousness has become a bridge between dimensions. It calls for a sacred integration of all parts of ourselves and the worlds we inhabit as multidimensional beings.

Common phrases in popular postmodern shamanic circles are *the healer is within* and we are becoming *the walkers between the worlds*. Shamanic philosophy teaches us that there are many unseen and seen dimensions. All are sacred worlds, not just the loftier ones. This viewpoint honors both the light and the dark experiences. It asks that we give up attachment to the concept of either/or thinking and start practicing a more holistic approach to living, thereby healing ourselves through embracing and embodying both the sacred and the profane in our lives.

This calls to mind the Serenity Prayer, which is as follows: "God (Creator/Great Mystery), grant me the serenity to accept the things I cannot change, the courage to change the things I can, and the wisdom to know the difference." The perennial wisdom in this simple, heartfelt prayer is an acknowledgment of our humanity and our divinity. It asks that we recognize both our power*less*ness and our pow*erful*ness. The most important thing to ask while praying is for the wisdom to know what is called for at specific times in our lives. In other words, which journey to make—to the higher or lower realms, or perhaps both.

During shamanic journeying, one frequently symbolically shapeshifts into a shamanic form and travels into the past to release energetic blockages. Some call this an extraction process wherein certain attachments are released in order to have a part of the self return. This is a reconnection between spirit, body, and mind, making more energy available for real change and transformation.

The journeyer may also travel into the future to gain insight or to seek a guide who will assist them in seeing the bigger story of their lives. This may allow them to make sense of their present suffering and a current dilemma. Earlier we discussed the power of the imagination. In a later chapter we will discuss *imaginal cells* and how the ability to download them is capable of rebirthing our psyches.

The late Lee Lipsenthal, M.D., was an internist, popular speaker, and author. He worked with Nita Gage for fifteen years, developing and delivering shamanic healing workshops and seminars for physicians and health care professionals. Together they taught that neuroscience has opened a new understanding of the power held by imagination to listen to the soul and promote physical and emotional health. Together they coined the term *Neuroimaginal* from their integration of the fields of neuroscience and imaginal psychology. In their workshops they used concepts from neuroscience, psychology, and shamanism. The workshops gave physicians an introduction to shamanism by allowing them to experience the healing power of altered states of consciousness through Shamanic Breathwork. Dr. Lipsenthal believed in the rigor of science and scientific investigation and lectured extensively about the power of the imaginal to impact healing. In his book *Enjoy Every Sandwich: Living Each Day as If It Were Your Last,* he says this: "We all have God or Spirit and the shaman within us. We just need to begin to practice, to scratch away at the old Neuroimaginal world we have created and build ourselves a new home."[2]

Shamanic energy medicine offers a potential healing balm for our world, and it is reemerging in a new form. Lipsenthal also stated that "as a student of many great teachers and as a teacher myself, I had many techniques that I could use to go within. One of my favorites is Shamanic Breathwork, which had been taught to me by my friends Nita Gage and Linda Star Wolf. . . . This technique seems to trigger the God spot in the brain. . . . In the Native American tradition, these experiences are interpreted as a connection with Spirit in which healing can take place."[3] The response to our collective soul's calling for a unique, sustainable solution for ourselves and our planet is all-inclusive and multilayered. It gives meaning to what many of us experienced as being real in the '60s. However, the message now says that it is time for an upgrade. There is an urgent need to take things to the next level—a higher octave of consciousness. In other words, we are not done yet!

This is where the shamanic practice of Soul Whispering comes in. But before we immerse ourselves in a detailed understanding of Soul Whispering and what it means to be a Soul Whisperer, let's focus on a more detailed discussion of trauma—which many of us suffer from in one form or another—to best understand how shamanism and its practice of Soul Whispering can aid in its healing and resolution.

2
Surviving Psychiatry
You Can't Keep a Good Shaman Down

Life is not a linear path to success and happiness. It is a spiraling journey from comfortable, naive unconsciousness to awakened, intentional living. Along the way, we all at times may experience what feels like a *loss of innocence*. This term is tossed out to minimize the deeper truth, more accurately termed *soul loss*. The infectious nature of soul loss results from trauma. We all experience childhood trauma to a greater or lesser degree, but it may not have been obvious to anyone around us. Our parents simply didn't validate what was meaningful to us. We slowly but surely learned to deny those parts of ourselves that were mirrored as not being acceptable. For others, the trauma was extreme and hidden, such as in molestation and abuse.

Many people seeking help find themselves in the medical psychiatric system. Psychiatry very often does not help but rather further traumatizes people through invasive pharmaceuticals and other treatments. Many people who have gone through the system have come out still traumatized and have found healing on their own or through alternative methods. Groups such as Hearing Voices, Psychiatric Survivors, and Spiritual Emergence Network support people recovering from adverse psychiatric experiences, people who consider themselves survivors of the psychiatric system.

We are not saying that psychiatric and medical treatments are to blame or are always toxic. We know and work with many holistic psychiatrists who are doing incredible work for people who are experiencing extreme states. And at times even medication is useful. We simply acknowledge that there are alternatives and recognize that much of what has been done in the name of the helping professions has not helped and has in fact harmed people.

TRAUMA AND A DEEPER UNDERSTANDING OF IT FROM THE SHAMANIC PERSPECTIVE

Just as the ocean waves flow in and out unnoticed, waves of energy from early soul loss lap at our consciousness unnoticed. No one is afraid of the ocean as it rolls in and out of the shore. We are habituated to a range of waves hitting the beach. It is predictable. When a storm or an earthquake underneath the ocean occurs—the water recedes, pulls back forcefully, and then lets go. A tsunami results. A gentle storm does not frighten us. It often is exciting. Yet, when it's a sudden tsunami, it's a tragedy—a disaster that causes destruction.

Storms in life are sometimes mild: a minor car accident, a root canal, or a friend's betrayal. Yet, when there is a major upheaval such as death, cancer, job loss, divorce, the sudden onset of hearing voices, hallucinations, racing thoughts—a tsunami may sometimes occur. We react with extreme emotions and often are labeled insane or out of control. A shaman utilizing the practice of Soul Whispering is able to intervene and redirect the retracted energy into an imaginal shamanic release rather than it remaining sustained as a tsunami of destructive emotions.

Trauma is complex. The American Psychological Association (APA) defines it as originating from a significantly horrible event, like a car wreck, or sexual molestation, or physical abuse, which results in an emotional response with long-term consequences.[1] For example, people might reexperience the event suddenly and viscerally much later in life.

The APA limits its definition of trauma as originating from a horrible event. Trauma actually occurs when one's safety or security is seriously threatened, even if this does not involve a terrible event. The external situation is only one component of a potentially traumatizing event. Your emotional reaction to an experience of the event is underlying the ongoing trauma.

You may be traumatized while others in your families are not affected. Perhaps you were extremely sensitive and more aware of your vulnerability. Anything that disrupts your sense of safety is traumatic. Unintentional neglect from a depressed parent can be traumatizing to some but not to others who may have bonded with a neighbor or an aunt. Loss of a grandparent can be traumatizing even if your mother and father are still living and apparently functioning well as parents. In another family or even to another child in the same family, the loss of a grandparent, while deeply sad, would not necessarily be traumatizing.

SOUL LOSS AND SOUL REMEMBERED

Soul loss is often subtle and obscured from the eyes of the uninitiated. Without wise adults around to contextualize, validate, and mirror true experiences for the child, we begin to view the world through the lens of "What do I need to do to survive?" Frequently these decisions result in dissociating from ourselves wherein a piece of our core self goes into hiding to keep us safe. Safety seems to require a splitting of the self—one part hides in the realms of the spirit body, and the other part forms the false persona (or, as it is more commonly referred to, the *personality*).

History is rich with stories of people who had a fragmented sense of self and were considered insane, but some of these individuals were in fact responsible for profound scientific and artistic creations. Two who come to mind are John Nash and Vincent Van Gogh. Nash was an American mathematician with fundamental contributions in game theory, differential geometry, and partial differential equations. He was the subject of a popular movie, *A Beautiful Mind,* and carried a diagnosis of schizophrenia. Van Gogh, one of the most important artists in history, lived on the street and in and out of mental institutions. Today many potential creative pioneers are labeled insane and then drugged. More than at any time in history, we have moved even further away from understanding the brilliance that is often being birthed through someone experiencing extreme states of mind. And they often have nowhere safe to go.

Will Hall is a brilliant and gifted counselor whose work as a therapist and group facilitator focuses especially on trauma, oppression, and working with extreme states of consciousness that get diagnosed as psychosis. He is himself the survivor of a schizophrenia diagnosis. In his work, "Letter to the Mother of a 'Schizophrenic': We Must Do Better Than Forced Treatment and Laura's Law," Will recounts one story of a young man whom he encountered in the course of his therapeutic work who needed attention, not treatment.

> A few months ago I met your son . . . I walked up to him and greeted him, unsure how this young disheveled man would respond to me. I had been told he was considered "severely mentally ill," the worst of the worst, so beyond reach in his delusions that clinicians were considering using force to bring him to the hospital for treatment. But as soon as we made eye contact I was surprised. There was a clear feeling of affinity and communication. . . . I lost the thread at different points in our discussion, but one thing was clear: your son is brilliant. I was not surprised when he told us he got a perfect score on the SAT. "It was easy," he explained when I asked. "Anyone can get a perfect score if they take the practice tests."
>
> . . . When he suddenly wove the author Kurt Vonnegut into the pattern, my eyes widened. Just moments before our meeting I was talking with my colleague, telling my own story of meeting Vonnegut. And now here your son was mentioning the author. I was amazed by the coincidence. As your son's talk became wilder and more complex, referencing the Earth Consciousness Coordinating Office, SEGA Dreamcast, and numerology, and as he did math equations instantly to prove his obscure points, I sensed an uncanny power and clairvoyance in the air. I was in the presence of someone in a different reality, but a reality with its own validity, its own strange truth. A different spiritual view.

Perhaps I am eager to emphasize your son's talents because today he finds himself so fallen. I don't romanticize the suffering that he, or anyone, endures. His unusual thoughts and behavior led to a diagnosis of schizophrenia, and seem to be part of deeper emotional distress he is struggling with. I don't romanticize because I've been through psychosis and altered states myself. I've been diagnosed schizophrenic, many years and many life lessons ago, moving on with my life only after I found ways to embrace different realities and still live in this one.

So when we met your son I was completely surprised. The "severely mentally ill man" I was told needed to be forced into treatment was intelligent, creative, sensitive—and also making sense. Like someone distracted by something immensely important, he related to us in bits and pieces as he sat in conversation. . . . What surprised me was the connection I had with your son. Because I took the time, and perhaps I also have the background and skill, I was quickly able to begin a friendship.

By taking interest in his wild visions, not dismissing them as delusional, and by telling him about my own mystical states, not acting like an expert to control him, we began to make a bond. I spoke with respect and interest in his world, rather than trying to convince him he "needs help." What, after all, could be more insulting than telling someone their life's creative and spiritual obsession is just the sign they need help? That it has no value? By setting aside the professional impulse to control and fix, I quickly discovered, standing on that cold sidewalk and then over hot tea in a cafe, that your son is able to have a conversation, can relate, communicate, even plan his day and discuss his options. Some topics were clearly pained, skipped over for something else, and he was often strangely distracted—but it was after all our first meeting, and I sensed some terrible and unspoken traumas present that were still not ready to be recognized. To me, clearly, he was not "unreachable."

. . . When I finally do meet the people carrying that terrible, stigmatizing label of schizophrenia, what do I find? I find—a human being. A human who responds to the same listening and curiosity that I, or anyone, responds to. I find a human who is above all ter-rified, absolutely terrified, by some horrible trauma we may not see or understand. A human being who shows all the signs of flight and mistrust that go along with trauma. A person who may seem com-pletely bizarre but who still responds to kindness and interest—and recoils, as we all would, from the rough handling and cold dismissal so often practiced by mental health professionals. Listening and curiosity might take skill and affinity, to be sure, when someone is in an alternate reality. But that just makes it our responsibility to provide that skill and affinity. . . .

Your son may be frightened, may be in a different reality, may spend most of his time very far away from human connection. But his life, like everyone's, makes sense when you take time to under-stand it. He deserves hope for change, and he deserves careful, skilled efforts to reach him and to connect—not the quick fix falsely promised by the use of force.[2]

Modern medicine is turning to shamanic models of health and sanity as scientific research unveils the positive impact of personally embodied spirituality. Indeed, Scottish anthropologist Ioan Lewis wrote the book *Ecstatic Religion* in 1971 in which he suggested that psychiatrists are really shamans. He claimed psychiatry was just one of the functions of the shaman, and he invited comparison between sha-mans and psychiatrists.[3]

Nita's Story

DOWN THE RABBIT HOLE WITH THE MAD HATTER
My Encounter with Psychiatry

I left home the day after I graduated from high school. At seventeen, I went on an odyssey that included an avant-garde college on the East Coast that was a radical departure from mainstream education. The college president, age twenty-three, was the youngest in the country. The teach-ers were professors from New York City who had dropped out and gone north to the countryside to form a college where education was based on spirit and freedom. Franconia College was a hippie haven where sex, drugs, rock and roll, and philosophy were on equal footing. I had found my tribe. During this time I stumbled upon the existential psychological writings of R. D. Laing and knew that I had to go to London to meet the man who'd said, "Insanity—a perfectly rational adjustment to an insane world."[4]

So off to London I went, where I met my first shamanic teachers since my reservation days—two Scottish psychiatrists: R. D. Laing and his lesser-known colleague Hugh Crawford. In the cloak of antipsychiatry were two men who were clearly walking between worlds and traveling in the transpersonal realms. Laing and his scene of alternatives to psychiatry grabbed my attention and held me captive for the next decade.

Given that I was suffering from existential despair at that time, I could have easily ended up in a psychiatric hospital on suicide watch, pumped full of drugs, and told it was all for my own good. In reality, medicating patients is most useful for keeping the *staff* calm while someone is displaying signs of disturbance that are disturbing to others. Call it good karma, luck, or destiny that instead I found myself in a safe sanctuary in a derelict house in North London created by a group of "hippie" psychiatrists and shamanic healers. Here my experience was soul enriching and profound, rather than soul deadening and bereft as it would have been in a psychiatric hospital.

Franconia, my hippie college, let me go to London as part of my degree. I trained as a psychoanalyst with Laing and his merry band of rebels. The training was a synthesis of reading Freud and studying shamanism, hatha yoga, pranayama yoga, meditating, rebirthing, and living with people in extreme states of consciousness. I later came to understand that it was another medicine walk with medicine doctors who were deeply connected to spirit, psyche, and soul. I was taught how to hold space for people in extreme states without intervening and yet offer love and compassion for their journey. My own journey of depression and underworld exploration was not separate from my training but rather an integral aspect of learning to be with people authentically. Facing my own darkest unconscious places in the company of loving, noninterfering, compassionate people prepared me to do the same for others.

We lived together in a community, eating together, studying, meditating, and engaging in psychospiritual practices of rebirth and psychodrama. There were formal training groups that some of us were involved in, studying the classical texts of Freud, British and French psychoanalysis, existential philosophy, Greek mythology, Eastern spirituality, shamanism, prenatal psychology, politics, mysticism, physics, esoteric science, and much more. The learning was a synthesis of intellectual rigor and lived experience. We explored what is sanity and what is madness and how all aspects of the spectrum are what it means to be human. In my world in the '70s, psychiatrists were the good guys—the shamans and the Soul Whisperers—who held space for extreme states.

Like traditional shamans, I was experiencing altered states and practicing symbolic death and rebirth in my own psyche as well as witnessing and holding space for the experiences of others.

During my time in London, my mother was diagnosed with brain cancer. I left London and the existential-phenomenology ashram of Ronnie Laing and his colleagues and went back to America to be with my dying mother. I was with her for six months. I was at her side holding space for her, making amends to her, telling her that I loved her, and forgiving her from the bottom of my heart. But when she did die, despite all the deep connection I felt I had with her during that time, I did not allow myself to experience grief. I was consumed with unspeakable shame. Unconsciously, I believed I had killed her. Not allowing that thought to come into consciousness, however, I quickly repressed it, and another piece of my soul left me at that time. After her death I went back to London and completed my training.

In 1980, I returned to America, where I found that psychiatry as practiced in mainstream medicine was not what I hoped it would be. Instead the world of psychiatric treatment was one of control, coercion, and misunderstanding and was bereft of anything spiritual let alone shamanic. My mission became to change the way psychiatry treated people. I went to work in a psychiatric hospital and started a small private practice. For several years I worked in a hospital, then an outpatient community mental health setting.

My unorthodox ways of working with people in extreme states were seen as both ridiculous and miraculous. Although many people made fun of me, I was the one called when a patient was "out of control" and displaying extremely disturbing behavior. I arrived and walked into the padded cell and met that person where he was, being with or listening to him, not interfering yet actively being present. In the vast majority of instances, the person felt safe, calmed down, and did not have to stay in the padded cell or be drugged further. Because of my ability to work with the most extreme of states, I gained the respect of the psychiatrists and medical leadership and was quickly promoted to positions of leadership myself. My private practice was successful, and many physicians and professionals sought me out, as did psychiatric patients who had met me in the hospital and felt seen and safe.

And I also encountered the wrath of mainstream medical personnel who saw me as a disruptive force who was undermining psychiatry and a danger to patients. I actively straddled the world of being respected for my unconventional approaches and being skewered for the same thing. Overall, from an outside perspective, I have had a very successful career in mainstream mental health. When I was in my early forties I was hired into a job at a prestigious psychiatric health care corporation where my office was on the top floor of a high-rise building in downtown San Francisco. I was on the executive team, leading the efforts to bring integrated mind/body approaches forward. Here I had access to all of the perks and privileges of corporate life. I was, by many people's standards, at the top of my game.

Star Wolf's Story
CUCKOO'S NEST TO SHAMAN'S DRUM

Soul Whispering abilities come from the fertile ground of defeat and collapse, which, if made conscious, blossoms into sweet surrender and strength. Shamans seek out challenging and even life-threatening experiences to open themselves to deeper and deeper wisdom. I certainly did this when I was attending college on my way to becoming a social worker.

For me the life-threatening experiences took the form of exploring many different psychoactive substances. My favorite weekend pastime involved combining drugs and music. Using drugs to reach an altered state and then going to a rock concert was unbeatable as far as reaching new states of heightened awareness and ecstasy. They didn't call it the era of sex, drugs, and rock 'n' roll for nothing!

I remember both the mixed feelings of fear and the thrill of "dropping acid," as we called it back then. There would be a period of waiting until takeoff and then the sudden, overwhelming rush of energy coursing through my entire body. My psyche then hurtled through space and time, losing touch with gravity as my normal senses became greatly exaggerated, usually accompanied with brilliant, cascading rainbows of color; a multitude of images flashing by; strong body sensations; and high-frequency sounds that would "blow my mind." This would last until my mind and body would finally move into some kind of orbit that circled around my life and settled into what was often called a "trip," which today I would call "a shamanic journey."

I would often have amazing insights during my regular weekend excursions into inner space, or wherever my journey took me. However, upon my return I was seldom able to even begin to articulate my experiences except to say, "Oh wow!" The experiences were profound, yet without tools for integration, many people in the era of psychedelics and experimentation in all forms of altered states were fragmented. We found our limits by going beyond them, sometimes over and over again. Yet there was important beauty born out of the chaos of those times, a deep wisdom that was generated, albeit often at the cost of great pain and destruction.

A Different Kind of Trip

It's interesting that Shamanic Breathwork utilizes various kinds of stimulating music to create an altered state of consciousness much in the same way that we used mind-altering drugs and plants and music in the '60s. The difference in the setting of Shamanic Breathwork is that we create a safe container to support transformational healing.

Journeying without substances allows us to maintain simultaneous consciousness instead of blowing ourselves out of control or "blowing our minds." As a result, we are able to consciously participate in dissolving old patterns, and bringing the gifts of the sacred altered state consciously back to the mundane world where they can "grow corn," as Twylah Nitsch (my adopted spiritual teacher and Native American Wolf Clan Grandmother) used to say.

In the early days we may have simply been interested in taking the journey and not knowing or really caring where it was taking us. Thinking we were inner space astronauts, we were possessed by naïveté and childlike omnipotence masquerading as courage. When we use altered states of consciousness we work with intention and we come back with solid information or guidance on how to make the changes that are needed to be happier and more "on purpose" in life. As my late husband, Brad, who was a shamanic priest and minister, once said, "If what we are doing doesn't translate back into our worlds, our lives with our loved ones and community, and the world, and into acts of loving-kindness and healing, I am simply not interested."

I made quite a few of these drug-induced trips over a period of several years while I was attending college, protesting the war, and saving the world. In our youthfulness many of us were determined to somehow save the world, create peace, and break out of all of the superficial boxes that confined us.

During my last trip in my altered state, I mixed several substances and ended up in the emergency room of a mental hospital. I was in college at the time, and several of my friends and I went to an outdoor concert where we pooled together our "medicine." We proceeded to share what we had with one another and prepared ourselves for an amazing evening with several bands that were known to "take you on a trip" with their music.

Sometime during the evening it became evident that I was in trouble; I was freaking out and also getting really sick. My friends panicked because they didn't know what to do with me. Remember, they were altered as well. That's when they came up with the idea to take me to the emergency room of the state mental hospital, which was actually not far from the college campus where the concert was. They wanted to take me here specifically because it was commonly known among college students that if someone who had overdosed on psychedelics was taken to the emergency room of the mental hospital, the police would not be called. At a regular hospital the personnel *would* call in the police, but if you went to the state mental hospital they would not. Don't ask me how we knew this . . . the tribe knew; we just did.

So that's what happened. They took me to the admitting area of the state hospital, rang the bell, and dropped me off. I was rushed into the facility and barely remember what happened next. What I do remember is several medical people around me putting me on a table and working on me frenetically, and hearing someone say, "I don't know if she is going to make it." Suddenly I felt a "pop," and things became very calm and there was light all around me. I was floating over a chaotic scene beneath me, and the body lying on the table seemed vaguely familiar. Then I realized that it was *my* body. I was nonchalant about that fact, and I felt a pulling sensation before I blacked out.

I woke many hours later, in a padded room, strapped down to my bed. It took me three days to convince the doctors and counselors there that I was not mentally ill and that I didn't know what I had taken, and it was not intentional that I had almost died.

It was during these three days of being in a locked unit at a mental hospital that I met a whole group of other patients who carried the diagnoses of schizophrenia, manic depression, and other popular mental illness diagnoses of the time. They were all heavily medicated; some were actively psychotic, and many were so drugged that it was hard to tell what was going on with them.

At first I felt very different and was afraid to be locked up with "crazy people." I spoke to anyone who would listen, trying to convince them that I wasn't crazy and didn't belong there. It was like the film *One Flew Over the Cuckoo's Nest.* The nurses and doctors were all behind strong unbreakable glass and walls, and the patients were lumped in together and lined up at the window where the medicine was passed out when they called your name.

It was here that I realized that as messed up as I might be, there was something horribly wrong with how these people were being treated. I started to communicate with my new friends—the so-called crazy ones. I began to relate and feel connected to the souls of these folks and to understand that I was truly just a few frequencies off from being exactly in their shoes. I did what I had to do over the next few days to get out of there in one piece, but I promised myself that I was first of all stopping drugs of all kinds and second that I was going to do something to help others who were sick enough to be in psychiatric hospitals. And of course, eventually, that's exactly what I ended up doing.

My parents were called, and they were relieved to hear that I was alive given that they hadn't been able to reach me for several days. Needless to say they were also confused by my actions and were quite angry and worried when they came to pick me up.

Upon my release, I was given back my street clothes along with several prescriptions that I was to continue taking upon my return to my parents' house, where I was ordered to stay for the next few months. Although I was quite blown away by all that had happened and was suffering from major anxiety at the time, something inside of me just knew instinctively that the medications were what were making me feel even more out of it. The medications were keeping me separated from the part of myself that could help heal and restore my energy field. Yes, I was a mess for sure, as well as a lost soul needing to do inner work on many levels.

At the same time I knew deep inside what my grandmother had always told me reassuringly as a child: that I had a great gift and psychic abilities and power inside of me that were special and that there was nothing fundamentally wrong with me. It was this inner knowing that gave me the courage to stop taking the medications the instant I left the locked floor of that institution. Instead I chose to begin to face my fears and look deeper for the answers that would unlock the past pain and suffering that had landed me in this perfect dilemma that had been set up by my soul. When I stopped taking the medications, my anxiety hit me hard, and I started to struggle with panic attacks and hyperventilation. They made me feel as if an elephant was sitting on my chest and that I would suffocate as a result.

I realize now that the feelings of suffocation were related not only to my drug overdose and near-death experience but also to the shock of the sudden loss of my beloved grandmother when I was twelve. The repressed grief, anger, and fear, along with dysfunctional family of origin issues and other painful events from my childhood, had been activated by the drug-induced, altered state. This was a very difficult time for me in that I was learning how to just make it through a day without feeling like I was going crazy. However, it was also the perfect setting for me to begin on the journey of healing that turned my world completely upside down yet again in my young life. I was nineteen years old, soon to turn twenty. I had the realization that unless I did something dramatically different I would not live a long life or I would end up in a psychiatric facility on a long-term basis.

For the next couple of months, I mostly stayed in my room at my parents' house or took walks at sunset, praying to some unknown force in the universe to help me not be so anxious and to give me direction about what to do and where to go next. I knew I could not stay with my parents forever as it was a total dead end for me. I had never really fit in there except when my grandmother was alive and holding that safe space for my vulnerability.

During this time of high anxiety I stayed up late at night writing poetry and short stories. I listened to music such as the Moody Blues, Pink Floyd, Jethro Tull, and Led Zeppelin, searching for the answers to my issues.

One day when I most needed it an angel named Margaret Jean appeared to assist me (actually she was my mother's first cousin). Growing up, I had spent nights with her on occasion, at which times she had confided in me that we were very similar in nature and that she too had "the curse" of knowing too much about people and things. She had been called "overly sensitive" her entire life, which included occasional miscellaneous unexplained bouts of illness that disappeared shortly after they'd arrived. She'd been prescribed a wide range of medications from various doctors to medicate her strange array of symptoms. Of course I had always known, as the saying in Kentucky goes, that "she ain't right," meaning she was a bit crazy. However, that had never bothered me at all, and in fact Margaret Jean was one of the few people with whom I felt an affinity. With her I could just be myself, without hiding or holding back. She introduced me to tarot cards and taught me how to interpret them and how to understand astrology and ESP and other psychic phenomena, although often I didn't understand it all.

Margaret Jean was the town psychic behind the scenes. She frequently gave readings for those who came to her back door late at night (to avoid prying eyes), and I was fortunate enough to be privy to those sessions. I sat on a stool and peered deeply over the cards that were laid out by candlelight in her small kitchen. On occasion, she even invited me to share my intuitive thoughts or messages with the good folks who sat anxiously, waiting to hear what fates awaited them. It was at those rare times that I felt at home with myself. She had taken more of an interest in me once my grandmother had passed away and took me under her wing from time to time until I left for college at the University of Kentucky to become a social worker.

When my aunt showed back up in my life after my near-death experience, she came bearing healing gifts. She brought me my in-depth personal astrological chart (which stressed that I was to become a healer of spiritual ills for humanity) and several dozen books that included stories ranging from those about the famous medium Edgar Cayce, accounts of past lives, stone healing, numerology, sacred geometry, astral projection, ETs, mysterious islands, and ancient cultures. She also gave me my very own tarot deck as well as a few crystals and other gemstones of sacred importance to her.

Over the next few years I would ravenously consume all the books that she had gifted me with and many more. My spiritual hunger was very great! It was during this time that I began to awaken and climb my way slowly back toward sanity. However, life is not linear or even simply rotating in a circle. It is a powerful spiraling vortex reflecting the greater mysterious workings of the universe, which we will discuss further in later chapters "The Nature of How People Change" and "The Five Cycles of Change."

I still had a long journey ahead of me to find my own ground of being and to keep the promise made to my roommates back in the mental hospital. So in that vein, spiraling around the vortex of my own life over the next year, I returned to college to finish my degree in social work. My becoming a social worker was the only way I could conceive of helping to change the world and make it a safer place, although at the time I did not understand how this related to my own personal sense of insecurity. I only knew that I wanted to help others and make the world a better place. That yearning to help others comes from deep suffering and confusion as a child when unconsciously we want to create safety for ourselves as adults. I know that I felt deeply compassionate toward the suffering of others, and I now know that it was touching my own pain.

The truth is that from our own suffering, compassion is born. Compassion is empathy imbued with a desire to ease the suffering of others. However, unless we also continue our own personal growth and healing, helping others can become quite murky. One remains wrapped up in one's own unmet emotional wounds, and working with others becomes primarily an avenue to enhance self-esteem. Confusion ensues as the helper's needs are overlaid onto the person seeking help. (We discuss this problem that plagues the helping professions in a later chapter, "Emotional Cancer.")

In any event, at this time I finished the course work that I needed to graduate with a degree in social work. I also met and married my first husband (our marriage spanned two decades), moved back to my hometown, and went to work (my first professional job) at the mental health center there. I was still recovering from my own anxiety disorder but was managing it the best way I could at the time—with my special spiritual tools.

I applied for a job as a mental health worker for the mentally ill at the clinic, and, to my surprise, I was hired over others who had more credentials than I did. I had even discussed my anxiety with them and had also shared some of my idealistic viewpoints about helping others. They were in a jam to hire someone right away to assist the already overworked and underpaid social worker on staff there.

My new job was to assist this social worker in running a hospital day-treatment program for people who were labeled chronic mentally ill. I was helping to coordinate and facilitate this program for roughly twenty patients on Monday to Friday of each week, usually seven to eight hours a day. Kathy, the social worker, was only a few years older than I was, and I was barely twenty-one. It was a new program created as a response to the deinstitutionalization sweeping across America at that time. It seemed like a good idea on some level but was a disaster on another. Thousands of individuals were put into nursing homes and on the streets, or returned to live with family who were unprepared to deal with them.

Our other team members consisted of a nurse, social worker, and psychiatrist who showed up at the day-treatment house once or twice a week for an hour to check up on us—to make sure that we were all still alive! The main thing they offered was medication support and someone for us to report the goings-on of the week to so that the program could be funded. Kathy and I worked forty to fifty hours per week and spent most of those hours directly dealing with between ten and twenty patients carrying diagnoses of schizophrenia, manic depression, or major depressive disorders. Many of these individuals were considered a suicide risk or were possibly too dangerous to be left alone.

We worked in an old white farmhouse on a couple of acres a few miles out of town and away from the main mental health center. We spent most of our time there alone with the patients and working toward being creative about what was meaningful to offer them during the day. This was not an easy task due to how heavily medicated the patients were. No one really seemed to have a clue what to do with folks who previously had been sitting in corners locked away in what were once called "asylums for the insane." There were a lot of hits and misses along the way. Whether we were teaching arts and crafts, reading, gardening, cooking, talking about personal hygiene, or listening to complaints about their living situation or treatment from others in their environment—we were doing what we were doing in the name of trying to help these folks create stability and better mental health for themselves.

Truthfully, I didn't have any idea what I was doing or what would work best for the patients. As well, I had virtually no directions from anyone else. No one seemed to know what to do except prescribe heavy medication. Once I figured out that the so-called experts were clueless about what to do, and knowing that I had barely escaped being one of the patients in a mental hospital and heavily medicated myself, I started taking more initiative to do simply what felt right, intuitively. This began with deep listening and meeting the patients totally in the moment—no matter how nonsensical or irrational some of their conversations might sound. Even heavily medicated, many had audio and visual hallucinations that I listened to, joining them where they were. As time wore on, I became more confident with my ideas and interactions. I cared for the people I worked with and started referring to them by name instead of as patients and diagnoses.

I found that the more I expanded my own psyche to embrace a larger field of "normal," the more "normal" they became. What I mean by that is the symptoms associated with their diagnoses quieted down, and in many cases I was able to successfully advocate for lower dosages of medications. The result was that they were present and aware in group activities! I gained a reputation as a *people whisperer* even back then, although I was barely twenty-one years old. I remember when the psychiatrist told me that I had a special way of working with "mentally ill" patients. He often called upon me to ask my opinion about what to do with certain patients, including what I thought about the effectiveness of certain medications for them.

Over the next fifteen years I would work in a variety of mental health programs. I also specialized in addictions as well as mental health and ran many family programs at treatment centers. During that time, the story was pretty much the same no matter where I worked or what state my husband and I moved to. I would quickly become the one that the clients related to the most. (The social services system started calling people "clients" instead of "patients" in an attempt to be more politically correct.) I would often translate what was really going on with the client to the professional with the more advanced degrees.

During this time, the state of Florida, where I was working, required that to be the supervisor of certain programs one must have certain degrees and credentials after their name even if they had been doing the job longer than anyone else in the workplace. I went back to school full-time on the weekends to acquire my degree to do the job I was already doing. This occurred a couple of times over my mental health and addictions careers, and each time I managed to jump through the necessary hoops to legally do the job I was already doing! Not only doing, but also receiving accolades for doing the work without having the required degrees or training in the first place!

There was a time in the mental health system when social workers and therapists were advised not to get too close to what was referred to as "the chronic mentally ill," because they were not able to bond with others and therefore lacked empathy. We were not to discuss their diagnosis with them, because it would be a waste of time and they wouldn't be able to understand it anyway because of what were their often extreme symptoms. Although some clients and the level of disturbances they were undergoing were more challenging to deal with than others, I found that by doing exactly the opposite of what I was taught, both the client and I fared much better.

For instance, I always sought to show anyone I worked with my respect and positive regard and to acknowledge their courage and inner strength for whatever they might be going through even if they seemed out of it. Once we had established a common ground I shared some of my own challenges and found most of my patients to be caring and concerned for my well-being, as much as anyone else was, including the professionals with whom I worked. I also informed clients of their diagnosis and why they were being given certain medications and what the side effects were. We discovered that many times the side effects were worse than what they were being treated for and that with medication reduction or adjustment, and sometimes stopping altogether, they improved on all levels. As an addiction counselor, the more I was able to introduce clients to natural altered states through meditation, music, art, and breathwork, as well as 12-step work, the greater the outcomes were for sobriety overall.

The common thread that ran through all the social services programs was that much of what I was being taught didn't actually work in real time. The more authentic and compassionate I was, the better things went on all levels. The more I gained the trust of those I served through compassion and authenticity, the more they opened up and shared on a deeper level. I loved working with the clients, and over the years I worked with clients of all ages and with every diagnosis and issue possible.

I was, however, becoming increasingly burned out with the outworn paradigms and patriarchal systems that presided over the truly sacred work that needed to be done. It was at this time that two powerful forces entered my life within a few years of each other. In an experience I will detail in the next chapter, I met an amazing teacher—a woman named Jacquelyn Small who rocked my world with her teachings and her book *Becoming Naturally Therapeutic*. Another one of her books, *Transformers: The Therapists of the Future*, grabbed me and resonated with me also.

I entered into Jacquelyn's training program at Eupyschia Institute (held at various retreat centers around the country) and dove headfirst into her style of Integrative Breathwork, an outgrowth of Holotropic Breathwork that had been founded by Stanislav Grof, M.D. The healing power of the breath, of any other substance or method I have ever encountered, possesses the greatest potential for self-realization and transformation. I have been an explorer for a long time in this arena, beginning at the Eupyschia Institute, where I would eventually become a lead trainer, working alongside Jacquelyn there.

To this day, breathwork is the main tool I utilize for my own journey of shamanic healing and is my first choice for most others that I work with for almost any issue. (How we use this work, and why it works, will be explained in later chapters.) In the training workshops at the Eupyschia Institute, I immersed myself completely in this healing modality, as well as participating in a variety of other transformational workshops on topics such as *A Course in Miracles,* transcendental meditation, yoga, crystal healing, chanting sacred sounds and words, color and light therapies, Reiki initiations, inner child groups, vision quests, sweat lodges, and Native American ceremonies and teachings. I also read volumes of books on a wide variety of psychological and spiritual subjects. With each thing I learned about myself and the universe around me, I became more aware of how asleep I had been and of course how asleep it seemed that most of the world still was.

The second event that changed my life was my fateful encounter with and meeting of the woman who was to become my adopted spiritual Wolf Clan Grandmother, Twylah Nitsch. I have written about the magical way that I met Gram Twylah in several of my other books, so I will not go into it here except to say that she called me to her in the dreamtime before I ever knew who she was in this reality. When we finally met she knew exactly who I was, calling me by the name that she had given me in the other dimensions.

Meeting my spiritual grandmother led me to embrace shamanism in a very real and elemental way. At that point, I walked forward out of my attempt at being normal once and for all. I accepted that I was a shamanic being and always had been. More importantly, I knew the only way that I was going to be truly free and happy was to authentically live my sacred purpose.

The psychic abilities that I had worked hard to get rid of or at least suppress began to reappear in my life. The very things that I had tried to deny and be rid of now became my greatest allies and gifts—not only for myself but for others as well. I began to realize that I was not defective and that everyone had things about them that were special, perhaps different. I also understood that it was only by bringing these things forward into the light of day and learning to love and accept ourselves that we could transform our wounds into consciousness and into loving, healing energies for the world.

I became determined to be more of who I truly was, not less. The more determined I became, the less shameful I was and the more I loved being alive and living on this Earth in a body with emotions that no longer overwhelmed me and which I could fully integrate. I became passionate about assisting others in learning to transform their personal wounds into healing assets so that they too could discover their path and purpose in the world.

This was a huge initiation for me in my early forties, and it has carried me forward ever since that time. I have never looked back. I have never regretted this path that I am on and I thank the Creator every day for giving me the life I have and all that I have been able to experience. Following my authenticity and walking away from the systems of mental health, I have created my own programs through my nonprofit organization, Venus Rising Association for Transformation. The organization is dedicated to merging ancient wisdom with practices dedicated to generating modern-day consciousness geared toward dealing with and resolving the complexities of today's world.

From the merging of breathwork, shamanism, Wolf Clan teachings, and psychology I have birthed a process I call Shamanic Breathwork. I have, over the past twenty years, kept my promise to myself and others back in the psychiatric ward that I would provide a place and a way for people to safely and powerfully traverse their own journey of emergence without unwanted or unhelpful psychiatric intervention.

3

Soul Whispering

The New Psychotherapy

Soul Whispering can be seen as an evolution of psychotherapy, which has traditionally been focused on healing the past. Soul Whisperers see self-healing as a necessary step on the path of transformation. The end game is that there is no end; rather it's a continual unfolding and responding to our ever-changing world—personal, collective, and planetary.

A RECLAIMING OF SACRED PURPOSE

The journey of our life is to step in to consciousness and sacred purpose. It may be that your sacred purpose is to simply find your way through the maze of your life fully awake. There are dead ends, monsters, false alleys, clowns, wicked witches, and white rabbits leading you the wrong way—endless distractions; some very dangerous, some just silly. Events happen to keep us awake. Too much comfort lulls us into complacency. Too little comfort distracts us as well. All of it is fodder for expansion and transformation.

The well-known British anthropologist Francis Huxley studied shamanism in primitive cultures and then spent his midlife career working with R. D. Laing teaching psychotherapy students the value of shamanism in therapy. Nita studied with Francis and remembers him speaking about the integration of modern medicine and psychological therapies being the same as shamanic practices.

As we know, in a shamanic context, expanded states of consciousness, which are often diagnosed and pathologized, are productive vehicles for healing. Shamanism lends itself exquisitely to so-called psychiatric illnesses. When someone is suffering from frightening hallucinations or deep depression, shamans look to find the lost soul part or the unseen demon lurking in the psyche of the person. Symptoms are indicators to be worked with in the process of finding the unseen issue. And with the newest research indicating that most if not all chronic diseases have their roots in adverse childhood experiences (ACEs)—in other words, trauma—then it may well be that soul return, the shamanic practice of healing trauma, has its place in all parts of medicine.

The turn to shamanism can be seen as a longing for our essence. In the late '90s, Nita asked her Native American teacher whether it was appropriate for nontribal people to be involved in learning shamanism, and the response she received was, "Honey, you white people have all lost your tribe just as surely as we [Native Americans] have, and it is time to reclaim the tribal roots to get back some wholeness!"*

The concept of wholeness is key here. Specifically, modern medicine is beginning to recognize that it's critical to see the person as a whole rather than merely addressing individual symptoms that may be presenting in that individual. Further, the medical profession is beginning to understand what indigenous healers already know: not only the whole individual but also the community and the environment are integral factors in determining health and well-being. The role that environment and social setting have on healthy development is well researched. The conclusion is that adverse childhood experiences (ACEs, or trauma) are the greatest predictor of physical or mental health. In this regard, ACEs are far more significant than diet, exercise, wealth, or the presence or absence of germs or toxins.

---

*When pressed, Nita's Native American teacher went on to explain to Nita that most white people are European, and their ancestors are from a Celtic tribe. As a result of this exchange, Nita embarked on a journey to learn about her Celtic shamanic roots through books and trips to sacred Celtic shamanic sites in Britain and Europe.

When we have been traumatized, our soul may choose to let a part of us take time out from life and wait—safely and serenely—like a caterpillar in a cocoon. When the time is right, the hidden soul piece emerges, transformed through struggle, breaking free and taking flight. Even if we are not experiencing the aftereffects of trauma, which impact us in myriad negative ways, we may believe our lives to be devoid of meaning and excitement. We may, like the caterpillar, be looking to break free from the cocoon and fly off into a new life of our own devising.

Shamanism is primary care. Developing your shaman within, your shamanic consciousness, is first aid for most maladies. Bringing awareness to unconscious and unresolved dysfunctional beliefs that poison your psyche and releasing these negative energies will improve health. Shamans are shape-shifters. Symbolically and imaginally they take on the energy of animals, plants, spirits, or other people to bring in whatever subtle energy is needed in the given situation. Being your own shaman means accessing the unconscious and the hidden by traveling symbolically to your own underworld.

Not everyone, however, seeks conscious transformation. Sometimes transformation seeks us, and we find ourselves unintentionally plummeted into an altered state of consciousness that can be frightening and unsettling. The problem is that in Western civilization adapting and assimilating are the standard of normalcy. If you do not fit into that standard you may not have any place where you feel safe or find meaning. You may be frightened and in need of safe sanctuary.

Just as a caterpillar needs a cocoon, some people need sanctuary for a time to reinvent themselves through a process of dissolving the old form. Caterpillars fully dissolve within the cocoon. If the cocoon is opened at any stage before completion the caterpillar will die and the butterfly will never emerge. Even when the butterfly is completely formed and struggling to emerge from the cocoon, if someone "helps" the butterfly by making it easier to emerge, the butterfly will fall to the ground and never fly. It must go all the way through the struggle to prepare its wings for flight.

Perhaps the butterfly is surrounded by spirits that encourage, support, and protect it without interfering. If you are a shape-shifter, like a caterpillar you will find yourself dissolving. Sometimes there are other Soul Whisperers around to guard your cocoon and speak words of support. Other times you are dissolving in that cocoon all alone. Either way you will dissolve, and you will emerge through and from the struggle. Trust the process, stop resisting, and notice the wings emerging instead of focusing on what is dissolving.

A tool that we've provided to help you get in touch with the intuitive wisdom of your soul is provided in the audio tracks that accompany this book. The five meditative tracks may be used for you to journey to access the whisperings of your soul. The tracks included are "Neuroimaginal Journey," "Creature Teacher Medicine Journey," "Turning the Light on Your Shadow," "Contacting Your Future Self," and "Inanna: A Feminine Tale" (one of our oldest myths). You will find more information about them, including how best to use them, at the end of the book (page 274).

What appears as suffering often has a purpose. At times, even though we are suffering, we are not victims. We all have the capacity of the shaman shape-shifting into a different octave of our true essence. Remember this all you shamans, spiritual seekers, unacknowledged mystics: You must come out of the closet today. The world needs you now!

THE PRACTICE OF SOUL WHISPERING

Soul Whisperer is a term that we have come to use for all the individuals who are guides for others who are on a journey of spiritual exploration, or for anyone who learns how best to listen to and be guided by the inner murmurings of their soul. Over the years those of us who are facilitators for others have referred to ourselves as counselors, psychotherapists, and psychospiritual mentors. As we have evolved, so has our understanding of the gifts we are offering to those seeking to heal and, in the process, become Soul Whisperers themselves. The term *Soul*

Whisperer addresses the depth and breadth of the work we are called to do and teach at a soul level.*

The process of Soul Whispering mirrors that of animal whisperers who succeed through love, patience, and a developed ability to communicate directly with the spirit or essence of the animal with which they are working. In this, Soul Whisperers embody characteristics similar to animal whisperers. Soul Whisperers may also be shamans who are wounded healers. These facilitators have faced their own inner darkness and released the energy connected to their wounds. Transforming wounds to gifts requires a process that includes releasing negative energy and embracing self-love and compassion.

Soul Whisperers, as facilitators/therapists/counselors/coaches/shamanic ministers, encourage and assist people to bring their symbolic story to life. Here we are talking about a type of interactive theater where the facilitator, through deep listening and thoughtful guidance, connects the individuals with their personal archetypal dramas. In so doing, the individuals are given permission to explore this potentially transformative realm as well as being provided with a safe container in which to conduct this exploration. They are also provided with support from the collective energy of other participants. The result is a bringing forth of the unspoken imaginal musing of the soul that had been leaking out in the form of unwanted symptoms, dysfunctional behavior, or other negative manifestations.

The luminous space between the dance/song and the dancing/singing is brought forward in holographic reality by the skilled Soul Whisperer. In doing so, transformation is fertilized. Calling this remarkable phenomenon healing sometimes demeans the process. We use healing to imply that someone is damaged goods. Transformation assumes wholeness that expands where metamorphosis is occurring.

A Soul Whisperer understands that actively engaging in energy work is effective only if the practitioner simultaneously disengages from

---

*In service of recognizing people who are called to serve through shamanism and Soul Whispering, the Venus Rising Association for Transformation offers certification for shamanic ministerial ordination.

an attachment to outcome. Additionally, the practitioner must even disengage from causality of any sort, particularly when the recipient of the work wants to attribute results to the practitioner. The goal is to create space for the recipient to fully embrace the outcome as resulting from his or her own transformative work. The Soul Whisperer intentionally teaches the recipient how to disengage from dependence on the practitioner and to experience the inner power of awakening his or her own inner shaman and to embody shamanic consciousness in everyday life. This form of empowerment constitutes the truly liberating appeal of this modality of transformational work.

The Soul Whisperer's primary skill set is the ability to be with someone deeply while bridging a connection with the collective field of the imaginal and symbolic together with ordinary everyday life. (The audio track "Neuroimaginal Journey" will help you to access this.) The collective field is where abstract and symbol reside. Often people are cut off from this field. They no longer remember that within them exists a deep well of imaginal knowledge. The Soul Whisperer shepherds people back to the land of their birthright. Grandmother Twylah Nitsch referred to this energy field as the "field of plenty"—the true source of creation and where all things originate from and to which they return.

As powerful as the collective imaginal symbolic field is, the true catalyst for transformation is the embodiment of this into everyday life. Many times people do not move through the imaginal, becoming enamored or even addicted to expanded states of consciousness. It's understandable when a person has deep, unresolved trauma that the world of the imaginal is preferable to the world of disappointing, abusive reality.

When one works with a facilitator who is versed in Soul Whispering, one learns how to become a Soul Whisperer oneself, eventually without the need of a facilitator. As the twelfth-century Spanish philosopher Maimonides said, "Give a man a fish and you feed him for a day; teach a man to fish and you feed him for a lifetime."

Let's now examine the world of psychiatric medical practice so that we may better understand what the modality known as Soul Whispering has to offer in comparison.

Nita's Story

DIAGNOSIS VERSUS UNDERSTANDING
Learning the Difference

Psychiatry is a branch of medicine primarily focused on what are considered diseases of the brain. Under the rubrick of psychiatric illness you will find personality disorders, mood disorders, addictions, dementia disorders, and many more. These psychiatric illnesses are typically identified by aberrant behavior displayed by the "ill" person. Positing that these symptomatic behaviors are caused by brain disease, the majority of research in psychiatry is looking for ways to treat the brain. The treatments today consist of psychopharmacology, psychotherapy, and more invasive procedures such as electroconvulsive therapy (shocking the brain) and surgical lobotomy.

Since its inception, psychiatry has had its share of powerful critics who decry what they see as the reductionist aspects of psychiatry. Among them are R. D. Laing, M.D.; Thomas Szaaz, M.D.; Stan Grof, M.D.; and more recently Will Hall, MSW, and Michael Thompson, Ph.D., to name just a few. All have written on this topic and in a variety of ways have spoken to the complicated nature of human experience and the problems with diagnosing human problems and behavior. Grof, Hall, and Thompson share a theoretical position that much of what is diagnosed by psychiatry is actually a spiritual unfolding for that person. This view is shared by shamanism.

Early in my career after returning to America, I started to use diagnostic language while regularly working in psychiatric hospitals. My earliest training with R. D. Laing in London had discouraged the use of diagnosis but was trumped by my attempt to fit in with my colleagues upon my return to the United States. And I knew even as I fell into using diagnostic terms, they were metaphorical. The truth was, however, it was easier to talk with other professionals when I used that language. I soon learned that others did not see it this same way; rather, a paradigm that utilized diagnoses was a license to objectify the person being diagnosed.

In addition to this, the practice of diagnosing a patient in traditional clinical psychiatry is problematic for many reasons. One is that the vernacular associated with it has found its way into everyday language. Particularly prevalent are the terms *depression* and *anxiety*. These are diagnostic terms that create distance between people. One person is labeling and the other is receiving the label.

In defense of psychiatry, let's note that at least in the *Diagnostic and Statistical Manual of Mental Disorders* (DSM), both depression and anxiety have a long list of descriptions; they aren't static conditions. The vernacular use of these terms has added to the numbing effect of pathologizing authentic responses. For example, if you are having a bad day you might say, "I'm so depressed"; or nervousness before a job interview is articulated as "I am anxious." Authentic emotions are dismissed as *conditions*.

And when we label ourselves in this way, we are creating more division: in this case between our experience (soul) and our intellect. Again, my early training with R. D. Laing absolutely discredited the use of any label or diagnosis. The intent was to create authentic connection between everyone with no labels or roles (patient, therapist, or doctor). The result was that a rich range of human experiences was welcomed in a home setting where people lived together. In this setting, *some* expressions of emotional experiences were disturbing to *some* people. Demonstratively there were no clear-cut categories of experiences that were inherently disturbing versus inherently pleasant. One might be horrified by another's expression of anger, while another person might be horrified by someone's expression of joy. Conversely, anger might be welcome and joy rejected one day by the same person or groups of people. The practice was one of authentic responses to changing experiences.

Without diagnosis or categorizing experiences as sick, healthy, good, or bad, what remains is openness to emerging experiences collectively orchestrated by individuals in a group—never dull, always unpredictable. Saints sometimes define enlightenment as the experience of the world as ever new. Reality is ever new, in that we don't actually know what the next moment holds. We don't know what is going to happen next, but we predict it based on the past. We do the same with people. We assume what their next behavior will be based on their past actions. We often choose to assume that certain things are predictable—the sun will rise in the morning, for instance—in order to have structure and to simplify our lives. There's nothing wrong with these assumptions, as long as we stay conscious of the possibility that things won't necessarily happen the way we assume they will. We can't know until they happen. Being in the bliss of "ever new" means embracing and trusting the experience of not knowing.

Trusting the place of "not knowing" is the rub. Not knowing is often terrifying. Not simply because we don't know, but because we don't trust our own ability to be resilient. Authentic trust is not an assumption of a *positive* outcome but rather an acceptance of *any* outcome. *Non-attachment* to outcome is another way of saying it, yet it is a passive way. *Acceptance* is active and implies intentionality. Trust and acceptance are not innate. Babies clearly do not trust that they will be fed; they scream when hungry. Survival seems to depend on a lack of trust and a ferocious determination to demand that our needs be met.

Learning to trust the optimal unfolding of the universe is both a spiritual path and an emotional maturation process. This is not a naturally occurring process. Rather it is the work we embark on when we are on a spiritual path. There is no emergence of spirituality without also developing emotional maturity.

WE ALL CARRY A DIAGNOSIS

Given that we all carry a diagnosis according to the venacularization of pathological terms, assigning a diagnosis is not useful. At best it is meaningless; at worst it sentences people to objectification, as mentioned above. Harmless as this may seem, the reality is that labeling and diagnosing our authentic responses is a slippery slope that ends in attempts to fix through drugs, other treatments, or "self-medicating" with all kinds substances and behaviors.

The approach we teach is a shift to collaboration with their soul. The Soul Whisperer hears, sees, and observes on a multidimensional level. What is obvious to the Soul Whisperer may be obscure for another by their own unconscious blocks to authentic feelings and thoughts. With a grounding of acceptance and trust with an attitude of curiosity, the Soul Whisperer may elicit powerful information that points to the longings of the soul that is seeking expression.

Nita's Story
POWER ANIMALS AND SKEPTICISM

The time came when my life was disrupted by my soul longing for wholeness, manifesting as serious depression. When I found myself unable to get up and *do life* at all, the only thing I could think about was suicide. Yet somewhere deep inside me a light showed the way through. Through grace, I found my way to a workshop on healing into wholeness. There I met Linda Star Wolf. On one particular day of the workshop, she taught us how to discover our power animal. You can have a similar experience by listening to the "Creature Teacher Medicine Journey" audio track. I felt the rightness of reconnecting to a Native American tradition; however, my personality was cynical, and for the most part I resisted this exercise.

"Everyone lie down and get comfortable," Star Wolf instructed. "Close your eyes, and take long, slow breaths. You are going on a journey to meet your power animal." Native Americans teach that we all come into this incarnation energetically tethered to a particular animal—a protector, guide, and soul friend. This animal is with us whether we know it or believe it. Different from totems, the power animal never changes and is with us always. Often, we dream of or have a fondness for a particular creature. This may be our power animal.

Being a good girl was my goal, and I went to the workshop to melt my ice heart and find out how to be nicer and sweeter so that I would be happy. As I lay on the floor, I hoped my power animal would be a bunny or a hummingbird; yet, I knew this was not likely.

"Let the drumming take you," Star Wolf encouraged us as the music began and the energy began to build. "Follow the energy, and surrender to the journey. You will begin to see or sense or feel an animal presence. It may or may not be your power animal. Ask it, and if it isn't, let it go." Star Wolf's voice guided us, accompanied by the drumming, as we all let go into the trance of altered reality.

My ability to journey has been with me all of my life, yet until now I had always labeled it daydreaming and felt some self-criticism when I indulged my imaginal world. Although being given permission to drop into that luminous space was wonderful, I again resisted the notion of finding a power animal. Finally willing to try it, I quickly began to encounter animals in my expanded state of consciousness. First, I saw a bunny hopping through a beautiful field of poppies, and I asked, "Are you my power animal?"

"No, silly, I am just a bunny," it quipped.

Next, I found myself flying high above the fields. Noticing I was soaring with a gaggle of geese, again I inquired, hopefully, "Are you my power animals?"

"Oh, my dear, we are your guides to the land where you will find your power animal," they cooed.

The geese flew me to a rain forest, and I began to feel trepidation. What if my power animal was a snake or a crocodile? I didn't want that! Suddenly, I was plopped down in the middle of the jungle. Running toward me was a magnificent tiger. My heart pounded out of my chest, not for fear that it would hurt me, but rather because I knew the tiger was my power animal. I didn't have to ask her. It was evident that she was mine, and my personality was so disappointed. I wanted a *nice* animal, but instead I got a ferocious one. I feared I would cause destruction. Despite my trepidation, I reluctantly surrendered and accepted it into my heart.

"Slowly find yourself returning to ordinary reality," Star Wolf's voice faded into my consciousness. "Let the drumbeat bring you back now," she said as the journey began to come to a close.

Embarrassed and disappointed but accepting my fate of having a tiger for a power animal, I listened to Star Wolf's next instructions: "Go out for a walk now in the woods and open yourself to see your power animal or to have an experience with it in some way."

Right, I thought. *That will work for people whose power animal is an owl or a bunny or even a bear, but, clearly, I am not going to see a tiger in the woods of rural Georgia.* Nonetheless, I dutifully set out on my walk by myself in the woods. Rather quickly, I heard what sounded like a tiger's roar, and I looked over and saw cows grazing the field. They looked quite frightened to me. Being the rational being I am, it immediately occurred to me that I was still altered and had heard what I thought was a roar because I was tuned in to my imaginal tiger. Actually, I felt quite pleased with myself. I had conjured up a tiger and even heard it! "Aren't I the shamanic one?" I said out loud to the cows.

With that, I sat down to write in my journal and drew a rough picture of a tiger, which looked more like a cow. The experience was very satisfying to me, and I felt a sense of lightness and release. I went back to my room, sensing that I had completed my task and gained the imaginal sense of a power animal. That felt great.

More was to be revealed.

That evening we had a sharing circle to talk about our power animal experiences. Jacquie Small was the therapist of the circle. My position in the room dictated that I would speak last, so I was proudly waiting my turn to report my experience. Halfway around the circle, one woman shared her experience. "My power animal is a bear," she began. "I was sitting deep in the woods by myself hoping to see a bear, when a group of horseback riders passed by me. The leader stopped and said, 'Miss, you shouldn't be sitting out here alone. Didn't you hear that a circus was passing through town, and a tiger escaped and is roaming these woods?'"

The group gasped, and Jacquie said, "Yes, I heard that happened."

At that moment, the room seemed to turn dark. I felt a seismic shift, and I was consumed by fear. I jumped up and started to leave the room. As I did, I said to the group in my panicked state, "Oh, my god! I am out of here! You people are involved in black magic. I imagined a tiger, and now it has become real, and it is going to kill someone."

Normally quite rational and grounded, I found myself in a fugue-like state of panic and rage. I was going to be the cause of someone's death. Why was I mixed up in this workshop?

I was determined to leave, but Jacquie said, in her elegant, calm, and wise voice, "Nita, I see that you are terrified, and I want you to listen to me." After a short pause, she continued. "What you are experiencing is deep *synchronicity*. You did not cause that tiger to escape. It is simply a synchronicity, no more significant than if you had found a toy stuffed tiger in the gift shop after our experience." She reached out to me and took my hand.

The combination of her touch along with her calm and compassionate attention to me dropped me out of my panic long enough for me to regain a sense of rationality. She was whispering to my soul. I stared at her for a moment and then fully grasped, of course, that what she was saying was true. The events as they unfolded for me had done so with a simple synchronicity.

But what a powerful synchronistic event for me! What are the odds of a tiger escaping into the woods precisely where I was, immediately after a journey to find my power animal—a tiger? Yet, the truth of it was undeniable. Synchronicity is a spiritual event happening at a human level. Like déjà vu, it is rationally explicable, yet there was a deeper purpose to my insight.

I sat back down, and the sharing circle continued. I felt puzzled in my newly regained rational state. *What was that about? Why did I have such a deep reaction of fear?* I wondered to myself. I sensed that something in me was up for healing—something was trying to break through to my conscious mind—and the synchronicity of the tiger event was the catalyst. Being open to a deeper meaning rather than dismissing it as happenstance, I sat with a keenly receptive heart and mind, allowing spirit to show me what it was trying to heal. Despite some inner resistance, some overriding force had brought me to the workshop that day, and I was determined to see the experience through.

Sitting in that circle, being held in safety, and guided by Soul Whisperers around me, a remarkable thing occurred: All at once it was as though the ceiling of the room opened to the starry sky. I could see the beyond and felt a connection to the universe and all that *is*. Out of the dark, starry sky, words began to form from the bright stars, flowing down through the night for me to see.

The words were as follows: "You did not conjure the tiger. It was simply a synchronicity, and here is the real truth: You did not kill your mother. She died, and it was a synchronicity too that your father always told you that you were killing her." These were simple, profound, and healing words that my soul needed. Floods of repressed grief washed over me, and I wept as though my mother had just died. Held by the group energy, I cried and released years of grief that had lived underneath my well-constructed barrier of shame.

I did not kill my mother. I *lost* my mother. I needed to grieve that loss. My soul had brought me there, knowing that this unresolved issue deep within me needed to be healed. My conscious mind had repressed all of it in a form of survival that had only put a Band-Aid on the issue. I told my small group what had just happened and what I now understood. At that point Jacquie again took my hand, looked in my eyes, and said, "Well done, my dear, you have healed that piece now."

Her words grounded the experience and helped it land fully into my being.

A piece of my soul came back that night and has remained with me ever since. I let go of feeling depressed, and I embraced my grief. The power animal brought that piece home to me, healing the layers of fear and shame. When we are on the right path, it will be marked with synchronicities all around us.

Pay attention. Spirit is waiting to whisper to us at every moment.

The authors both followed an unconventional path of training as has been revealed throughout this book. Both of them stumbled into the field of psychotherapy somewhat unintentionally while on a path of self-discovery. Nita was initially taken by the political and philosophical allure of R. D. Laing's work. She went to London to learn more about social revolution and discovered her own longings for wholeness. Star Wolf was specializing in the fields of mental health and addiction while also following a deep inner calling to acquire more knowledge to enhance her skills as a counselor. This culminated in a series of synchronistic events that brought a path of self-discovery and shamanic consciousness to her full embrace.

Part of the wonder of Star Wolf's path was in finding the women who would act as mentors for her on her own journey as a healing arts practitioner. In an earlier chapter we discussed Star Wolf's fateful encounter with healer Jacquelyn Small. As well, we mentioned her connection with Grandmother Twylah Nitsch. Next she will elaborate on her meeting with Jacquelyn, and we will also be introduced to another seminal person on Star Wolf's transformational path, Alice Miller.

Star Wolf's Story
REMARKABLE WOMEN AND THEIR IMPACT ON MY WORK

Kindred Spirit Jacquelyn Small

During the 1970s, when I was training to be a counselor, I was probably trained the way most psychotherapists were trained, and that was to keep a strong boundary between patient and therapist. Later on as I worked in the mental health system, as previously noted, we stopped calling people "patients" and began calling them "clients" in an attempt to form a partnership and collaboration with the person. But it made little difference what we called the people who came to us for help. The main objective was to listen, evaluate, and diagnose. With the rise of easily accessible psychotropic medications, diagnosing became the arbiter of which medications the psychiatrist should and did prescribe.

My own background consisted primarily of working initially with those diagnosed as chronic mentally ill. These were individuals who were diagnosed with chronic mental conditions such as schizophrenia, bipolar disease, major depressive disorders, anxiety, and personality disorders. The vogue treatment during that time was medication and behavior modification. These were the tools of the trade to bring people into some sort of maintenance to control their mental illness.

As time went on I began to work with other types of populations, such as women and men who had been sexually abused. As well, I ran groups for those diagnosed with chronic depression and anxiety. Eventually I entered the addictions field, specializing in working with alcoholism, drug dependency, and codependency. Later I worked with adult children of alcoholics and other dysfunctional family systems. With each group, the basic protocol was to interview, listen, diagnose, and offer a treatment plan. This often consisted of the prescribing of medication and developing strategies to change the behavior through goal setting or other types of cognitive behavior modification therapies.

Right from the beginning I strayed from the rules. Perhaps it was because of my own difficulties with fitting in to mainstream society or because I had been a hippie or knowing that I too suffered from anxiety and was medicating with alcohol through most of that time myself. As I stated in other chapters I went on to recover from addiction. I did my own personal healing work and discovered new types of integrative therapies that addressed body, mind, and spirit. Therefore it was natural for me to want to share these things with my clients. From the beginning I talked to my clients about my own struggles but kept these matters from other clinicians, knowing that what I told them would no doubt be frowned upon.

I found it difficult not to be more personal or to be totally objective. I found myself hugging my clients when they'd come into the office. I also couldn't help holding their hands and discussing things outside the realm of what was usually acceptable, such as spiritual experiences. I asked them about their relationship to a god of their understanding. Ironically, even though I was young and perhaps not as sophisticated as some of my colleagues, my track record in working with various populations of all kinds was quite good. As noted earlier, people seemed to get better and made great changes with my unconventional methods. This did not go unnoticed by the directors of the clinic treatment centers. I was promoted and given greater roles within the system.

I mentioned my initial meeting with Jacquelyn Small briefly in the previous chapter but want to take the opportunity here to detail it, because it was a highly significant event in my life. In 1980, I had the opportunity to go to a drug and alcohol conference, which is where I met Jacquelyn for the first time. In meeting her, I had finally found another therapist who felt like a kindred spirit!

I'll never forget, in a large conference room with perhaps five hundred people, when she came up onto the stage. While the other presenters had been somewhat interesting but rather dry, Jacquie marched up onto the stage and proceeded to ring Tibetan bells and tell us all to close our eyes. She then proceeded to take us on a guided journey, with the music of Tibetan monks chanting in the background. This created a powerful altered state for me through music that I'd never heard before. Immediately, I felt very altered and nervous. It was a state of consciousness that I had tried to avoid, afraid that I would lose control.

Next Jacquie had us imagine a problem that we were experiencing in our personal lives—imagine that, therapists having problems of their own!—and to assign that problem an image or a symbol. She then had us imagine the most positive outcome around that problem and give *it* a symbol. Then she asked us to imagine a triangle and on the left side, assign this same problem to it; on the right side the most favorable solution. Next we were to gradually have those two symbols rise slowly to the top of the triangle until they merged to create a third symbol. From that third symbol she asked us to then see the solution to the problem. I remember being amazed that I had the answer to something I was struggling with at the time.

When the presentation ended, I waited until everyone had left and Jacquie was signing books onstage. I wanted to be the last person to walk past her so that perhaps I could speak to her for a few moments. She had written a small book called *Becoming Naturally Therapeutic: A Return to the True Essence of Helping,* and it was written for all counselors but specifically for addictions professionals. In that little book she spoke about the qualities of a naturally therapeutic counselor. As I glanced through the book I was amazed to see that many of the things she spoke about were exactly how I treated my clients. And I was very excited that this amazing woman traveled on the same wavelength as I did in relating to others who were suffering.

She'd been noticing me waiting to speak to her. As I walked toward her, she put her arms out to me, hugged me, and said, "Hello, kindred spirit."

I burst into tears. It is quite likely that without this synchronistic moment, I would not be where I am today, writing this chapter. Even though Jacquie was obviously at that time light-years away from where I was in my understanding of certain things, she saw who I was and held that for me. She thus gave me the courage to be more authentic and less apologetic for loving others in assisting them as a kindred spirit on their journey.

Years later, I met Nita under similar circumstances, only at that time I was the teacher and Nita the student. What unfolded was initially a deep healing experience for Nita, and later a bonded friendship and working relationship that has been enduring for both of us. Having experienced a similar collaborative friendship with Jacquelyn, who was a Soul Whisperer to me, I paid forward this same dynamic to Nita.

Over the years as I studied with Jacquelyn Small and her organization, the Eupsychia Institute, I continued to do my own personal healing and transformational work. I slowly began to really understand that my own healing was the teaching and lessons that I most needed, both for myself and to best assist others.

It's always worth remembering that no one person has a monopoly on spiritual wisdom; it's in each of us. If you are called to Soul Whispering, you are privileged to share your personal healing and transformation with another person by being present for them. Their journey is unique. You are only the teacher insofar as you reflect possibilities of personal transformation to them. It is a profound privilege and responsibility to witness and be the supporter of another's transformative experience.

The Formative Influence of Alice Miller and Her Foundational Theory of Wounding

Maturing physically is no guarantee of emotional or spiritual maturation. Trauma is arrested emotional development while the physical body continues to develop. Childhood mistreatment often results in a deep emotional disturbance, creating an internally frozen state. Mistreatment is defined by the person receiving it, not the person delivering it. Parents do many things out of love or for the child's own good that in fact are wounding. As children we adapt to the wounds of childhood through denial. We deny our feelings in order to survive, and then we repress the feelings and forget.

Alice Miller is a psychoanalyst who specialized in childhood wounding and how we unconsciously carry these wounds into adulthood. She puts forward the concept that, overall, we tend to idealize our parents, thus keeping ourselves locked in our false personas in order to protect ourselves and our parents from the truth of their negative behavior with us. Alice Miller's books detail this foundational premise.

Soul Whispering is the process by which, among other things, we deconstruct this false persona that we have constructed in the process of discovering who we really are on the soul level. I thus encourage anyone and everyone who is interested in the practice of Soul Whispering to read Alice's books, for they are pertinent to spiritual seekers who are on their path, as well as those of us who are professional spiritual facilitators in some form or fashion, and/or anyone who is in training to be a spiritual practitioner or facilitator. Particularly for working professionals or those in training to be professionals, Alice's books may be a tough read if you have not already discovered that you may well have gone into the healing arts to heal your own wounds. If you do not know that you *have* wounds, it's an even tougher read! Yet, despite this, it remains a *must-read* for anyone in the profession of working with others on a soul level.

In her books, Alice Miller explains how uncovering our personal truth is painful and so it's avoided, yet it is the only way to become whole and awake. The road to emotional maturity or emotional intelligence is a journey of rigorous and honest self-awareness. Not for the faint of heart, it requires that we bring to light the buried enigmatic whisperings from our denied soul truths. While challenging, this journey is quite possible for anyone willing to embark upon it. And although Alice Miller's work thematically involves the subject of childhood wounding, she did not, in her work, develop this further to include the concept of the wounded healer, which is what many shamanic practitioners and Soul Whisperers may be referred to. Thus I have made that connection here for the reader. In so doing, I want to underscore that the wounds we are seeking to heal through helping others can become *our* greatest gifts if brought to our conscious awareness.

We have heard from people we work with over the years how their journeys of self-discovery led them to be able to go on to assist others as Soul Whisperers. The story below is a typical, and particularly poignant, example of this. Laura Wolf is a gifted Soul Whisperer and an advanced student of Star Wolf's. She tells her own story of transformation—her path to awakening and stepping up to assist others—below.

My Life Did Not Always Look This Way

Laura Wolf

Today, I love my life as a transformational life coach and shamanic guide. I feel very blessed that I get to help people heal the trauma of the past and learn to unconditionally love themselves in the present. My life did not always look this way.

Before stumbling onto Shamanic Breathwork ten years ago, I struggled with depression, anxiety, and a sense of being overwhelmed on a regular basis. Driven by my desperation to feel loved, I chronically created dysfunctional, codependent relationships with unavailable men. I was afraid to speak my truth and didn't know how to ask for what I wanted. I hid out in unfulfilling jobs, because I didn't feel worthy of doing what I loved or of having abundance in my life. I thought I was broken.

At that time I had no idea how to love myself or how to offer a generous connection that wasn't desperate or needy. I also did not know how to tap in to the infinite wisdom of my soul or how to discover my sacred purpose. That all began to change when I first experienced Shamanic Breathwork.

At my first Shamanic Breathwork journey at Venus Rising, my inner child appeared as a frightened toddler who felt very alone and lost. This part of me just wanted to be loved, held, rocked, and protected. I reclaimed that very young aspect of me that day and committed to caring for her and loving her in whatever ways she needed.

I experienced a lot of abandonment as a child. My mother suffered from depression, anxiety, physical health challenges, psychotic episodes, and alcoholism. When her inner turmoil became more than she could bear, she would check herself into a hospital or drive ten hours to Chicago so that her mother could take care of her, leaving us kids at home with my father for months at a time. Dad escaped into work and was seldom home. Like much of the latchkey generation, I raised myself. I felt alone throughout my childhood and carried that feeling well into adulthood.

Through Shamanic Breathwork, I began to heal the abandonment of the past. By actively allowing my inner child and inner adolescent to feel all the stored up feelings of hurt, anger, loneliness, and disappointment, I gradually released layer upon layer of the old, toxic energy that had been trapped in my body for years. I believe that repressed energy is what caused the severe depression and anxiety I experienced throughout my twenties.

Through the Shamanic Healing Initiatory Process (SHIP)* I also learned about the concept of the inner beloved—a loving presence that could hold me, reassure me, and always be there for me in a way that no human had ever been there for me. During that time, I broke up with the unavailable man I had been dating and went into a period of intense grief. I cried hard every day—but because of SHIP, I now knew that the grief pouring through me had something to do with the much deeper well of grief related to my family of origin and to every breakup I had ever gone through.

This was the first time that I had any such awareness. In prior breakups, when I felt intense grief, I believed that the solution was to try to get the man back. If only I could get him to see how perfect we were for each other, then everything would be fine. This time, as I grieved, I called upon my inner beloved to hold me at night, stroke my hair, and comfort

---

*SHIP is a highly experiential program developed by Venus Rising Association for Transformation for individuals who wish to awaken the shaman within. SHIP utilizes many shamanic rituals and tools to support students on their personal and collective journeys.

me—and it worked! I felt comforted. I felt held and loved. I didn't need to try to get him back. This experience changed my life.

Around this same time, Star Wolf began teaching me about chakras and the purpose of each chakra. I'll never forget the day that she said sexual energy and creative energy both emanate from the second chakra. They are essentially the same energy, or chi, just channeled in different ways. Some people have shut down their second chakra energy due to early sexual wounding. When this happens, creativity often gets shut down at the same time. At the other extreme, some people channel all of their second chakra energy into their sexuality and have little left over to channel into their creativity or life purpose. She must have been talking to me, because I suddenly realized that I had been sending out sexual energy from my second chakra all my life in desperate attempts to get love and approval.

When I first realized this, I felt intense shame. I made a commitment to learn how to contain my second chakra energy instead of letting it run rampant all the time. This was much harder than I anticipated! I had been seeking attention with my second chakra energy for so long that I had no clue how to hold my energy in my own body and not go flouncing it all over the place. I practiced and practiced holding my own energy and felt frustrated and embarrassed when I would suddenly realize, Oh, shit! I just did it again. I just energetically bounced my energy toward that guy without really even meaning to!

It took me about a year to really trust that I could contain my own energy and not unconsciously use it to seek attention. Now please understand me—I am not saying that there is anything wrong with second chakra energy or with flirting or with using that energy to connect and play. The problem for me was that I bounced that energy around unconsciously, compulsively, all the time. I was so busy using my second chakra energy to seek attention that I didn't have any energy left to be creative in other areas of my life. I usually had about four part-time jobs, which brought in no real money. I felt anxious, stressed, and exhausted all the time. It wasn't until I stopped incessantly seeking attention and consciously focused on channeling my life-force energy into my own creative projects that I began to experience more stability and fulfillment in my life.

While doing all that inner child, beloved, and chakra work, I began to receive many visions in my breathwork journeys about who I really was and my sacred purpose. My visions showed me as a priestess or medicine woman in many lifetimes, which is my calling and destiny in this lifetime as well. In one particular journey, I saw a post-apocalyptic scenario in which I walked among terrified and traumatized people, helping them to release their fear and connect to their understanding of God so that they could summon the courage to go on with their lives.

This is essentially what I do today. We aren't exactly living in a post-apocalyptic world—at least here in the United States—but we do live in an incredibly stressful world. Many people on our planet are suffering from depression, anxiety, being overwhelmed, disconnection from themselves, and feeling separated from God. I am blessed to have the opportunity to support people in healing the hurts of the past, releasing the pent-up stress and fears held in the body, learning to truly love and trust themselves, deepen their spiritual connection, and discover their sacred purpose.

I am so grateful to have stumbled into Shamanic Breathwork when I did. The shamanic-psychospiritual path helped me shift from feeling depressed, anxious, broke, lost, and miserable to feeling happy, whole, and loving my life. I learned how to heal the past, love myself, channel my energy into the creation of my dreams, and live my sacred purpose. I am incredibly grateful to Star Wolf for the foundation and mentorship she gave me, which supported me in becoming the woman I am today.

GUIDES FOR THE JOURNEY

As demonstrated in Laura's story, Soul Whispering is a practice of serving others in their journey toward wholeness and transformation. It is not a practice of fixing someone or treating them, which implies a superior/inferior relationship. Instead, it is a relationship between equals who are meeting each other for a purpose. It is a relationship in which one person holds space for the other to dive deeply into their journey of self-discovery. For a healer to be effective they must first take care of their own emotional, physical, mental, and spiritual needs and show up with compassion, not pity, for the people who seek their support.

Mariko is a true Soul Whisperer living in Sedona, Arizona. She is the founder of Living Breath of Venus Rising, a global community dedicated to peace within and peace upon the planet, serving as an anchor for personal and planetary growth and evolution. In the story that follows, Mariko shows how paying attention to her own and others' Soul Whisperings led her to her path of fulfillment.

Living Breath and the Dream

Mariko Yamamoto

Around age two, my path presented the initiatory journey of great change and adjustment when my father, who was my anchor in this world, became a fugitive to life, carrying unbearable shame upon his heavy shoulders and an empty void that could never be filled. He made promises to show up, which he could never keep, then disappeared from the face of this earth. As I forever wondered if he was dead or alive, he ended up dying alone.

This original wounding lay dormant within me, yet showed up in my teens in underlying grief, feelings of unworthiness, suicidal thoughts, and disassociation from others to protect my heart from being wide open and broken. I remained painfully quiet, afraid of life, and ashamed to take up space. This generated a relentless soul search, and my senses were hyperalert and hyperaware.

In the very core of my being, there remained a longing and distinct feeling that "one day, I will return 'home,'" not really knowing what that meant or how that would look. This inner sense became my soul compass, which, twenty-eight years later, would lead me on a solo journey to the Hopi villages. When I first arrived atop the mesa, a Hopi grandmother waved to me and invited me into her ancient earthen abode. Her first words were simply, "Welcome home!" My knees buckled, and I wept. Her soulful eyes looked straight into me as she placed her hand upon my shoulder and whispered, "I know." From this silent, windblown plateau of sacred ground, overlooking infinite sky and multicolor desert, I knelt with my heart wide open and sent prayers of peace out to the world—to the land, the waters, the trees, the animals, and all peoples—which felt like a familiar love song resounding in my bones. Had I been to this place before, or was it my future self peering through the present, or both? An ancient future of a distant past. . . . Years later, my beloved medicine teacher, Star Wolf, granddaughter of Seneca Wolf Clan Elder, Grandmother Twylah Nitsch, would give me my spirit name, "Peace Wolf."

I came to the conclusion that the past and future were not so linear and separate from this moment but rather somehow dancing and woven into this very present. This seemed normal, yet I felt like a stranger in a strange land. I asked, "God, what is the purpose of being shown these things?" Not really expecting an answer, I touched into a knowing that someday perhaps the deeper meaning would be revealed. In college, these Soul Whisperings would propel me to attend personal growth seminars and workshops to stay in an atmosphere of remembrance, to learn and grow while juggling school, relationships, family, and work life. For many years I even worked in my dream career, the wild dimension of broadcasting. Having grown up in front of the TV screen, it looked to be quite fun and fulfilling. Even being told that it was mission impossible to find an entry point into this field, following a course of inner Soul Whisperings opened the doors. I dedicated myself to the work and simultaneously dove into the holistic, shamanic, energy, and consciousness fields.

Though my inner life was rich in many ways, and my outer life appeared like the ideal movie script—with the perfect job, partner, and place to live—there was a storm of unrest and emptiness brewing beneath the surface. Waves of depression, separation, heartache, and unresolved emotions crashed upon the barren land. There was a sense that I needed to deal with things that were much deeper than what I was consciously aware of, things that were keeping me from fulfilling my true purpose. My soul hungered and longed. I did know that some of what I was looking for included contributing to lives in a way that made a profound difference, opening the heart of compassion and living a life full of meaning. Yet for this to occur a major breakthrough needed to happen.

I searched, read, meditated, participated in retreat and healing programs, and apprenticed with teachers from a full spectrum of spiritual *backgrounds, many of which were of Native American tradition, which I felt deeply connected to. It was not until I was first introduced to the power of the breath in the 1980s, while working with a medicine woman and wisdomkeeper, as well as diving into a type of breathwork known as Rebirthing during that time, that I had a groundbreaking experience. Diving deep into the ocean of the breath was the key that would instantly propel me through multidimensional doorways into new frontiers of self-awareness and the familiar, dreamlike landscape of transcendent wisdom and healing states. The terrain was infinite, including healing original birth traumas and old imprints carried forward from childhood wounds and soul contracts, shining light into unconscious decisions and beliefs that had been impacting my entire life. In these eternal moments, new perceptions and life-enhancing choices were made possible and miraculously birthed into being. During a two-year period I experienced more than fifty powerful breathwork journeys, some of them on land and some in the water, which activated an accelerated path of growth and awakening and opening to Soul Whisperings.*

Fast-forward thirty years. During a critical initiation of facing the death of loved ones, a strained and deteriorating marriage, and the death in my arms of my most loyal four-legged companion and best friend, life took a turn, unraveling to the point of hopelessness and despair. It took all I had to remember what I carried in my rainbow medicine bag of years of healing tools and modalities. At that divine intersection point Linda Star Wolf and her beloved Brad Collins were to offer a Shamanic Breathwork weekend in Sedona, where I reside. Shamanic Breathwork works with the pure power of the breath, evocative chakra-attuned music, art, and group process within ceremonial space. Within this sacred journey one can access perfect sacred medicine.

Learning of this, the Soul Whisperings turned to Soul Thunders, and every ounce of my being knew to dive heart, mind, body, and soul into the living sacred waters of this experience. I discovered this to be an entirely new octave of being with the breath, allowing me to reach new depths, states, and heights of dancing with Spirit. The beauty was that in partnering with Great Mystery one does not have to know or have all the answers. Phew! *Just answering the call by showing up and breathing seemed to be more* than enough. The breath—being nondenominational and a God-given inheritance to every one of us—has a way of magically drumming forth the perfect and miraculous medicine for each soul, regardless of age, creed, color, gender, or belief system.

Through the sacred ally of the breath, Spirit would guide me within this first journey and all those to follow. The whos, whats, whens, wheres, whys, and hows would be "downloaded," often in a holy instant and sometimes all at once, not only releasing and clearing the old and returning soul parts but also activating sacred purpose and destiny. Soul Whisperings through the power of the Shamanic Breathwork journey are a conscious tool for direct soul access and experience, one of the most powerful vehicles for transformation that I have ever experienced. Nothing less than everything changed!

There came the recognition that this was my life's work—not only for my own access to the depths of Soul Whisperings and transformational journey but also for potentially being a vehicle for others to receive direct access to their eternal Soul Whisperings and infinite wisdom and to be supported in living their truth, vision, and sacred purpose. I went through the accelerated SHIP (Shamanic Healing Initiatory Process) program with Linda Star Wolf and Brad Collins at Venus Rising. I apprenticed, master apprenticed, and became a master Shamanic Breathwork facilitator and ordained shamanic minister.

I feel a return home to a life that nourishes, supports, awakens, and celebrates our spirit and humanity. I am grateful for the opportunity to live the dream and walk with integrity, dignity, love, and wisdom with, through, and between the worlds.

As Mariko's and others' stories throughout this book will show, Soul Whisperers are guides along the journey. We are not Sherpas. We will not carry your bags or protect you from discomfort. We will, however, nudge you in the direction of discovery, encourage you to traverse this territory as many have before you, help you build your own cocoon for transformation, guard the cocoon until you are ready to emerge, and celebrate your transformation with you!

4

Steps in the Journey of Becoming a Soul Whisperer

Becoming a Soul Whisperer is far more complex than training to be a psychotherapist or counselor. Becoming a Soul Whisperer first and most importantly is a calling. The path chooses you, and if you respond to the call it means embodying spirit and developing a deep connection to your soulful purpose. Second, it is a path of training that is a spiral; as you dive into your own discoveries, you will learn from masterful people if you remain humble and teachable.

Soul Whisperers come from a variety of backgrounds. They are poets, soldiers, mothers, fathers, ministers, psychiatrists, nurses, teachers, dancers, singers, farmers, builders, and many more diverse professions as well as young people just starting their path of work in the world. They are people who know in their hearts that they are drawn to a path of authentic connection and service to soul purpose in themselves and others. The path requires shining the light on all that is painful in yourself to heal and transform. Equally demanding is the requirement to embrace your gifts and step in to your authentic power and let go of limitations. And with this power comes responsibility for your thoughts, feelings, and actions as you serve others from a place of authentic altruism. It is not for the faint of heart. It requires bravery and trust in the unknown as you accompany and hold space for people traversing their own darkness to find their way to their light.

PUTTING YOUR PERSONALITY IN PERSPECTIVE

To authentically assist others in a way that is enhancing to their transformation, we must first understand that who we take ourselves to be is actually a false persona developed from childhood wounds and reaction formations. Specifically, our personality is anything *but* personal as it is a map of reactions to our adverse childhood situations learned from other people.

The personality is known by other names—ego and superego—and may be mistaken for our conscience. It is cunning, sneaky, and tricks us into thinking it is our true higher self. Its job is to keep us in our comfort zone and maintain the status quo. Robotic in its mission, it does not differentiate between positive or negative change. Therefore, when we attempt to step out of its domain to follow our soul calling, the alarm bells go off and its defenses rear their ugly heads to pull us back into a set of reactions that are familiar, albeit dysfunctional, in the present.

The right-hand supporter of the personality, his henchman, is our dark, critical voice—the personal critic. The personality uses the personal critic to do its dirty work of filling the mind with negative judgments about what you are doing or even just who you are. "You can't do anything right—you are a bad person; give up now. Who do you think you are, anyway?" says the personal critic.

The personality steps in to assuage the sting of the personal critic, at times by over-flattering you and seducing you to listen to its guidance. "Of course you are not a bad person; you are very, very good. Just keep doing good things and you will be safe," it will say.

Seductive messages are soothing and meant to keep us from trying something new or taking a risk. And if its warnings go unheeded, it will even create great pain at times to deter us from following our soul voice. Like an abusive lover, it attempts to segregate us from others through shame and threats. The personality advises us not to discuss our desires, longings, or dreams with friends, saying they will think we are stupid. The personal critic mocks us and dares us to step out of our safe zone and then trips us on the way out the door, saying, "See, it's dangerous to try something new."

Depending on the degree of our conditioning and our childhood wounds, we may give more credence to one of these voices, but both are false. Our soul voice is neither critical nor seductive; it is supportive, loving, and grounded in truth. It is a sober voice gently guiding us to make choices that will lead us to expansion rather than contraction. If we have spent a lifetime being guided by the personal critic and the personality, moving out of this container is not easy. It requires that we shift our perspective, and it can mean leaving behind friends, places, and jobs.

The personality is often pulling our life in the opposite direction from where our soul is calling us to go. You can begin to distinguish between the voices of the personality/critic and soul by the quality of the messages you receive. Here are some of the differences between the personality and the soul.

- The personality is urgent, demanding, and critical.
- The soul is patient, compelling, and supportive.
- The personality doesn't want us to be conscious of our belief system or wounds. It wants us to keep things hidden, particularly the truth.
- The soul wants everything out in the open; it loves the truth.
- The personality tells us to mistrust the soul's urgings and avoid self-examination.
- The soul loves us through self-examination and even reveals painful memories to help us heal.

A Soul Whisperer knows when the directives of the personality and critic are active and dominating a person. The Soul Whisperer finds ways to speak and listen directly and recognizes the authentic soul voice. It is utterly normal to be afraid to even look at our beliefs, let alone do something that runs counter to them. So, a Soul Whisperer teaches and acts to role model how to be compassionate and gentle with yourself. You can quiet the voices of the personal critic and personality, but you may find yourself needing or wanting support and encouragement from one who knows the pitfalls and signs on the path.

Recognizing and neutralizing the personal critic and personality is the path to hearing your soul's voice, the voice that will lead you out of the darkness and into the light of your true purpose. Unless you bring these false voices to consciousness you cannot know when they are speaking to you, and you will remain a prisoner to their power.

BEING PRESENT FOR YOURSELF

Being present for yourself means that you take care of you first and listen to your inner guide about what you need, then face your pain and embrace it as your medicine. Some Native Americans define *medicine* as anything that contributes to your healing and wholeness. Pain, be it emotional or physical, is a great teacher and not a sign of weakness. Knowing yourself fully means that you take the good, the bad, and the ugly, and love yourself till death do you part.

Before you can be truly present for another, you must first commit to bringing your inner truth forward so that it is mirrored in your outer world and there is a clear reflection between your soul and the person you are in the outer world. Clearing the obstacles discussed below will ready you for this sacred marriage of your soul and your life path as it evolves.

A Soul Whisperer will help you listen to your own Soul Whisperings and encourage you in:

- Looking at yourself with radical honesty, fierce compassion, and tough love
- Seeing and letting go of beliefs that fuel harmful habitual ways of being

For some, this means:

- Facing buried memories of childhood trauma
- Facing addiction

Soul Whisperers know how to have a relationship with their personal inner truth. Like the stalking practice of shamans, Soul Whispering requires:

- Intention
- Practice
- Attention
- Action

Intention

Intention says you are willing. You may be fearful about looking more deeply at yourself, and that is understandable. Simple willingness sets intention, which ignites the process. The practice of listening to your inner truth can be done daily and may also require taking time out for retreat, away from your daily routine, to kick-start the process. Daily practice develops the ability to pay attention to what is true for you right now. Action follows naturally when we set intention, practice paying attention, and live in the present no matter what is going on around us in the moment.

Setting an intention that we are willing to face and discover our deepest truth is a commitment that should not be taken lightly. When we make this commitment we give permission to our soul, our higher self, to take charge and move us along a path of self-discovery. It's not a path that someone else has smoothed out for us. Much of it will be bushwhacking as we embark on a new adventure into the unknown of our psyche. "If you know where you are going, it ain't nowhere new!" said Seneca Wolf Clan Grandmother Twylah Nitsch when others complained that they were afraid of the unknown.

Practice

Practice is the daily work of self-examination, connection to your soul messages, communication with nature and nature spirits, and practicing forgiveness and compassion. Soul Whisperers develop the muscles of curiosity, stillness, and centered beingness.

Attention

The attention to be effective and potent in your life requires practice. We are all distracted and distractible. We constantly and often unconsciously seek to not look at difficult or painful emotions and memories. Shamans engage in practice called "stalking," which is the process of the sacred witness seeking out those aspects of consciousness that need to be transmuted to higher levels of awareness. The stalking aspect of the psyche is sometimes called "the double" or "the spiritual warrior." One of its roles is to seek out undeveloped, shadowy, and ill-formed aspects of personality.

Action

Action following the voice, once you hear it, will strengthen your action. Imagine if you went to a teacher, guru, or AA sponsor and asked for and received helpful guidance yet never followed through with taking the steps required. Soon your support team would lose interest in giving you guidance that you clearly had no real intention of taking into consideration or following. So too our soul voice will give up after a period of time and retreat into silence if we don't act on its guidance with sincerity, commitment, and clarity.

LIVING CONSCIOUSLY IS A PRACTICE

Most people have not lived a life of listening, believing, or following their own Soul Whisperer or inner truth. The inner truth, or intuition, guides a mother to run upstairs for no apparent reason to find her two-year-old about to fall out a window. But outside of extreme moments, the inner truth, the knowing, is often ignored. Early life experiences often teach us to deny our inner truth.

We become co-opted by the norms of behavior taught to us by parents and society. Maturation does require a certain amount of conforming to social expectations, yet social norms are also often repressive and destructive. Being alive is a continual spiritual practice if you allow that we are here for a reason. We don't know the reason for life. Though there are endless theories, it is all speculation. Simply accepting that there is a reason is a powerful surrender to seeing life as an adventure, a journey, and an opportunity. Curiosity replaces fear; wonder replaces worry; and self-compassion replaces regret.

We are familiar with the notion of meditation or yoga being a practice; however, living consciously also requires practice. Spiritual traditions teach the importance of disciplined practices. You can also practice conscious awareness. Just as there are specific poses, or asanas, in yoga, there are poses you can practice in life. As you make these practices routine, like brushing your teeth, you will experience a deeper and more satisfying life.

Practice Presence

Practice keeping your focus on the present moment, free of worry (focusing on the future) or regret (focusing on the past). Catch yourself worrying or regretting and bring your attention back to something in the moment to engage fully in the present. It could something as simple as your breathing. Regardless of what else is going on, focusing on your breathing will not only get your focus off the past or future but also has the added benefit of shifting and releasing stress hormones and clearing your emotions and your thoughts. Then you can also focus on what is happening in the moment with greater ease.

Practice Forgiveness

Start to practice forgiving self and others as a daily exercise. This is not the cheap forgiveness that is easily given yet carries hidden resentment and vindictiveness. Practice consciously trying on forgiveness, and notice your actual emotional reaction. If you imagine forgiving someone who has harmed you, and you feel anger as a result, explore that further by fully going into the anger and rage.

Practice Healthy Expressions of Anger

When you allow yourself to fully express and embrace your anger and rage you have a better chance of moving through it. The same applies to self-forgiveness.

Practice Accepting Pain and Suffering as Part of Life

Embrace the really bad times in life by recognizing that pain and suffering are a normal part of life. When we compound the pain and suffering with beliefs that create more stress, we are exacerbating the problem. Blame, resentment, and self-pity are some examples of exacerbating the problem. Self-love and self-compassion give us a soothing response and accelerate healing.

Practice Self-Compassion

We are all flawed and stumbling through life, and most of the time the transgressions or mistakes we make are not intentional. Even when you do act out of anger or vindictiveness it is not you, it your false personality. There is always room for reflection and curiosity about your own behavior. Blaming ourselves on top of the suffering keeps us stuck in the suffering. Physiologically, blaming creates brain grooves that lock in the experience. You can remember the transgression and learn from it, and at the same time let it go. Give yourself the same loving touch and attention that you would a child who is hurt.

Practice Gratitude

Take time to focus on gratitude and make "thank you" your mantra and "I feel grateful" your affirmation. Again, physiologically, gratitude releases stress, improves heart rate, and strengthens your immune system. Gratitude also makes you feel better emotionally—if not in the moment, then over time.

Practice Appreciation

Develop a habit of telling others how much you appreciate them. Simple. It might be an e-mail, a phone call, or in person. Make it part of a conversation, particularly with those closest to you. The practice of appreciation has been shown to shift brain responses and calm stress while generating a positive outlook.[1]

HOLDING SPACE
AND BEING PRESENT WITH OTHERS

It is often essential to acquire the support of someone other than yourself to help point the way out of the illusion of separateness and despair. Soul Whispering is the new psychotherapy—or perhaps a return to a deeper, soulful type of healing transformation—offered by facilitators who are themselves constantly evolving in roles such as life coaches, enlightened ministers, and counselors. We don't know anyone who has totally broken out of their negative patterns of behavior and moved in to their soul's purpose without a measure of support from soul friends and professionals. These professional facilitators want you to love authentically and live vibrantly.

The Soul Whisperer hears, sees, and observes on a multidimensional level. What is obvious to the Soul Whisperer may be obscured for another by their unconscious blocks to authentic feelings and thoughts. Standing on the ground of acceptance and trust with an attitude of curiosity, the Soul Whisperer may elicit powerful information that points to the longings of the soul, which is seeking expression. The job of the Soul Whisperer is to provide a facilitating environment that allows for authentic soul expression.

Soul Whisperers also know when it is the right time to give someone guidance, information, interpretation, and advice. It's not the content of the information or guidance given but the timing, intention, and connection to the spirit of the giver that supports transformation in another person. Soul Whisperers also know when *not* to speak or suggest anything and how to assist others in discovering their inner truths themselves.

As facilitators, Soul Whisperers do not use diagnosis or psychological assessment tools. Instead they engage in shared inquiry with the person so that they may learn about their capacity for joy, curiosity, connection, acceptance, and trust.

A prevailing assumption from a shamanistic perspective is that if the soul is not allowed expression through art, dance, poetry, music, and expressions of imagination, it will speak to us through symptoms of disease. The soul only communicates through these mediums, and without communication with the soul, true healing is not possible and transformation will not occur. In many cultures the shaman was also the poet and artist—and art, song, dance, and healing were considered to be synonymous. In Sanskrit, *shaman* means "song."

The four questions asked by a shaman, according to some traditions, when a person is dis-eased are:

When did you stop dancing?
When did you stop singing?
When did you stop being enchanted by stories?
When did you stop finding comfort in the sweet territory of silence?

Something moves in most people who hear these questions. There is soulful poetry in the questions, comfort in knowing that somewhere on the planet they are still being asked. The stories that people tell in response to them give the information needed to understand most emotional and physical diseases.

Another question that we feel is pertinent in these postmodern shamanic times is, When did you stop playing in the dirt?

Alienation from nature has become a diagnosis itself: nature deficit disorder. Mainstream attention is being drawn to the dearth of nature activities not only among busy adults but also among children who often spend most of their childhoods primarily indoors. Aware of the damage caused by too much screen time and too little swing time, physicians have actually begun to write prescriptions for children to get outdoors and play.

Take some time to answer the four (or five) questions for yourself. Write them at the top of a page and allow yourself to write a few pages in answer to each one; let it pour out of you. Perhaps your first responses will be that you never danced or sang, or that you have no talent for either. However, *all* of us danced and sang as children, so start with your childhood memories. You will likely find that you have stopped dancing and/or singing many times in your life . . . find the commonality among those times. Look back over your writing and circle the themes and notice what you are feeling in your body. In the days and weeks ahead, try to incorporate these joyful activities into your everyday life.

A DEEPER LOOK AT THE QUALITIES OF A SOUL WHISPERER

Soul Whisperers use shamanic energy medicine as they assist people in shifting energy at a physical, mental, emotional, and soul level. Most important is a deep noticing about what is happening and a curiosity about it in oneself and others. R. D. Laing taught that we are trained out of our natural ability to perceive truthfully what is going on around us. So we become dull and pretend not to notice out of a strategy to survive. We then become convinced that our numbness is just our personality.

Expanded abilities and skills that Soul Whisperers embody may include the following:

- Can access and trust intuition
- Discerns the difference between ego agenda and soul longing in self
- Is self-reflective and self-examining on a continuous basis
- Possesses the ability to connect to the collective field of the symbolic and the imaginal
- Pays attention to intuition and allows higher wisdom to come through (sometimes this is called channeling—we prefer to call it revelation; *revelation* comes from mystery, "what is being revealed")
- Possesses the ability to assist people in concretizing the symbolic and imaginal in their lives
- Possesses the ability to expand beyond ordinary consciousness with self and others
- Has a well-developed sense of compassion, not codependence
- Is openhearted and not rigid; flexible but tough

- Is a dancer, singer, poet, artist whose dance, song, poem, or work of art is in service of weaving the soulful imaginal field with the field of the ordinary
- Is skilled in diving in and out of other people's energy fields without violating them
- Is mature and has an expanded grasp of human psychodynamics
- Has a love of all living beings and systems
- Is unafraid of deep darkness or brilliant light
- Possesses a willingness and passion to serve the highest good in themselves and others

SUPPORTING PEOPLE
AS THEY HEAL AND TRANSFORM

When someone comes into your life seeking your assistance to heal, it will serve you and them if you see that this is really their soul seeking transformation. With this in mind, the work that you will do with them is considered to be a sacred contract. Some would say that the contract was made at a soul level, perhaps in another dimension, before birth, or in another incarnation. Even as a metaphor, knowing that it is a soul contract of service shifts it from being a situation where one person is fixing another.

Most of the time the person seeking assistance has experienced some trauma in their life. If the person is disturbing or disturbed, then it's easy to assume that they have suffered serious external events such as abuse, incest, and/or molestation. But this is not always the case. They may have had a childhood that by outward appearances was decent or even good. However, as we have established elsewhere, ordinary childhoods are often experienced as being wounding in some way, and mild trauma is still trauma, the effects of which may be very real and very powerful.

The initial soul loss may result in a distorted reality that builds on itself in ever-spiraling layers of inauthenticity that appear real based on an original distortion. The traditional view is that events we call "traumatic," and the state of being traumatized, are unnatural occurrences that unfortunately damage people at least emotionally, if not psychically and even physically.

Consider the notion that the events (labeled traumatic) occur to knock us off course to take us on a journey. Alice (in *Alice in Wonderland*) is a good example of this. She falls down a rabbit hole, and from then on her reality, in one sense, is highly distorted. In the context of Wonderland, however, it is perfectly constellated. Alice gains insights and wisdom that would never have been hers had she not been subject to the trauma of falling down the hole. Dorothy (in *The Wizard of Oz*) landed in Oz due to a tornado—seemingly a disastrous event—but it was in Oz that she found her authentic self.

Alice and Dorothy both were trying to avoid pain by respectively running away, down the rabbit hole, or in Dorothy's case, begging the universe to take her over the rainbow. This avoidance is another manifestation of disease. It is often in the pain and darkness that we find answers to our suffering and furthermore find our greatest gifts. As R. D. Laing says in *The Divided Self*, "If one could go deep into the depth of the dark earth one would discover 'the bright gold,' or if one could get fathoms down one would discover 'the pearl at the bottom of the sea.'"[2]

The "geographic cure" brought relief from the ordinary, and yet it also brought newer and more painful, and at the same time enriching, experiences. As well, it brought both of them several key Soul Whisperers on their travels. Some of the characters' roles were that of guide, or way shower. Alice had the Caterpillar and Cheshire Cat; Dorothy had Glinda. These characters held the respective experience (that they were undergoing with Alice or Dorothy) in such a way that showed Alice and Dorothy what they needed to discover in themselves. The paradox in both stories and in many fairy tales is that Alice and Dorothy, the ones who were accidentally thrust into the strange places, were the ones who assisted the residents of these worlds in finding purpose and self-love. While tumbling through their own transformative world of chaos and discovery, they had the innate ability to listen and reflect wisdom to others.

The Soul Whisperer archetype is in Alice and Dorothy, and it came alive to assist others. And they were helped by the Soul Whispering archetype as it came through the other characters in their story who showed that the way out was through their own heart and efforts. Psychotherapist Nathan Schwartz-Salant says, "Allowing the process between analyst and analysand to exist in a 'third area' is an imaginal act, creating in fact an imaginal vessel, that contains and allows for experiencing fragmenting parts of a personality without distorting their mystery through an analysis of ownership of contents and historical origin."[3]

In other words, the therapist joins the person and supports them in reimagining the original event. The imaginal world of the traumatic event becomes the ground for healing and transforming the perceptions. The Soul Whisperer allows the adult to relive and create a different response to the childhood event. That individual is now free of the bondage of isolated soul parts yet has also the experience of living through the alternate reality caused by the distortion of the childhood event—dual tracks accomplished simultaneously. This distortion is not viewed as pathology or damage. Rather it is seen as powerful medicine for the soul. In that cosmology, there is not good or bad, just experience.

Our cells carry painful childhood memories manifesting in how we look, move, and feel. Our feeling nature or our emotions develop unconsciously in response to, and leaving us stuck in, childhood wounding. Our personality is a mixture of our thoughts and is dictated by unprocessed emotional material giving us the illusion of a fixed personality that is immutable. Our inner critic is made up of internalized, useless missives, spoken and unspoken, from our parents, caregivers, teachers, and religious leaders that originate from their own unresolved trauma and resentment. We mistakenly take the inner critic to be our conscience and empower it to guide us. Our true essence, our soul, waits for us to wake up and surrender to lead us in joy, altruism, and fulfillment through wisdom and love.

Soul Whisperers are interested in expanding our capacity for joy and giving us access to our own heart. Healing childhood trauma and wounds is the first step. Even people who are bighearted are often cut off from feeling their own heart and self-love. They may be masters of loving others, yet they feel empty and unloved or unlovable. In *The Wizard of Oz,* Tin Man, who had no heart, was the most loving of the group, yet he believed he was irreparably damaged. He was under the spell of the wicked witch (the inner critic) that kept him stuck and separated from his essence.

Like the Tin Man, many people are unable to find their heart. It is locked away in a protective fortress built to shield them from the pain of being separated from their own spirit and under the spell of unconsciousness. The skilled Soul Whisperer, like Dorothy, shows love and compassion and encouragement to bring life back to someone who is shut down. When the person is gently led to find their own feelings, they realize that they have had a heart all along, and they dissociated from it a long time ago because feeling pain was more than their child self could manage.

BOUNDARIES ARE A CONTAINER FORMED BY LOVE

In our early training and working as counselors we all realized that having healthy boundaries with those we were assisting was important. Over time we saw that the true cure for all of us was love and caring respect. Too often boundaries between us are really walls that keep us from intimacy. Healthy boundaries come from a deep connection to our essence but allow closeness to others. We are all related. As the native elders said, "*Om mitakuye oyasin.*"⁹ *Becoming naturally therapeutic*, a phrase coined by Jacquelyn Small (and the title of one of her books), is what the authors of this book have named Soul Whispering. The psychotherapist of today can best serve others by a continual process of self-knowledge, healing, and transformation. The knowledge must include that of both their light and shadow: unearthing from their unconscious their past wounds and imagining their future as positive healthy beings. All this is necessary to be more present, as well as more authentically available to people who seek support on their journey.

We can't take anyone else someplace we're not willing to go

ourselves. We all need to be witnessed by others and receive love and acceptance to truly recognize ourselves. One of the Soul Whisperer's main tasks is to support, listen, and reflect back to the individual that their true transformation and power lies within them and not within the therapist or a pill or a reward system. The true reward is in knowing oneself and feeling an inner empowerment. We all have the ability to change and to reenvision and reinvent ourselves each day toward greater octaves of love and wisdom.

Soul Whisperers do not take advantage of others. They do not need to steal their power or give their power away in caretaking. The reward is in passing on what they've learned and seeing others transform and become empowered. Many times in the process, as individuals heal and enable their own empowerment, the boundaries begin to slip away between therapist and client. In this we find our soul friends and kindred spirits, just as Jacquelyn Small acknowledged Star Wolf from the very beginning as her kindred spirit.

Friends, it turns out, soul friends, come from what we may have thought were unlikely backgrounds. Being the peaceniks we are, the authors were surprised when the door opened for Soul Whispering with the military. Paul Henderson came into Star Wolf's workshop to find healing and transformation for himself. He became a friend and a colleague who has taken Soul Whispering and shamanic awakening into the military.

Soldier, Veteran, and Shamanic Warrior

Paul Henderson

When I came to breathwork in 2002, it wasn't for the purpose of becoming a facilitator or a shamanic minister or a teacher or anything that had to do with being a spiritual guide or healer. I got there the way most do—my life had come apart, and I was in crisis. I was looking for something— anything—that would offer a solution or at least some relief from the pain and confusion. And, I had been knocked down sufficiently to realize that my old coping mechanisms of alcohol, drugs, relationships, work, and the endless pursuit of stuff just weren't working any longer and might very well kill me before long.

So at the invitation of a friend, I attended a Shamanic Breathwork workshop in Oregon that was facilitated by Brad Collins, the late husband of Linda Star Wolf. Needless to say, everything shifted dramatically (although in ways I could not initially realize), and my life began a dramatic change.

For the first few years, I still had no interest in Shamanic Breathwork beyond the therapeutic and healing effects it had for me. I attended some local workshops and a couple of eight-day programs put on by Venus Rising. I got to know and work with Linda Star Wolf. I always recognized the power of breathwork to plunge deep into my being and expose me to truths that I could not otherwise access.

In 2007, I took the plunge and attended the Shamanic Healing and Initiatory Process (SHIP) in North Carolina. My transformation accelerated after attending the teachings and experiencing powerful and shattering breathwork sessions. It was then that I first became interested in moving in to the field of being a breathwork facilitator myself. This seemed like the next logical step. As I went through the apprenticeship process and learned the necessary skills, I discovered a whole new level of healing. By sharing my gift of breathwork, I connected deeply with other practitioners. At times I was profoundly shaken by the experience of connectedness and the exchange of emotional energy that resulted.

In 2010, I began a process of reconciling my war experiences and the resulting psychic trauma that I had carried with me. Since the late 1990s, when my PTSD became an overwhelming and destructive force in my life, I had subscribed to the medical model that pathologizes PTSD and tells war veterans that they have an anxiety disorder that is permanent and the best they can hope for is to learn to manage its symptoms. Through an organization called Soldier's Heart, I came to recognize military service as part of an ancient tradition and, for millennia, part of a process of initiation that cultures have dealt with and processed for the ultimate benefit of the individual and society. Psychic war trauma is very real, but it is also capable of being healed. And, like any transformational or shamanic process, it can ultimately lead to a new consciousness that is expanded, connected, healing, and committed to service. War veterans are wounded, but they are not broken. Their archetypical destiny is a life of service as elder warriors, but they need the tools and the guidance to get there. It became almost immediately apparent to me that breathwork had an important part to play in this healing process.

I worked with Soldier's Heart at veteran workshops and warrior journeys. I incorporated breathwork into the process as part of the purification phase of healing. War toxins stay in the entire body, and cultures traditionally use a purification process utilizing one of the elements— air, water, earth, fire. I chose air and facilitated breathwork sessions in addition to other methods and rituals including isolation and tending, storytelling, reconciliation with the civilian community, and commitment to warrior principles. I became a veteran workshop facilitator as well as a breathwork facilitator and was able to combine the two. I have conducted workshops for both veterans and active duty military in the air force and the army. I was invited to do a workshop on PTSD and conduct a breathwork session at Robert Bly's Minnesota Men's Workshop. It appears that I will be introducing breathwork as part of a graduate program in veteran's work at a university on the West Coast.

Breathwork is a healing tool. It is a process whereby humans can transcend their limited perspectives of life and open themselves to a reality that would otherwise remain obscured and beyond reach. It can pierce the veil of limited perspective and expand personal horizons. As a breathwork facilitator I have been able to participate in that process. I don't personally change anyone's life, but I can help to open a portal to transformation that allows them to expand and connect beyond what they thought possible. In the process they heal, I heal, and the whole world heals.

5

Avoiding the Void

Shamanic Energy Medicine and Addiction

Spirituality is not a theory. It has to be lived.

THE BIG BOOK (OF AA)

Shamans and Spirit Whisperers do not label conditions in human beings. We name things based on connections or lack of them, between the natural world and the experience of a person or group of people. The shamanic energy approach addresses suffering as initiation or transformation. Addiction is a label. Working to humanize and destigmatize addiction over the past century many compassionate people decided to call it addiction and classify it as a disease. Being a disease paved the way for treatment to be developed and funded, and yet it reduced a complex topic to a set of symptoms.

ADDICTION IS A STRIVING FOR WHOLENESS

Calling the constellation of issues of addiction a disease is somewhat misleading. The soul is thrashing in the body of someone labeled an alcoholic or an addict because it is out of touch with the natural world and has been blocked from full expression. The body is accepting poor substitutes for love and misplacing its longing for passion. Attempting to fix our dilemma of suffering, *we long for a fix.* The person identified as an addict is on a journey to wholeness. Along the way, scary, dangerous, and tragic events happen until we surrender to the "no-fix"—the void—and step into it with energy.

Viewing addiction through the lens of the disease model creates humane treatment at times. At other times it forces treatment that is often not effective and is dehumanizing. At best it could be said that addiction is a chronic illness, no more or less mysterious than other chronic illnesses. Addiction went from relying on a purely spiritual cure comprised of 12-step programs to being labeled as an illness to get insurance to pay for "treatment"—and treatment in the early days was largely AA based. Eventually it became popular to see addiction as a result of faulty thinking and faulty beliefs. Treatment modalities, which taught people to reprogram their thinking to lead to better choices, abounded. More recently the biological/neurobiological understanding is that with addiction, brain receptors get compromised and faulty decisions occur as a result. The addictions field has become polarized over the years between theories of harm reduction and abstinence as the best option.

The reality is that some people, as with any chronic disease, will change behavior dramatically, and some less so. In any event, awareness and compassion are the key. The most serious addiction today is with legally prescribed drugs, yet we still focus on alcohol or the scary drugs such as meth and heroin and increasingly new designer drugs that can be purchased on the Internet.

THE SHAMANIC PERSPECTIVE
Desperately Seeking Ecstasy

Looking at addiction from a shamanic perspective, it is often a way to enter into ecstasy and get away from ordinary or normal reality, which is too painful. Using drugs or alcohol is a craving for ecstasy, an urgency for an experience of divinity. Even the horrific pain and discomfort that unfolds in the lives of people using compulsively can be a shamanic initiation. To be a Soul Whisperer it's vital to step out of judgment and view the addictive behaviors as the soul seeking expression.

Seeking the divine spark means going into an altered or expanded state. And many indigenous shamans administer some type of substance to induce that altered state. However, substances are not always necessary or even desirable to achieve expanded consciousness. There are many ways to enter the expanded state and experience the void consciously and intentionally. We avoid doing so, most often out of fear of the unknown. Mircea Eliade is a world-famous and highly respected shaman who, in his book *Shamanic Archaic Techniques of Ecstasy,* makes the point that the use of narcotics is not the optimal way to go into a journey. Sacred plant medicine is not the same as narcotics, though chemically induced altered states have become popular and are believed by some to be a shamanic experience. Naturally achieved trance states, without drugs or plant medicine, are powerful and perhaps preferable as they can be called upon at any time by the trained person.

Anytime that we move out of our ordinary reality and go into the void, we are going to a place we don't know—a place that's formless and without boundaries. It's a dark space where we cannot see the next right step. People talk about this next right step, but, so often in the void, it's elusive and is a step that the ego personality is terrified to take. To go into the void truly means *death* to the ego. However, it doesn't mean the entire ego dies, but rather a piece of the ego must be sloughed away for us to enter this place of authentic surrender.

Much has been written about how a consumer-fixated society drives and thrives on the compulsive desire to distract oneself from the pain of being human. These attempts at distraction are universal and are also why so many people use legally prescribed medications to numb themselves. As a culture we believe that suffering should be avoided at all costs.

Soul Whispering with someone who is labeled an addict is a natural fit. Speaking directly to the soul is often easier in someone who has suffered through compulsive addictive behaviors, because they are broken open and vulnerable. Gabor Mate, M.D., has written extensively on the subject of contextualizing addiction in culture, in particular in his book *In the Realm of the Hungry Ghost*. An important concept is that a person not be defined by their compulsive behaviors.[1]

Star Wolf's Story

MY PERSONAL EXPERIENCE
OF FACING THE VOID

I'll never forget the day, while living in the rural foothills of western Kentucky, that I walked into the bathroom of our little country home, looked into the mirror, and said to myself, "Hello. I'm Linda, and I'm an alcoholic." This admission, which I had been avoiding because I felt like it would surely send me spinning out of control, turned out to be the exact catalyst that my ego needed. For more than a year, I'd been running from this inevitability, avoiding it at every turn, saying, "No, no, no—I can control it. I'll just drink on Saturday nights playing cards," or, "I'll only drink a glass of wine at dinner." I finally just let it go, and I dropped into the void.

One of the questions that arose when I finally realized (with great relief) that the admission was not nearly as bad as I had feared, was, "Why did I fight this so hard? If I can go into this, own it, and get help, then I can be free! I can find myself again, and I can heal myself!" The next thing that came up for me was the fear of becoming lost in the void. To admit that you're defeated by something strips away the false feelings of control, leaving you to ask, "What if there's no help? What if there's no real answer?"

Denial delays the inevitable confrontation with your fears—the fears of being defeated, alone, and powerless. When I first got sober, my sponsor said to me, "You're so strong-willed and stubborn!" I replied, "If I'm so strong-willed, why can't I quit drinking?" She said, "Well, you're about as strong and stubborn as any person I've ever met. That may tell you something about how powerful this addiction is. If you want to win, you must surrender to win." I've never forgotten those words, and although I didn't immediately understand how surrendering was

winning, I instinctively recognized the truth of this assertion. I imagined being in a battle and having to surrender—wave the white flag.
My sponsor said that this was the only way to win, otherwise I would
face butt-kicking after butt-kicking and still be no closer to victory. *In
surrender is where you will win.* She asked me to, literally, tie a hand-
kerchief on a stick, hold it up, and say, "I surrender." I can't tell you the
extent to which that went against everything in my being—the fiery
lioness/wolfy girl that I am—I almost couldn't do it. It took awhile for
me to finally get to that place where, again, I just had to surrender and
do it. When I did, I knew what she was talking about. I felt it. I felt
myself let go.

To me, surrender simply meant acceptance—the acceptance of not
knowing the eventual outcome of a situation. It didn't necessarily mean
that things would even turn out the way I had hoped—not at all! In
fact, I lost my attachment to affecting the outcome as well. "What,
you don't have an agenda?" my ego protested. "You don't know where
we're going? You don't know the direction? You're not going to make
something happen here?" I replied, "Nope. I've surrendered, and I don't
know where I'm going. I don't have an agenda, and in fact, I'm not even
attached to the outcome. It's one breath at a time—one day at a time."

I love the poem "Little Gidding" from *Four Quartets* by T. S. Eliot,
which has multiple vignettes, each seeming to spiral in upon itself, leading us into the void. The poet talks about finding the still point within
ourselves and how, in this point, there is both stillness and movement.
We are neither going nor coming. We are simply in that place of noth-
ingness. It also talks about coming back to the beginning and knowing
that place again for the very first time. There's new awareness that is
born each time the void is entered. Over and over again, we continue
to start anew. This is another major reason that we avoid the void: It
makes us think, *Wait a minute. I've built an identity. I've built up my
circle of people. I've found who I think I am!*

I've been so many things in my lifetime. I could tell tale after tale
about my various incarnations in this one lifetime. Obviously, because
of these eclectic parts of myself, I have much experience dying and being

reborn into many different personalities and ways of being on the Earth. Every time, I think this process is going to get easier, but now I'm not so sure. In the past, I taught that it gets easier each successive time one enters the void; however, I think perhaps I was fooling myself. I realize now that each time we go into the void, we let go of a huge part of ourselves, and what we create on the other side is bigger. Naturally, when something is bigger and better, we tend to be a little bit more attached. Each time that our identity becomes tied up with who it is that we are, we start to feel a bit restless, as if we need our boat rocked. (A word of warning, however—do not have that thought unless you really mean it. It is the kiss of death!)

Two months before Brad, my beloved, was diagnosed with cancer, I thought that things were really good and that I needed a little something to shake things up. I needed to change again. I didn't know what I needed to change, but I felt like I'd been in the teacher role and in the North station of the medicine wheel for too long. I felt that I needed to be in a place of humility and innocence like the dove again and to see things with new eyes. The leap from being the teacher to being innocent and not knowing is a big leap. Many times we get stuck on the wheel of transformation because we choose to stay with what we know because it's comfortable.

For almost two years now, I've lived without a vision, which is excruciating for me because being a visionary is so much a part of my identity. I love being a visionary. I love being able to see intuitively and psychically. As a child, I was afraid of and criticized for it. As a teen, I suppressed it. As an adult, I was finally able to learn to develop it.

Recently, the very gifts that have allowed me to be a visionary have become a burden on my soul. Despite focusing on the positive, each time I touched into my visions over the past few years I could see that my future more than likely was going to be without my beloved husband, Brad. I tried using positive thinking and projecting an outcome for him to get well. In fact, everyone was praying for Brad, but in the deepest part of my heart, I was not praying for him to get well; rather, I was praying for his highest good. That was extremely difficult for me to process, but I knew, in every part of me, that praying specifically for wellness was futile. I have experienced the energetic power of prayer and the positive influence it has on reality as we know it in this dimension. However, I knew Brad's initiation was a powerful one and that it was not okay for me to interfere with his soul's journey, no matter how it affected me.

For almost two years I let my visions go, because I sensed that I needed to direct all of my energy toward Brad. I couldn't begin to entertain the thought of him leaving the planet, or having to deal with what that would mean for me as far as a new vision for my own future, which no doubt would mean another lonely voyage into the void. So, we entered into our own void during that time. I couldn't get too excited about anything, and what I did find pleasure in were things like taking him to the beach or seeing him have a good day or being able to eat. This was all very Earth-centered, *one day at a time* living. We were in a limbo that felt like a void; yet, it was rich, and there was neither agenda nor vision.

After he passed away in August, I wanted to leap out of the void and immediately start creating and being fruitful again and bring back my vision. I realized, however, that even though I could do it and be excited about it and feel happy, it would somehow remain a re-creation of the same vision. It felt like, despite his passing, I was trying to revert back to the way things were when he was in my life.

By December, it became clear that I had lost my mind, and I finally started my descent into the underworld. I understood that, by doing that, I was not only saying good-bye to Brad, but I was saying good-bye to our way of life and to the amazing way that we, together, were able to create and achieve our lives in a way that I know I will never experience with anyone or anything else. What had been my soul's purpose had truly become my ego's agenda. Sadly, it was time for me to let it go.

I descended, knowing full well why I had been avoiding it. Despite the delay, I knew that things would not look or feel the same when I emerged on the other side. Just as when I had become sober, I was afraid that I wouldn't survive. No wonder I was afraid of saying that I was an alcoholic! For me it was, in the truest sense, putting myself in the hands of God. I use the word *God* to mean the Creator of this universe—a genderless and powerful force to which I absolutely give myself—the raw material that I am: Water. Earth. Fire. Air. Spirit. I say, "Take me. Do with me what you will. Show me who I am now."

Returning into the void means merging into the formless, letting go of my identity and attachments, and dying. I know now, once again, what I've learned from the many stops on my spiral journey: if I don't go into the void on a regular basis, I will physically die. However, I'm not ready to do that—not yet. I'm not done. Although the void is amorphous and fluid, it is not a place of depression or numbness. The void is at once empty and pregnant. There is nothing there, but there is a way in which the seed of yourself is fertilized—the very seed of who you will become as you emerge and continue on the next round of your spiral path. To become a small seed again is frightening when you've been a redwood.

My original and metaphorical womb experiences have not been great. My mother got pregnant right after my father had returned from the Korean War. He was suffering from PTSD, and they didn't have much money. I feel quite certain that the news of my conception was not good news. There were financial worries and, more than that, just a general air of heaviness while my folks struggled to make ends meet. Both of my parents had grown up without much money during the Great Depression. Living and growing in my mother's womb at that time was probably confusing for me in utero. While I had been created by the love I know my parents shared for each other, it felt like that love was withheld from me as a result of my unexpected arrival during such an inopportune time in their lives. Ultimately, it wasn't about me; rather, it was the compounding effects of their own immaturity, fear, and other internal and external travails of the times. Nonetheless, it made a deep imprint upon my psyche.

I grew from that small seed in a dark, uncomfortable womb, without feeling safe or secure. As I became a young woman, I always seemed to have problems with my own womb. I had difficulty with my moon cycles and never quite trusted them. Now, I realize that it was a mistrust of the feminine.

The place where I finally began to feel more comfortable going into the void was with my teacher, Seneca Wolf Clan Grandmother (Gram) Twylah Nitsch, as I have discussed earlier in this book. She talked to me about how to approach going into the void as a journey into the Womb of Creation. I said to her, "I'm not sure I trust the feminine and the womb, because it's been a negative experience for me overall." As a child, I trusted my maternal grandmother more than I did anyone else. With her, I allowed myself to be in the water and earth cycles. When she died, I, at the age of twelve, was left with a sense of betrayal that tied into the same faithless energy that I had experienced growing up. I also felt that I had betrayed myself, because I couldn't keep my own womb, having to let it go through surgery at the age of thirty-two.

Then Gram Twylah said, "Well, I think that happened so you can go back more deeply and be more in touch with the womb of the universe. Instead of drawing power from your own womb, you're drawing from the Goddess." She also said that I wasn't here primarily to be a mother; rather, I was here to be a grandmother. I didn't understand, but then she explained that I'd been a grandmother since I was thirty-two. I had the hysterectomy and let go of my physical womb. It was not about age—age was an illusion. It was about having been delivered to the planet to fulfill my destiny as a wisewoman. The world didn't need more children—unwanted, unclaimed, starving youth abounded all over the world. The world did, however, need more wisewomen, and that, according to Gram Twylah, was my soul's purpose—my bigger story.

With that, everything changed for me.

I forgave myself. I forgave my mother. I began to see the bigger story. Suddenly, I began to realize that my true mother was not of Earth and that her womb was the void. Goddess's womb was the void from which we all come.

At peak moments, I remember that going into the void is coming home, and then, when I'm born again and emerge on the other side, I realize that I'm just visiting.

SURRENDERING INTO
THE VOID

Instead of collapsing, Star Wolf surrendered to the void. Consciously choosing to work with herself and the circumstances presenting for her, she shows that life presents opportunities for initiation. Dynamically this means working with our emotions rather than having them work us. Feeling is central to this process, not a false sense of stoic rigidity. Rather, working from a shamanic energy perspective, bringing consciousness to a difficult experience, positions it as an initiation rather than an annihilation. Another person might have started drinking or using drugs after the death of a loved one. It would have been perfectly understandable to take that action. Developing a capacity for *dancing in the void,* rather than *avoiding the void,* can serve to keep us conscious during challenging times.

We have developed a spirit-driven rather than ego-driven capacity for holding the intensity of experiences, which then allows our soul to communicate and emerge. We have worked at this capacity for years. In the same way, someone who practices yoga for years or runs marathons is able to endure far more than someone who has not practiced and built strength and capacity. What do you do if you have not developed this capacity? What if your own ego-personality is not able to hold your soul bursting forth?

Soul Whisperers are people like us who have developed the capacity to hold their own soul process as well as work with and hold others who may not have that same capacity. Often what a person needs is time, and safe space, along with a Soul Whisperer, to allow the soul to emerge. It doesn't mean that you have to be in crisis, but if you are, then you need the safe retreat even more. You can use the retreat with the Soul Whisperer to develop your capacity when you are not in crisis. You will learn to be your own Soul Whisperer and have a healthy ego structure to allow your soul to communicate, emerge, and create the rejuvenated you!

THE HEALING GROUND
OF THE TRANSFORMATIONAL WORKSHOP

Historically in every culture, seekers take retreat, time out of the ordinary to heal, transform, and reconnect to spirit, nature, and their soul. Transformational workshops are structured to release you from the pull of day-to-day living and allow you to drop into reverie and reference. They are titled many different things but carry some common components. Meals are prepared and served, and you only have to show up and eat. Activities are planned and scheduled, and you just wake up and attend whatever is planned for you that day. Many activities are designed to assist you in making friends with the group. Safety is created by agreements such as confidentiality and a commitment to staying with the group and activities—all of which engender deeper bonding to each other as trust is fostered by these agreements. Group leaders assure you that if you need them, they are available to talk, support, and guide you during the workshop.

A healthy, safe, and worry-free environment is the foundation of the experience for the duration of the workshop. One might say that it is an ideal childhood re-created for the workshop; a time and place in which you may rediscover your lost longings and creative capacities.

The foundation of a successful transformational workshop is one of safety and nurturing. Yet these alone would not facilitate transformation. The next necessary part of the equation are skilled facilitators—Soul Whisperers—who are able to get underneath your personality and whisper directly to your soul, coaxing it to communicate and come to light.

Safety, support, nurturing, time out of ordinary reality, skilled facilitators—all provide the basic ingredients of a transformative experience. What motivates people to attend such a workshop, and what exactly is one aiming to transform? Is it one's belief system, or dysfunctional behavior, or self-defeating ways of living, or one's socioeconomic circumstances? Generally people who attend transformational workshops are seeking relief from emotional pain, increased creative agency, deeper personal meaning, connection to oneness, or a combination of all. Activities are designed to allow you to recognize your individual and collective longings, woundings, and creative strengths.

Just what is it you are afraid of losing in the darkness of the void? Avoidance is primarily the fear of dying and losing everything you've been and everything you've known, including the people, places, things, and situations that together tell your life's story. The truth is that you don't know. There is no guarantee that, after going into the void and coming back out, you will still be married to the same person, have the same bank account, and still enjoy the same things. Remember, it is a complete surrender but, all in all, a very rich place.

When you get there and wonder why you avoided the void for so long, remember this: Your attachment to an outworn belief or personality trait is dying. You no longer will be the same person. Grieve the loss of those parts; dysfunctional though they may be, you grew attached to your familiar parts and mistook them for your essence. You don't remember this when you're in the light projecting, operating in the world from the personality. The void often feels like going into the womb or a chrysalis and dissolving and reforming. When you go fully into the grief, as Star Wolf spoke of above, you will emerge to celebrate your newly formed self. The new self may look completely different, or slightly different. Either way, it was formed from the rich experiences of your life. Your new self is empowered with self-awareness and purpose. The process of renewal follows the trajectory of facing the void over and over in an ever-spiraling path of self-awareness. The path seems to encompass surrender; reviewing and embracing all of you; feeling the truth of your buried emotions; and building a capacity for forgiveness, reparation, and compassion.

THE POWER OF A 12-STEP PROGRAM

Addiction as disease is a useful notion if we understand that all disease and symptoms are metaphors for the soul working to burst forward to lead us to truth. As Alice Miller says in her seminal book, *Breaking Down the Wall of Silence: Liberating Experience of Facing Painful Truth,*

"What is addiction, really? It is a sign, a signal, a symptom of distress. It is a language that tells us about a plight that must be understood."[2]

Self-help programs such as AA and Al-Anon work with a 12-step approach to self-awareness. Steps are effective because they build on each other. The first three steps are about surrendering to what is in your life and turning control of your life over to your higher self, the soul. Steps four to six are about taking an inventory or an honest appraisal of yourself and asking your higher self for acceptance. Steps seven to nine examine your self-destructive behaviors with love and compassion and engage in the work of self-forgiveness and reparation with others. Steps ten to twelve are for the daily practice of humility, reparation, gratitude, and altruism.

An important component of this process is to understand that your ego personality will cling to the unforgiving state, because it has been a survival tactic for you. When you bravely push past the tape loops to say, "Hey, I am not perfect, at times I am actually bad, yet I deserve acceptance and love," your soul and the higher functions of your mind rejoice and release you from the stranglehold of self-loathing.

You do not have to be an alcoholic to use the structure provided by the 12 steps. The 12 steps are a powerful set of psychological and spiritual tools for living each day authentically and fully. For some people there are parts of the steps that don't work for them. For example, some people don't subscribe to a concept of a god that is outside us. Other people feel that there is an inappropriate emphasis on accepting powerlessness and making amends when what they have experienced in life is real abuse and victimization as children. Even with these reservations, the 12 steps can provide you with a reference point for moving through self-loathing to self-forgiveness.

The famous Swiss psychoanalyst Carl Jung provided inspiration and guidance to Bill W., one of the founders of the Alcoholics Anonymous movement. Letters between Jung and Bill W. are the central focus of a book by Jungian analyst David Schoen titled *The War of the Gods in Addiction*. In it Jung explained how addiction is a spiritual hunger and likens it to evil, or low-level urging. He also articulated his belief that recovery constitutes a spiritual healing.[3]

Jung, it seems to the authors, was an important facilitator of the writing of the 12 steps; it's no surprise that utilizing the methodology of the steps is one way to work with your shadow systematically. It is a psychological and emotional healing exercise with a spiritual foundation. This is a spirituality that is without dogma or morals. It is a spirituality of humility, gratitude, and compassion. There is no other spiritual practice in Western culture that has illuminated the importance of total acceptance of the darker side of human behavior. If, on the path to becoming a shamanic Soul Whisperer, you would like to begin working with your own shadow energies, you may undertake the guided experience offered in the audio track "Turning the Light on Your Shadow." In it, Nita Gage will guide you through the exercise that will put you in touch with these shadow energies in the interest of freeing them and releasing them.

Remember, the ego personality has kept you locked into a way of being that has become untenable. You may feel empty and try to keep busy to avoid this emptiness. You may have tried to fill the emptiness with obsessive behavior such as overwork, over-giving, or being a do-gooder. You are not alone. By facing and embracing the emptiness you have sought to avoid, you can come home to yourself.

You will be amazed at what happens when you surrender and go into the void. You will often immediately have this thought: "Why did I fight this so hard?" For invariably there is a relief that comes with true surrender.

The following story is from Nikólaus Wolf, who followed his heart from an early age, which led him to step off the path of addiction and onto the path of shamanic consciousness. This amazing transformation resulted in his becoming a Shamanic Breathwork facilitator and teacher, co-leading workshops with Star Wolf in Venus Rising's training programs around the world.

Entering the Underworld

Nikólaus Wolf

Growing up in the Midwest, I moved many times when I was younger so I got to see that much of city life is the same no matter the specific area. By this time McDonalds and WalMarts were everywhere, along with chains like Applebee's, Staples, Petsmart, Walgreens, and so on and so forth. Each city was quite generic with a few unique quirks. This was similar to my life—I had two sisters, a mother, and no father around. My single mother had a difficult life before I showed up, and it didn't seem to get all that much easier afterward.

From an early age, I remember experiencing physical abuse, neglect, and above all, the spirit of disappointment. This escalated in my teen years when my mother lost herself to addiction, and my sisters went on their separate ways. I found marijuana as my saving grace. It wasn't long before I began drinking myself into a stupor and making my life's purpose to sustain my high. Pills, psychedelics, over-the-counter medication, cocaine—you name it, I did it. My rule was this: Every day I prayed to die, yet the only way I could kill myself was if I ended up in jail for a long period of time. No touching meth, crack, or heroin. No invoking death by stepping out in front of traffic or getting into a provoked fight that ended my life. I knew that as much as I wanted to die, it had to come of its own accord. Until then, I decided to live my life in a trance.

The day came, sometime after my first LSD trip, that I realized there was something within me that I needed to find. Through all of my experiences I was able to get glimpses of magic within that told me that the so-called real world all around me was fake and a lie. I began to realize that there was way more to life than what I was taught in school or could find on the Internet. After multiple experiences that left me utterly devastated and heartbroken by the age of nineteen, I knew I had to do something out of the ordinary to find sanity and get out of the pain. I had no idea what to do though, except to have faith and follow the signs around me that seemed to be pointing the way. These omens led me into another life crisis, heartbroken and alone.

Miraculously, they also led me to Linda Star Wolf's book Shamanic Breathwork on the day of my lowest low, just when I had made up my mind to walk to California from Missouri on my upcoming twentieth birthday. Two weeks before I planned to set out on my journey to California, on which I hoped I would either die or find a new way to live, I spontaneously wrote an e-mail to Star Wolf. I had no real expectation of hearing back from her, and yet when I did it changed my life in a wild way that I never could have imagined.

On October 1, two days after I wrote the e-mail to Star Wolf, I received a call from her partner, Brad Collins, offering me an internship at Isis Cove in North Carolina. I was shocked to hear from him, and even more shocked to find that we shared the same birthday. From here I found an uncle I never knew of in Asheville [North Carolina]. I went to live at Isis Cove as an intern and dove as hard and deep into shamanism as I could.

To my surprise, as a shamanic minister and Shamanic Breathwork facilitator, I became the youngest graduate of Venus Rising's training program. I apprenticed with Brad for a full year, learning about the land at Isis Cove, Venus Rising's programs, Shamanic Breathwork, ceremony, and counseling. I also took advantage of all the opportunities available to me while being exposed to community members who were professionals in a multitude of fields. After participating in two monthlong training programs, multiple Shamanic Breathwork weekend workshops, a Priest Process, and other mind-altering experiences, I was ready to explode! I needed to find people closer to my own age, to travel and see the world, and to integrate all that had been poured into my psyche in an extremely accelerated time frame.

The signs brought me to Isis Cove, and when the time was right, they led me away. I followed my heart across the United States, seeking happiness and love. I found way more than I ever expected. As my journey evolved I found opportunities to support myself financially, meet people from all walks of life, and learn what passions I carried besides getting high on substances. This journey led me to the greatest high of my life. I was in love, happy, and lived every day full of magic and mystery as a result of following what I felt in my heart. At the peak of it all, I found myself in Hawaii on December 12, 2012, where I prayed that all that was in the way of me reaching my true potential would be removed from my energy field.

Well, as the old saying goes, "What goes up, must come down," and down it went.

There is a well-known spiritual saying that goes like this: "Be careful *what you pray for." What it really means is that when asking for change, remember that with each change in our lives there is a letting go of the old. Sometimes it is something we wish to release, such as an old self-defeating pattern or addiction. But sometimes, when it is someone we love or a lifestyle that we have grown comfortable with, it feels more like a sacrifice. In my case it was a combination of both, and I found myself needing to let go of what formerly was sustaining my happiness and life in order to embrace my deeper longing connected to my soul's purpose. This felt devastating, and I felt powerless as I watched my love relationship and lifestyle dissolve around me. I realize now that I was undergoing a shamanic initiation that I had invoked somewhat innocently. I do believe, however, that it was truly what needed to happen for me to move forward on my spiritual path. Although I loved the woman I was with and the journey we were on, I also intuitively knew that something greater was calling me, and I could not avoid that deeper calling any longer.*

Everything in my life started falling apart. Dreams, relationships, lifestyle—it all began to crumble around me as I fought to hold it together. My heart was shattered open, my world gone as I knew it, and I tumbled down into the underworld. Over the next few months a new prayer was born while practicing all I had learned to heal and re-member myself. An attitude of surrender began to take hold as I prayed to wake up and remember who I was. As I let go I simply began to chant my name, Nikólaus, and allowed its power to fill me up and lead me on a journey within the vast void.

Slowly the knowing came that it was time to go live in Virginia with my birth father, Paul, whom I'd never had much of a relationship with, and dive in to my family of origin. When I arrived in Virginia, I decided to go to college. I had always hated school and swore I wouldn't go back, yet I knew no other direction to go in and figured at least I could get some money from student loans to help support my way. I did all the work to get enrolled for the summer term, began going to school, and helped out in the house where I could. My family's house was a mess, not in terms of cleanliness as my stepmother is a great cleaner, but in terms of unprocessed emotions. My stepmother was deep into her addictions; my little brother had been diagnosed with multiple disorders and was on nasty medications; and my father was completely shut down and emotionally unavailable. I began teaching my stepmother about meditation, sage, and chakras, and all of the things I had learned when I shifted my life from a place of emptiness to one of connection.

We began working with healthy boundaries for my little brother instead of letting him run the house like the adult. I tried to engage with my father about the sorry state of affairs he and his wife were in, individually and collectively, as well as his son's! Externally, I was doing great in school, getting very good grades, acing my tests, and being active in every class, which was totally different from my straight Ds in high school. My teachers loved me, and truthfully I enjoyed talking with them more than any of the students.

Even though outwardly I appeared to have it all together, inside I was increasingly depressed, bored, wanting to die, and was in a place of complete disillusion with the world around me. I felt hopeless, yet I refused to fall back into my addictions of smoking marijuana, drinking, partying, and engaging in addiction in any way as I didn't want to run from this bottom I was coming to. I had a feeling that I was in the process of undergoing a major life transformation.

At this time almost all of my thoughts consisted of leaving the planet. I reached a point where I began mixing different kinds of poisons within my head every moment I was awake. I hardly moved, I was such a prisoner within my psyche. Not only did I consciously agree to enter a cage by coming to Virginia, living with family, but I went into a cage within a cage by going to school, fully aware of what it was! Now, I reached a place of surrender, for I knew I was going to do the only other thing that I promised myself I would never do: place myself into the cage of a mental hospital!

One evening I told my stepmother that I was going to admit myself into an inpatient program. In the hospital I told them that I was suicidal but couldn't hurt myself, that yes I did hear voices but I wasn't crazy, and yes I did see things that weren't physically there from time to time. I expressed every truth of mine even though I knew by their standards it was diagnosable. I shared my journey with the intake people: how I saw things, and where I was in that moment. They decided not to mention the voices or my seeing things as I guess they didn't feel I was schizophrenic but admitted me for being suicidal. I felt like I had entered into hell, a place that brought much more harm than good. I refused to take the medications after realizing that I wasn't going to get any help except pills, and I asked to be released. They tried to hold me against my will and sent in a professional to evaluate me. After multiple hours of talking with the hospital staff, it only took five minutes of sharing with the evaluation professional before she decided to release me.

At least the hospital experience got me an A+ paper in my psychology class. In the next semester, my brother calmed down considerably, my stepmother stopped drinking and went to Isis Cove for support, and my father was showing up as a really good friend, helping me to make it through this dark time in my life. Even so, the pressure was building inside of me, and I knew I was done with school and living in Virginia. I was guided to invest everything I had saved up into a trip to Thailand to learn massage. It made no logical sense, but it called to me and I followed that call with every ounce of effort I had left in me. I asked for support from my communities, I pulled as many resources out of school as I could, and I made the leap.

Coincidentally it just so happened that Star Wolf reached out to me at the same time, asking if I was interested in visiting Isis Cove and attending a Soul Return workshop. I decided to attend the workshop with the intention of leaving for Thailand directly afterward. At the workshop my body started shutting down, and I began feeling extremely exhausted and increasingly inflamed. The PTSD acquired over the course of my life had finally caught up with me, making it impossible to take the training in Thailand.

Fast forward nine months later, and I no longer feel the need to physically die as I'm learning to walk through the cycles of death and rebirth consciously, which have led me to a sustainable lifestyle.

I am now Star Wolf's personal assistant and living life on a higher octave. I have made many changes in my lifestyle, not only in the way that I think but also in the way that I carry myself in the world. I have begun to learn how to dress differently, eat healthily, and communicate more effectively. My heart is slowly healing, and I am allowing happiness to replace the disappointment that had rooted so deeply within me from *childhood. My entire being and life has shifted, again, without any Western medications, and I am now living from a place of service where I am able to share with others who are seeking to find their own shamanic energy medicine within.*

Through the power of Shamanic Breathwork, I was able to embrace the parts of me that needed to die away for me to step more fully into my sacred purpose and personal power. It seems the universe answered the prayers I had made in Hawaii—to remove all lower vibrations from my energy field so that I could awaken and realize more of who I came here to be. The universe continues to teach me to be careful for what I ask for and to be appreciative of all the ways in which my prayers are answered.

6

Shamanism's Inconvenient Truth

Transform Yourself and Heal the World

Learn how to see. Realize that everything connects to everything else.

LEONARDO DA VINCI

Shamanism is the practice of living from the perspective that what we do to nature we do to ourselves. Indeed, if we have deep, unconscious self-loathing we treat ourselves and nature as loathsome creatures deserving of punishment and disregard. Transforming into self-love is not a prerequisite to healing the planet; it *is* actually healing to the planet from a shamanic or systems view of life.

Physicist and systems theorist Fritjof Capra, Ph.D., writes:

Within the context of deep ecology, the view that values are inherent in all of living nature is based on the spiritual experience that nature and the self are one. This expansion of the self all the way to the identification with nature is the proper grounding of ecological ethics. . . . The connection between an ecological perception of the world and corresponding behavior is not a logical but a psychological connection. . . . If we have the deep ecological experience of being part of the web of life, then we *will* (as opposed to *should*) be inclined to care for all of living nature.[1]

Planetary change will only happen when consciousness shifts. Mandates, laws, collective guilt, and even a certain amount of pain have failed to impact behaviors that are hurting people and the planet. This is not a new concept. Ecopsychology posited this truth twenty years ago—that is, an evolved person is a person who will not willingly harm themselves, others, or the planet.

Star Wolf's Story
STANDING UP THROUGH DARK TIMES

Many are fearful, because politically and ecologically the world seems to have plunged into darker times. Many feel betrayed and confused by seeing animals on the brink of extinction, politicians leading with hate and revenge, and increasingly more people in desperate situations with no hope for a better life. Despair can breed apathy, disassociation, and giving up. And yet the human spirit does prevail.

It is important each day to pay attention to the news and hear the reality of what is going on in the world, of the destructive actions occurring everywhere: devastation of the natural world, atrocities visited on people in the name of religion and nationalism, and on and on. I believe that we must be aware of all that is happening so we can do our part. And I give equal attention to all that is beautiful and life-affirming—the people who are fighting for justice and standing up to greed and oppression. I see the incredible unifying power of thousands of people from all over the world at Standing Rock in North Dakota who are bravely and tirelessly showing up to protect the water. The human spirit is resilient and powerful and darkness can and is balanced by the forces for light.

It is in times like these that we have the opportunity to lean in to our sacred purposes and remember why we are on Earth in the first place and to have courage, which means to take heart.

I realized a long time ago that I had to make a choice to either participate in life or be a victim. I stood up against the injustice I witnessed during the Vietnam War; I stood up for the civil rights and women's rights movements. As a naive teenager I did the best I could to stand up. Today I am no longer naive, but I am still standing—because I know if you don't stand up for something, you stand for nothing.

RETURNING TO INDIGENOUS WISDOM

In a desperate thrust to save the planet, scientists and activists alike are turning to indigenous elders for help, for they are beginning to realize that indigenous tribes have maintained a deep connection to the Earth while the rest of the world focused on materialism. Now like King Midas, the gold is meaningless, and being able to touch the Earth is the "new wealth." Increasingly the affluent are opting for eco-vacations where they can run barefoot through the jungle or swim in pristine waters.

What was natural has become precious and limited. Seeking answers to saving the planet and our own health, we are turning to shamans, medicine people, and/or elders for guidance and answers. Often the response is that to save the planet we must look inside and heal our own darkness and our destructive natures. Rather than a formula for political action, the answers lie in personal responsibility to heal our wounds. Facing the inconvenient truth that we are wounded and only we can heal ourselves is often the first and most profound step to healing the planet.

The wounded state of the planet is a reflection of our internal state of being. Simultaneously, the state of the planet impacts our state of being, creating a loop of problems. Where to start?

Let's begin by recognizing and admitting our own loss. Rather than looking to the destruction of the Amazon only, let's look inside for our own destruction and devastation. During the turbulent era of the 1960s, many people, including the authors of this book, got lost or detoured. We were not mature or grounded enough in our bodies and psyches to deal with and integrate multivaried explorations into altered states of consciousness into our everyday, ordinary lives. Most of us didn't have elders or mentors who could safely guide us through these rites of passage, and there were many pitfalls and a lot of damage done without wise support from someone to help hold the space that was needed for healthy psychic change and integration. On another level, perhaps a shamanic one, the confusion and disillusionment, as well as the excitement of that time, brought a whole new wave of consciousness with it.

RESPECT YOUR ELDERS!

Respecting your elders means learning and springboarding from their place of consciousness. It is the integration of wisdom with innovative new experience and understanding. Respecting your elders doesn't mean crawling in the coffin with them by being stuck only in their reality. Shamanic wisdom comes from traveling through all dimensions and harvesting the fertilizer from the past and planting the seeds of the future. Transforming what stinks and rots into fertilizer supports new growth and requires an alchemicalized psychological process of discernment, surrender, and trust.

Nature spirits show humanity how to be in harmony with our own consciousness and that of the planet. To develop a shamanic consciousness means to pay attention to nature and listen to our elders, ones we may not have even recognized in the past. Seneca Grandmother Twylah Nitsche emphasized again and again that we need to learn from our grandmothers and grandfathers, our elders, and their wisdom. She wasn't just talking about human beings; she was really referring to Grandmother Mountain and Grandfather Sun, and Father Sky and Mother Earth.

She said, "If someone tells you that you're as dumb as a bag of rocks, thank them, because they've just told you that you are as smart as the wisest beings on the planet, the ones that have witnessed all that's happened on this Earth." She believed that we had it all wrong thinking that human beings are at the top of the evolutionary mountain and that after us are the animals, plants, and then the mineral kingdom.

Grandmother loved to ask, "Does it really make sense that humans, the newest kids on the block, are the smartest?"

We need the wisdom of our nature elders, and we need to trust the new and the unknown. Looking to nature we can see how nothing is wasted, but much is discarded freely. Leaves are dropped from the tree to go into the ground to fertilize and mulch it for the rich new growth that will follow. The tree isn't clinging to dead leaves, screaming, "I will not let go of my leaves; these are the leaves of wisdom." Instead the tree lets go, knowing that true wisdom is in allowing death and rebirth over and over.

As the new kids on the block, as Grandmother Twylah called us above, we human beings have great ideas and have the potential to take things further than our ancestors. However, we're building upon their strengths and wisdom, and we need to pay attention to the wisdom of those who've gone before us so we don't have to reinvent the proverbial wheel. When we disconnect from that wisdom, we lose the rich foundation that has been given us. We may find ourselves ungrounded, or missing out on key elements or perennial wisdom. There is a mix of learning from the old while downloading the future and then grounding it all in the present.

In *Shamanic Mysteries of Egypt: Awakening the Healing Power of the Heart,* which Star Wolf coauthored with Nicki Scully, an author, shaman, and priestess who has been visiting Egypt since 1978, one chapter pertained to the reconciliation of the opposites. Star Wolf and Nicki articulated the archetypes of two Egyptian deities—Sobek, the crocodile deity, and Horus, the hawk-headed deity—and relayed how in the mythological stories they were continually battling with one another.[2] Neither one of them ever won in a decisive way. The story and rituals, as developed in the book, demonstrate how to reconcile these two powerful energies within ourselves. The crocodile represents the old wisdom of experience and what has been learned, so to speak, from the ancestors. The new energy represents the soon-to-be pharaoh and lord of the land, Horus. Horus is symbolized by the hawk, the one who delivers the bigger picture and the new story.

When these two archetypes can be reconciled within us we can create a new reality that is infused with the wisdom of the old story and the creativity of the new story. The integration is more powerful than either alone. You can also imagine this as balancing the left with the right, or the reptilian brain with the cerebral cortex. Truly this can be seen as the reconciliation of all opposites. Reconciliation of the opposites is a shamanic task, because when we break things down to black or white we can get stuck and lose half of ourselves.

In this place we don't find a wholesome solution and may settle for something less than the bigger truth that is trying to come through. If we can find the third thing, which incorporates all opposites, we are moving into a realm that's new, alive, and vibrant. Typically we can find ourselves caught in an extreme experience as we vacillate between thoughts, caught in "either/or" consciousness. To be caught in that either/or dilemma is to feel that there's absolutely no graceful way through or out of a situation. However, if we can embrace both the old and the new, the dark and the light, and all the opposites we are struggling with, then we often suddenly find ourselves on the other side and can hardly believe that we made it through. The other side, holding "both/and," doesn't look like what we thought it would, because the state of being is new. A more integrated outcome will be a completely new creature or reality unto itself.

UNITING THE WISDOM OF THE PAST WITH AN EXPANDED VISION OF THE FUTURE

As discussed above, in stressing the value of listening to our elders, often we can glean profound insights from the past. As noted earlier, many of us did a lot of "psychedelic fieldwork" during the past century, specifically in the 1960s. Many of the most powerful lessons we have learned had their genesis in these experimental times. For in the '60s, the paradigm was shifting away from individualistic to collective, and naturally it was the coming-of-age group who were nudging that shift through personal exploration. We used our bodies as chemical laboratories, not really caring about the potential consequences. We had been raised on the certainty that a nuclear bomb would wipe out the planet, so living for today fueled our passionate drive to change the world by changing ourselves.

Astronauts who take an incredible journey into the unknown of outer space do so with the knowledge that they are not sure where it will take them or even if they will make it back home, and if they do they will certainly not be the same people who left. Edgar Mitchell, *Apollo 14* astronaut, was one who was forever changed by his experience. For him, it was the visual of coming around in the space capsule and seeing the Earth rise. Beyond the moment of extreme awe was the cognitive dissidence created by this staggeringly beautiful view of the place he had taken for granted. It was as though he was outside of ordinary consciousness and understood that taking consciousness for granted was no longer tenable. He was inspired to found the Institute of Noetic Sciences (IONS) in 1973—a nonprofit research and education organization. He chose the name *noetic* because it means "intuitive mind" or "inner knowing." The mission of IONS is to support studies and experiences in transformation through consciousness research.

Exploration of the unknown and going to the edge of consciousness drove the collective youth consciousness of the '60s to break through the bubble of fear and the illusion of security that the '50s represented. Moving on from the '60s, many people like Edgar Mitchell continued to explore and create new ways of thinking and approaching existence.

There is value in remembering that the origins of what today are considered serious scientific endeavors, such as IONS, began from wild and unruly young people breaking out of the box. Forgetting these vital chaotic roots, the accepted science of today becomes calcified into established and revered theories. Today the wild and seemingly crazy ideas are popping up everywhere, and the times are, once again, changing.

COMPASSION, GENIUS, OR MADNESS?
A New Generation of Change Agents

Currently we are witnessing many people waking up and beginning to really care for our beautiful planet Earth. Everywhere there are stories about incredible people who are doing amazing things in the world to help heal the Earth and her creatures.

Very often these individuals have been through a lot of suffering in their own lives. Frequently, they are sensitive and very conscious about how they are walking on this planet. And yet even though they have great empathy for our troubled Earth, many of these individuals have not been able to find their own place in the world or their sacred purpose.

Others may even look at them as being unrealistic, ungrounded, and therefore irrelevant. Sometimes those who are the most tuned in to what's really happening on more subtle levels, precisely because they are so sensitive or wounded, are unable to create sanctuary or healing for themselves. Somewhere in childhood many people lose their personal power, submitting to the norms created by the family in order to survive. Many people find survival methods that label them insane or mentally ill.

Many of these sensitive individuals find it difficult to live in today's world and feel like they do not belong here and that their true home is not of this world. Although they may be touching on some greater cosmic truth about our origins (who knows . . . we may all originate from some distant star), that longing to go home may actually detract from their full embodiment here.

These individuals may feel like the only way to be here is to engage in creating an altered state of existence rather than trying to enter into what mainstream reality offers. This they choose to do through engaging in the use of recreational drugs, especially marijuana, psychedelics, and alcohol. Another way they escape is to disassociate through imagination and fantasy, which can occur in a number of ways, including the watching of video games and fantasy films and the reading of fantasy books.

Who can blame them when much of the mainstream world seems to be still asleep, in denial, and ignoring even what world-renowned scientists are telling us about the accelerated planetary decline that is happening on every level around us. So, what is the answer to healing ourselves and healing our planet at the same time? We can't do one without the other. In other words, focusing on generating good deeds in the world will take us only so far.

THE NEED FOR ACCELERATED HEALING NOW

Albert Einstein is often quoted as saying, "No problem can be solved from the same level of consciousness that created it."

If this is true, we must learn how to evolve, to accelerate our consciousness to the next octave to discover or download the solutions to the problems of our time that perplex us in our present state of awareness. One way to do this is to access the audio track "Contacting Your Future Self" and undertake the meditative journey it offers. Doing so will help you to open to your greatest potential and evolve your consciousness to the next level on the great spiral of change.

As we undertake this very profound work, the following points are important to bear in mind.

1. **Raising personal consciousness is everyone's responsibility.** Planetary change will only happen when consciousness shifts. Destruction comes from repressed emotions, unhealed trauma, and unconsciously motivated action. When you do your personal work, turning the light on your unconscious darkness, you will live in harmony.

2. **We are connected to everything.** Separation is an illusion. What happens to one of us is happening to all of us. What we do to a tree, person, or even inanimate object reverberates through everything. We have to try to help as many people as possible to experience this shift in consciousness and have the realization that we are all interconnected.

3. **Time may be running out; action is needed now.** Ecologically it doesn't look good. The problem with this ideology is that it backfires and inspires apathy. If the end is near, why do anything? Let's party. In fact, the end is always near; tomorrow is always an illusion. Death is with us personally at every minute, so it follows that the end of the planet is just as immediate. We confuse the notion of living in the present with a post-hippie philosophy of "la, la, la, live for today . . ." meaning live as though your personal enjoyment

is all there is. Living in the present, consciously, is a capacity for riding the energy of birth and death. In those luminous moments, people always describe having a connection to oneness, loving everyone and everything. Compassion, right action, and right motives are natural in a state of presence and luminosity.

4. **Love is all that matters.** Again the flower children were correct, yet they knew not what love actually is. Love is the energy of being present and connected. This is a state that we are hardwired to experience. Hormones and pheromones will produce it temporarily. Accessing the state of connection simultaneously with the luminosity of being fully conscious and present is just as obtainable, yet so few tap in to it. Jill Taylor-Bolte, a neuroscientist who gave a powerful TED Talk and wrote a book called *My Stroke of Insight,* gave the world a great gift when she shared her experience of having a life-threatening stroke. Essentially her left brain turned off and gave way to her right brain, where luminosity and presence are the norm. What we don't know is exactly why we have a mechanism called the left brain that seems to be bent on raining on the parade of higher consciousness. Clearly there is an evolutionary purpose to thwarting a consciousness of oneness. Perhaps we as a species must evolve other parts of our body and consciousness prior to attaining unlimited access to this wonderment of bliss and connection.

5. **We are waiting for something to happen to change everything.** Is this our modern-day Godot, after which we will be fully alive and connected? While we wait for this happenstance, it is happening constantly. Life is evolving itself; our day-to-day thoughts, feelings, and behaviors are creating us and everything every moment. Godot never comes, and that is irrelevant. What we are doing while we wait for the thing to happen is creating the thing. Stop, breathe, drop into your heart, and be present now.

It seems that we are programmed to heal ourselves and, in so doing, to transform ourselves repeatedly throughout our lifetimes. It appears that by transforming our inner landscapes, we become more effective as change agents to help heal the world. One way to start you on your own inner healing is to listen to the audio tracks that accompany this book. The five meditative tracks will help you put aside the constructs of your personality to access the higher wisdom that your soul is longing to express.

Let's hear from change agent Wendyne Limber, who recounts her own incredible journey on the shamanic/Soul Whispering transformational path and shares the pearls of precious insights that she has learned along the way.

Imagine Healing

Wendyne Limber, MA, LMFT, RDT-BCT

I am honored to have been asked to contribute to this book, and I too am one of the baby boomers who have experienced a grand shift in consciousness over these years, having been right in the middle of it all and privileged to have been the honored guest at so many healings and transformations. Many incredible shamanic stories have risen from my experiences and nudge me to be told. I will tell a few in this chapter, along with what I learned about shamanic energy medicine, as requested by my dear friend and colleague Linda Star Wolf.

I had to heal and transform myself first. Certainly I had a diagnosis, probably several. Without knowing all that, I began my personal healing journey in the late '70s and '80s with a giant intention to transform my life. I was ready to heal my body and commit to something for myself. It worked. My whole body changed in what seemed to be a very short amount of time.

What I learned: Intention is a powerful, dynamic life force. Attention gives energy to what you are focusing on. Intention is the part of the mathematical equation that is responsible for the transformation. These principles are as valid as science and mathematics.

In those days I navigated many dark nights of the soul and spiritual emergency for myself, moving through the middle to the other side. Psychospiritual processes and Shamanic Breathwork were my therapies, along with a small group that I participated in where I saw my life on the chalkboard every week, to my amazement. I became aware. Group work was amazing to me and for me.

What I learned: The energy frequency vibration of love and connectedness gets activated when we work together in groups. We long for the Divine and look for it through people, places, and things. Our addictions are that search for the sacred, that connection to something bigger than ourselves.

In 1987, after what seemed to be my first initiation from the cosmos—I began to communicate with the universe in new ways, not aware that I was downloading from the future. I began to have visions and knowings about things. One day while meditating, I visualized the future. I saw a geodesic dome with people sitting in a circle inside of it, doing healing work. It was clear: I knew that I must work with people in this way, and that someday I must build this dome. This was my assignment, and I agreed to take it on.

Not long after that vision, a series of amazing and what appeared as supernatural events occurred: I received the Imagination Process—a shamanic healing and transformational journey program that I was to do someday. The next day I was asked to work in a teen addiction program. Thus, I quit my teaching job to start this new life.

What I learned: The universe will contact you and will support your decisions and dreams if you follow the signs and symbols. Your thoughts/feelings create your life as you create the future template.

I was pulled toward different processes and techniques of healing, which were considered "far out" in those days. I became interested in risk taking, going to the edge of reality, taking people to new places of being, experiencing pain and joy, and breaking through the old and transforming into the new. I took courses to become a licensed marriage and family therapist, doing shamanic work, drama therapy, meditation, and altered states work.

People healed and transformed way past the initial diagnosis/ prognosis.

Longing to be on my own without a boss telling me what I could do, I was ready to take the next risk, a thing I love teaching about today. I was soaking in the universal laws and spiritual principles and became keenly aware once again that miracles will happen if I stay connected to the bigger story, the universal mind, and if I co-create whatever I keep in my mind, thoughts, and feelings. So what did I want? . . . My own healing center.

One afternoon I drove right to it—a quaint little office with one large room, a small room, and a bathroom. It was in downtown Stuart, Florida, on the water, a perfect location, and in a building I had always loved. I had to have it.

But I had no money. By Monday morning I would need first month's rent, last month's rent, and a deposit of around twelve hundred dollars. I told no one about this. After all, was I being realistic? On Sunday afternoon two different people, unknown to each other, called me saying, "God told me to give you one thousand dollars." By Monday morning I had the money, and I was even able to have power and a telephone. It was a sign. I was on the right track. I called my new business Solutions Center for Personal Growth, Inc.

What I learned: The energy from the universe in the quantum field is influenced by your thoughts and by the power of your focusing and will arrange the solid objects, situations, and people in your life to come together to match your intentions/vibrations like a radio channel. This is why it is important to see all things as perfectly part of the process, and to have gratitude for everything. It is the lower system that holds us to the idea that something is good or bad. We say in our shamanic work, the good, the bad, the light, the dark—no difference.

I am quite sure that Albert Einstein decided to pay me a visit back then. For a period of about two months his energy seemed to be around me constantly. Everywhere I turned, the man was beckoning me, leading me to the secrets of energy and the healing process. Every other day I would see a quote of his, or a person would walk in with something that had Albert Einstein on it.

During the last week of his visit, I had these encounters: On Monday, I received a thank you letter in the mail with a wax seal on the back, imprinted with an image of Einstein. On Tuesday, I went to a realtor's office and on her desk was a picture of Einstein with $E = MC^2$ under the *picture. On Wednesday, I met a* different *realtor at a house I wanted to see. To my amazement, I saw over the fireplace an original painting of Einstein!*

Thursday, I was in a mall, where I rounded a corner to see a very large framed poster of Einstein looking at me, with the phrase Imagination is more important than knowledge. *Somehow he was validating my work, my vision—beckoning me to understand imagination and energy . . . shamanic energy medicine, really. I bought the poster.*

What was he trying to tell me? I searched in books, old and new. Finally, on that Friday, a woman with a book on Reiki and energy healing came in for an appointment. She said she just knew I needed this book. I opened the book randomly as I often do with books, and of course, I had opened it to a chapter on Einstein and how his theory on energy applied to healing work. It was the only chapter in the book about Einstein. I read and discovered what he wanted me to know. That was it.

He left after that day. I am grateful for his visit. He is in my heart and soul. His picture is on the wall in my office, as I remember each day to thank those genius minds who opened the work up to the world, to me.

What I learned: We are energy and information. The cells and tissues in our bodies have a memory of everything that has ever happened to us in our life beginning with conception and birth as well as other lifetimes. It is important to clear out any imprints that may give us the impression that we are not worthy, intelligent, creative, beautiful, or important. It is important to implant new ideas that remind us that we are all unique, special, wonderful, talented, and can create our dreams and passions.

I now understood for certain that I must facilitate the expression and release of past trauma, reverse negative old beliefs in the subconscious through reprogramming and feeling new feelings, then teach the universal laws of energy for manifestation and creation. I get it! We can't reprogram if the old stuff is still in our energy system.

And so it came to be after that most incredible and magical beginning that I followed the vision and the instructions. I am so glad, grateful, and honored to have received the Imagination Process, which has expanded and evolved over the years now with workbooks, trainings, and new projects. We are integrating psychology, a variety of incredible healing modalities, consciousness studies, quantum physics, neuroscience, spirituality, shamanism, and technology. Those who partake experience shamanic energy medicine extraordinaire and continue to take quantum leaps in the field as we all keep breathing, breathing, breathing!

What I've learned: The universe will bring together the most incredible designs you could imagine when you let go completely and walk the path of trust. As you surrender to your personal shamanic spiral path, all the necessary pieces and parts will show up to create your magical, mysterious masterpiece. Keep your eye on the prize, and it will all come to you. Open your heart, mind, and soul to receive information from other dimensions. Love whatever shows up first, and keep your energy vibration high. This will accelerate evolution, and all your dreams will come to you.

It's the law.

7

Emotional Cancer

Depression and Narcissistic Altruism (a.k.a. Codependency)

Modern epidemics abound. Cancer, depression, anxiety, autoimmune diseases run rampant, and there appears to be an endless loop of pollution of mind, body, and planet. Empathic support rather than prescribed solutions allows people to access their soul wisdom, which leads to sustainable personal and planetary change. Accessing personal truth to the path of direct experience is necessary for a sustainable life for the individual and the planet.

STRUGGLING TO REACH THE HIGHEST OCTAVE

If you plant a flowering plant in a dark corner of your yard and don't water it, it will not survive. It will twist itself into bizarre shapes to try to get some sun and water. Would you blame the plant, or say it is a mentally ill plant that is not adapting well? If you dig it up and plant it in the sun and water it, the plant will thrive. No blame should be assigned in the former case; rather, we need to recognize the right condition needed to nurture and support the plant, the person, and the planet.

Knowing what a plant needs and then doing the right action is very similar to knowing how to work with people. They are programmed to grow. Given the best ground to thrive in, they will not only grow but also transform and reach their highest octave and sacred purpose.

In the shamanic model, illness—both psychological and physical—is not an enemy to be eradicated; rather, symptoms or disturbances of mental or physical health are messages from the soul, or otherwise indicate obstacles to *hearing* messages from the soul.

Nita's Story
MY STORY OF DEPRESSION AND NARCISSISTIC ALTRUISM

Depression has been my companion for most of my life. As a child I was depressed off and on, which primarily manifested in physical illnesses, because that is what got the attention of my parents. At eighteen I hit a deeper depression and began to consider suicide. Going to my parents was a disaster. My mother grabbed her heart and sobbed, and my father yelled at me and said the words I had heard all my life: "You are killing your mother with this talk!"

My friends thought I was silly, saying, "Oh, you're just bored; life is great; just find something you enjoy doing and keep busy . . ." or words to that effect.

Depression, in the late '60s, was still not in vogue, and no one was going to therapy in rural Arizona except for "poor Harriet; she has gone crazy." Harriet was my mother's friend who was married to a really horrible man, and I suspect once Harriet hit menopause she just snapped. My mother had a psychotic brother, Bub, which didn't help things. He snapped at the age of twenty-four. He had PTSD, though no one called it that at the time. He had served in the war and was discharged with a diagnosis of schizophrenia brought on by shell shock. He was hospitalized and remained in a psychiatric ward for life. When I had my meltdown at eighteen they worried that I was turning out like Uncle Bub, but instead of getting help, they retracted into fear and denial. So, basically, I was on my own.

Clueless, my strategy became keep busy, have oodles of fun, and keep depression at bay. That worked great during my twenties, mercifully. I did not inherit my dad's alcoholic gene, so I had no addiction issues to deal with, at least not an addiction to substances. Instead I developed relationship addiction, otherwise known as codependency or, as I now call it, "narcissistic altruism."

Stumbling through my late twenties with the birth of my first child, I stopped drinking completely, floundered silently through serious post-partum depression, and fantasized about suicide as my only means of escape from the unbearable emotional and mental pain of depression. Looking into the eyes of my precious and innocent baby kept me from ever seriously considering killing myself. At that time I was in therapy three times a week, and my depression was analyzed away as my "unconscious, unfulfilled desires to marry my father."

My depression raged on, and again I was on my own with it. As detailed earlier, my twenties were spent living in London, England. During the '70s, I swear the sun never really shone at all. When the Beatles sang "Here Comes the Sun," with the line "it feels like years since it's been here," they weren't being metaphorical!

When I moved back to California, being in the sunshine every day lifted much of the depressive symptoms, and for many years I was free of it—or so I thought. The reality was that the depression was always there, on the back burner, simmering in my unconscious, building steam for a later day. After the reprieve of my thirties, my old friend depression came screaming back with a vengeance. Like a spurned lover, it caught up with me and promised to destroy me.

In my early forties, I had just left an abusive marriage. During the marriage I had quit my job to help my husband with his business. I fled the marriage with a suitcase, jobless and broke. My carefully constructed way of being in the world and my personality came unglued. I tried in vain to hold it all together. Ignoring my mental, physical, and emotional exhaustion, one day it dawned on me that I was seriously depressed.

My ability to carry on with tenacity masked my deep-seated depression. Truth was, I was ashamed of being depressed. Despite my professional training, or perhaps because of it, I was unable to admit my disease and hid it like an alcoholic hides drinking. Even though I did talk to my friends about my depression it was years before I could admit that not only was I depressed, but I was suicidal as well. Suicidal ideation was my escape valve. There were days, even weeks, when all I could do was lie in bed all day and obsessively worry about how I was going to work and survive. In some odd attempt at comfort, I would remind myself that if it got too much worse I could kill myself. Knowing that was my out, I found I could carry on another day.

Depression with suicidal thoughts was my secret. My personality did not allow for depression. Instead my personality included seeing myself as a victim, but the twist was that I felt like a *heroic* victim. "Oh, the things I have survived . . ." was my mantra. Running from self-loathing and depression fueled my mission of taking care of other people. My Mother Teresa complex kept me from feeling the deep longings of my own soul.

My strategy worked for a long, long time, and when it didn't work, I collapsed. The deep exhaustion I experienced on every level of my being put an end to my ability to pretend to be a really, really good person. I didn't know it at the time, but I was hitting what the literature speaks of in the 12-step world as a "codependent bottom." This is the moment when one's way of being in the world is no longer working. I was familiar with the concept of codependency but thought it only related to how one behaved when living with an alcoholic.

No longer able to work, I was forced to rely on the kindness of my friends. This was the greatest gift my depression brought me. Broken and hopeless, I found myself on the couches of a few good friends at different times over the next few years. I still owned my home, but I would stay with friends because I didn't feel safe being alone. My suicidal thoughts were beginning to be more pervasive.

One fateful day, I awoke and something in me had shifted for the worse. There was a dead calm within me. I felt anxiety-free and numb to my depression. I knew this was the time to end my life. Having some small presence of mind, I heard a voice in me say, "Okay, Nita, do you really want to die, or do you just want out of your life?"

In the moments that followed, I found myself speaking out to the universe, saying, "Today I am going to shop for a gun, and I will also go to a bookstore; if anyone is listening, help me find the right book first."

Looking back, it sounds so silly—a book or a gun—but it was my moment of truth. Did I want to live? Part of me did. Kmart is a great full-service store, everything you need, including handguns, is there for the choosing. I found myself at the gun counter discussing which gun to buy with the clerk.

"Women usually like this one," the clerk said, holding up a cute little pink thing.

A cute little pink thing didn't seem quite right for the task I had in mind, and even in my temporary psychosis of the day, I could see the humor.

I thanked him and even said, "I'll probably be back, but gotta go to the bookstore first."

Walking into the bookstore in Yuma, Arizona, a very small rural town in the Southwest, I was not expecting to find any book that would help me, but my soul knew better. The bookstore stocked bestselling novels and fish and game books, mostly. I had been in the bookstore hundreds of times over the years; I had never noticed anything that even resembled a self-help section. That day, I walked in, almost trance-like. I looked straight ahead and there, sitting on its own, was a book titled *Awakening in Time*. I ran to the shelf, grabbed the book, and began to read it. *Awakening in Time: From Codependency to Co-Creation* by Jacquelyn Small was the book that saved my life that day.

And there was that concept again: "codependency"—what did that have to do with depression? I took it home, read it cover to cover, wept though most of it, laughed through some, and felt the life force coming back into my being. When I finished it, I saw the author's phone number in the book. I called her, and to my shock, Jacquie answered the phone as though she was my best friend and waiting for my call. I blurted out my story, thanked her for saving my life, and was prepared to say good-bye and hang up when she said, "Nita, how are you now?"

She actually seemed to care, and I responded, "I want to live, but I am scared that I will stay depressed."

She told me about healing workshops and retreats she did, and I signed up for one on the spot, not knowing how I would get there or pay for it.

Books, people, and songs seem to come to us just when we need them. I did go to the retreat with the gracious help of a close friend who paid for it. I was not prepared for the profound impact it would have on me. I found myself in the safest, most nurturing environment imaginable. Jacquie and her staff embraced me in all of my brokenness with dignity and genuine excitement. They knew, as did my soul, that I was about to discover how to access my own deep healing and creativity. They held the light of hope for me until I could find it myself. I could begin to trust in the process of my own life, though it took years before I could live continually in a state of trust and grace. The retreat was the first experience of many that altered the course of my life.

What was underlying this deep depression for Nita?

CODEPENDENCY AND CHEAP COMPASSION
Narcissistic Altruism

Don't compromise yourself. You are all you've got.
JANIS JOPLIN

What does *codependency* mean? It's a confusing and unfortunate word. Many people, like me, think it has something to do with being dependent on alcohol or drugs, or living with someone who is an alcoholic.

Narcissistic altruism is a more accurate name for the condition referred to as codependency. It is when we are caught in a misguided attempt to get our needs met by taking care of others. True altruism has no hidden agenda; it puts the needs of the other first with compassion. Cheap compassion is a form of "idiot compassion," which Buddhism teaches as false compassion. Compassion, to be authentic, comes from deep understanding and embracing of our own hurt, anger, and shame. We must first bring our wounding to consciousness and express the emotions attached to our early wounding so that we can move through to forgiveness. Without going through the deep, difficult emotions to find our own essence of self-love we can't be free to be compassionate to others. Sympathy and pity are confused with compassion. Coming from a place of subtle superiority we look upon someone who is less than us and feel sorry for them.

Authentic compassion and altruism are based on a foundation of strength and self-love. The outpouring of genuine concern and desire for another person to be relieved of suffering characterizes compassion. Altruism is defined by acting from a place that benefits the other without benefiting oneself.

Nita's Story
MY STORY CONTINUES

There's a great joke that goes like this: "When a codependent person dies, someone else's life flashes before them . . ."

The first time I heard this joke, I didn't get it. I didn't really know the difference between my life and someone else's. And furthermore, my life depended on me taking care of other people. The joke brought the same feeling of disbelief that I got on airplanes when they make that announcement about your oxygen mask: "Be sure to put your air mask on first before assisting anyone else . . ."

How could I do that? How could I leave my child, father, friend, or even the stranger sitting next to me unattended while I took care of myself first?

Put myself first? Not possible. What I learned next was the most shocking revelation of my life: If you don't take care of yourself first, no one else will, and you will not be able to take care of anyone. The instruction from the airline attendant is simply saying, "Put your mask on first, so you can keep breathing, and unless you do, you won't be able to help that person next to you . . ."

Ah, I get it, I am human too, and I need to breathe just like everyone else. Okay, now I was really depressed for I had to admit that I was one of them, part of the everyone crowd, the ones who suffered and were not perfect. With that realization, I curled up in a ball on the floor of the retreat center with loving, nurturing people surrounding me. I surrendered control and wept, without much letup, for three days. I wept at every group session; I wept in the hot tub in the evenings; I wept in my bed; and I wept at every meal.

I had cracked, and what was underneath was a whimpering, sobbing, mushy, vulnerable being without a clue of who I really was. Surely I would die. Shockingly, everyone at the retreat was not only kind and supportive, but they were actually celebrating my collapse as well. It felt like I was dying, and my grief was real. Yet it wasn't me who was dying; it was my personality, false self, the codependent hero, the narcissistic altruist, the Mother Teresa complex, my controlling and domineering self who was dying.

Narcissistic altruism thinking goes like this:

- I am okay.
- You are not.
- You need me to fix you.
- I need you to let me fix you so that you will take care of me.
- I don't have to see that I am not really okay.

That thinking no longer worked, and what was left was the ugly truth:

- I am *not okay;* I am depressed and bereft, and I don't know who I am.

THE MYTH OF VIRTUOUS SELF-DENIAL
Put Your Own Oxygen Mask on First

Where does the tendency start when we deny self and believe that we are serving others and being good? If we are honest, it starts out from a conscious place, but from a place of unconsciously adapting to the demands of our family and society. Codependency is said to be an honest mistake. It is a misguided attempt to please others where we think we are doing it to serve and be good; narcissism masquerading as altruism. Shockingly the reality is that we are trying to please others in order to be loved. We accept the meager substitution of being needed for being loved. We indulge in all manner of addictive behaviors in the pursuit of satisfying the insatiable drive of our own unmet primal needs.

Attending to personal wounding and unmet needs leads to clarity of motivation. Our motivation is clouded with unconscious resentments, cravings, and drives geared to feed our false personality structure. When we operate from an authentic (not narcissistic), altruistic position we are simultaneously taking care of others and ourselves. When the giving and caring for others is from a place of lack in the self, it is inauthentic, unsustainable, and leads to a breakdown in the relationships and projects. Someone is left feeling betrayed, everyone is left confused, and no one's needs are met.

Narcissistic altruism happens when we operate from unmet needs and overindulge in caring for others in a misguided attempt to feel good about ourselves. Our actions often do not match our intentions, and we find that we are unappreciated and often accused of being controlling and uncaring. It's so confusing because the intention comes from a genuinely caring place, that "honest mistake." Narcissistic altruism develops in response to sacrificing our essential self and longings to be loved and accepted.

The problem is that our intentions and actions are not aligned, because our unmet needs are unconsciously driving us. The unmet needs are like large gears that cause our intentions to go in one direction and our actions to go in another.

One woman describes how her actions didn't match her intentions: "I believed that I was helping my daughter with everything I did for her. It seemed that she didn't appreciate anything! Later when I did some personal work, I realized that I was doing things for her to make me feel better about myself. Things that I did weren't things she needed or wanted, they were things that I wanted someone to do for me. Now I do those things for me and give to her what she wants and asks for. I am not resentful, and she is grateful."

THE IMPORTANCE
OF LISTENING TO THE HEART

You've always had the power.

Glinda the Good Witch of the North, *The Wizard of Oz*

In learning to listen to our hearts we can find new ways of responding to life events that are not driven by emotional responses from childhood. Glinda taught Dorothy to speak from her heart, and in doing so Dorothy found her way home, home to herself. The symbolism in *The Wizard of Oz* is potent, and through an allegory the story speaks of the journey that many people take finding their way back home through their hearts. I believe Dorothy was not only bored, but she was bereft and depressed as well and was looking for her truth. She needed the journey to find compassion for herself.

Dorothy was living a life of narcissistic altruism. As she met each new character along the way, her only concern was getting them to the Wizard for help. Her own needs came last, and it wasn't until she was locked away in the tower of the Wicked Witch that she truly cried out for help for herself. Yet she continued to put herself last. When they were all at the Wizard's, she waited until everyone else got help before she could ask, "What about me?"

It was in the asking that Glinda came forward and showed her that what she needed was with her all along, she just had to want it badly enough. In other words, she had to admit her needs before she could access the magic of the ruby slippers, a metaphor for the heart. She had to leave home and journey for her own healing.

BE WILLING TO HEAL

Saying something out loud can set intention, so try saying something like this, "I am willing to heal and to be whole." If you can be more specific than that, great, but a simple statement of willingness gives your soul permission to take charge. The intention to heal into wholeness requires courage. Remember, bravery doesn't require fearlessness but simply willingness to do something even when we are scared to do it. Setting the intention, you are giving permission to your soul to come forward with the truth, and though it may be uncomfortable at times, I promise that you will be rewarded for your efforts.

We have to examine the obstacles to our hearing our wise soul voice. In our psyches are disowned dreams and unhealed trauma. Surviving by trying to be good is a response to external pressures and expectations, coupled with a deep belief that we are in danger. The narcissistic altruist tactic is being good in order to survive. While it may work intermittently, overall it keeps us locked in despair and unrealized potential. Our truth is stored deep within our psyches for safekeeping. We then forget we put it there.

Our personality eventually begins to disintegrate, and what is underneath demands our attention. It demands our attention, because buried underneath what we loathe and disavow about ourselves is our creativity and greatest gifts. Acknowledging that we have been hurt, wounded, or abused is never easy. Resistance to looking at pain and hurtful events of the past is normal. We erect our personality to mask our pain.

In the case of severe childhood abuse, often the memories are buried and arise unexpectedly. When the memories of abuse do come to consciousness the tendency is to minimize or even try to forget them again. And let's be clear, the determination of severity of childhood abuse is subjective, not an objective fact. While we might deem some events objectively horrifying, such as satanic ritual molestation with a young child, it is very difficult in most cases to claim whether what a person went through as a child was severe.

Remembering is the first step to healing. Acknowledging is a step beyond remembering. When we acknowledge that something painful was done to us we often reexperience the shame and fear that led us to repress a memory of the events in the first place. Lodged in the depths of our unconscious is the memory of the feelings about the wounding event. From the unconscious feeling memory, we formed beliefs about the world and who we are, and from these beliefs we react in present reality. We set up rules that we try to follow and expect everyone else to follow and are continually disappointed when the rules are broken or when we break our own rules.

Clearing our psyche of the beliefs requires that we uncover the feelings and bring them to consciousness for healing. We do not have to have an exact memory of the wounding event to heal the feelings that drive the beliefs that control our reactions today.

FEELINGS ARE REAL

There is some confusion in the healing process that we must be exactly correct about the events of our past and be certain that our feelings about our past are justified. This is the powerful lie that the personality holds on to in a misguided attempt to keep us safe. Breaking through the cycle of dysfunctional reactions only requires that you suspend belief about the accuracy of the details and pay attention to the feelings. The feelings are the bread crumb path to finding our way out of the forest and into the light of consciousness.

Remember, we developed the personality initially to protect us when we were vulnerable and in danger. Taken to an extreme, protective behavior is inhibiting and ceases to protect us. And this is the reason to bring it to consciousness. The personality is developed in a sequence as follows:

1. I am being hurt by someone.
2. It must be my fault.
3. I deserve to be hurt.
4. I am damaged.
5. I must hide that I am damaged.
6. I cannot trust and must vigilantly keep myself safe.

From here the next step seems to go in one of two directions:

1. I will be very, very good to pretend that I am not damaged by assuming the role of:

    a. Valedictorian

    b. Nun

    c. Beauty queen

    d. Perfect mother

    e. Successful executive

2. I will be bad and pretend that I deserve to feel bad by assuming the role of:

    a. School dropout

    b. Criminal

    c. Drug and alcohol abuser

    d. Negligent mother

    e. Self-sabotageur of my career

Both personality types keep us from healing. Both are fueled by the same goal, and both want to keep the memory and the feelings associated with it locked away. Both personality types are crying out for someone to notice them and, hopefully, recognize that they are in pain. The following are steps one may take to unravel this false personality we have created.

Steps to Unraveling Our False Personality

1. I must stop hiding and admit that I feel damaged.
2. I really am damaged by the abuse done to me.
3. I did not deserve to be hurt.
4. It was not my fault.
5. I was hurt by someone.
6. I trust and surrender that I can take care of myself.

YOUR INNER PERSONAL CRITIC IS NOT YOUR SOUL WHISPERER

Self-loathing results from an internalized—be it actual or perceived—negative message that typically is embedded in early childhood. As we have established but bears repeating here, your parents may have been basically kind and well-intentioned people. They even may have appeared to support you, yet you still were subjected to their unmet unconscious needs that landed on you as judgment and criticism. Depending on how you embodied those messages, you will now have them running in your head in the form of a subliminal monologue, ever reminding you that you are not perfect or even good enough. If your parents were abusive, the messages will be even more severe and more deeply embedded.

Take a moment and listen to the running monologue in your mind that spews negative messages. It may say things like "Who do you think you are?" or "You are so silly" or stupid or bad, or "Don't listen to this nonsense." Just observe and listen. Then write down a few things you hear. When we start to identify this voice we can discern that it is not our conscience, and certainly not our soul speaking. Our soul is always supportive, loving, and wants us to expand and grow. Our inner personal critic is judgmental, harsh, and wants us to contract and remain stuck. The inner personal critic is not useful in any way, it does not keep us in line, nor does it keep us from indulging in addictions and other self-destructive behaviors. Rather, its criticism is often what drives us to self-sabotage.

Another origin of self-loathing happens when we reject the authentic human experience of hate. Children hate with abandonment, and move on to love with equal passion. Hate is a powerful and passionate force, and it is not necessarily destructive. Embracing our experience of hate is to walk into the eye of the hurricane. Allowing the healthy expression of hate will bring us to a place of calmness. Denying it throws us onto the edges of the storm and tears us apart. When we deny our experience of hate toward someone or something, we turn it inward. And only then does the experience of hate become destructive.

Seeking safety and security, we do not express hate for fear of alienating the people we needed (to take care of us) as children. We learn to hate ourselves for feeling hate. Our hate is split off and banished to an unconscious holding tank and becomes a dark motivation for revenge and punishment of ourselves and others. Unconscious hate fuels our self-destructive behaviors, and it interferes with our natural impulses. Passion is dampened as our self-hatred stops us from knowing what we want. Eventually we must journey to reclaim our split-off self and embrace hate, lest it destroy us.

Healthy people experience hate and move through it. Hate is an authentic response to injustice and is the warrior face of compassion. Hate is meant to be disruptive and loud. It is meant to point out incongruities between what we value and what we are experiencing. In another vein, hate is simply our authentic response to feeling limitations and not getting our needs met. Recognition of hate serves us by showing us our needs and limitations.

Denying the authentic experience of hating fuels the inner critic's self-sabotaging and destructive behaviors, which lead to further self-loathing. Destructive behaviors can range from things as benign as denying ourselves pleasure in life to more serious and far-reaching behaviors such as addiction and abuse. The more destructive the behavior, the more shame we experience. The more shame, the deeper the self-loathing becomes and the more we engage in destructive behaviors. It is an endless cycle of self-defeat.

Firing the inner critic and forgiving ourselves is the antidote to self-loathing. Authentic forgiveness is only possible when we first admit that we have something to forgive ourselves for, which means admitting that we have been destructive toward others or ourselves. The inner critic will distract us from a loving self-examination by amplifying shame and causing us to contract rather than embrace our sometimes painful truths. Often we must face that we have hurt others, and usually the other is someone we are or were very close to, like our children or partner. Many times we have justified our destructive behavior because it was in reaction to a terrible wrong done to us; we don't count it as needing forgiveness because we feel self-righteous.

The inner critic fuels self-righteousness by goading the personality with increased accusations of wrongdoing. The personality reacts defensively and creates stories of being wronged by others to justify one's own destructive behavior. Self-righteousness always is an indication that we have something we feel shameful about, and we cling to the position of being entitled to the bad behavior because of what "they" did to us. Sadly this position fuels self-loathing. Unpacking the self-righteous baggage will be some of the most painful and most rewarding personal work we will ever do. Forgiveness is a result, not an action. We can say we forgive, but saying it doesn't make it so. Forgiveness emerges when we face our pain and surrender, *turning it over* as it is termed in the self-help language of Alcoholics Anonymous. This means letting go and accepting what feels unforgivable about oneself. After surrender, an honest appraisal without judgment becomes possible.

THE SHAMANIC PATH TO FORGIVENESS

When we take an honest look at things we have done that we are ashamed of, we have started on the road to self-forgiveness. Forgiving others is often easier than forgiving ourselves, but without self-forgiveness forgiving others can be inauthentic. If we unconsciously hold on to judgment about ourselves, we will lack deeper compassion and remain stuck in a loop of getting angry, forgiving, then getting angry again at the same type of behavior in others that we don't like in ourselves. Though we may forgive someone, we will not live fully in a state of forgiveness.

A state of forgiveness is one of openheartedness, of compassion for others and for ourselves. When we approach the world in a forgiving state of mind, daily living becomes much easier and more satisfying. A state of forgiveness assumes that things will go wrong, that we will do things we wished we hadn't, and that we will occasionally be hurt.

Forgiveness is about taking our power back. We are not perfect, but we give ourselves permission to admit mistakes, make apologies, and move on, rather than staying stuck in self-admonishment. We all know people who can openly admit their faults and take responsibility without beating themselves up. These folks seem lighthearted about their transgressions and personality flaws. They accept difficulty with grace, and because they are flexible and forgiving they are energizing and refreshing to be around.

Accepting life on life's terms means rolling with what is happening rather than being prisoner to unconscious beliefs you have about how things *should* be. What we take to be our system of values and beliefs are most often rigid laws that are unrealistic, and when we or others break these "laws" we revert to punishment. These laws were developed as a result of our wounds, what we saw in the world as children, or what our parents or religions taught us. The "laws" are meant to keep us safe, yet the unrealistic expectations set up by these self-created laws create the very pain that we are trying to avoid.

An example of an unreasonable law can be gleaned from Marsha's comment at a women's retreat. "My parents didn't see me, they didn't encourage anything about me, and I had to find my way in the world and that is why I am so controlling. No one else is going to take care of things; I have to do it myself."

Marsha's law was driving her victimhood and tendency to blame others. "Oh, I get it; I believe that parents are supposed to have the skills and wisdom to give us what we need."

While her law seems reasonable, the reality is that most parents stumble into parenthood without skills or knowledge and so expecting it to be otherwise is unreasonable. She understood she could not go back and change the way her parents raised her. She could, however, work with this new realization as she uncovered how the unconscious law had driven her behavior. "Wow, I have wasted a lot of energy and time trying to get the world to see that my parents were not there for me. And, in the process, I have become a control freak, something I am deeply ashamed of, and have never admitted until right now. Admitting it, and having the group accept that about me, and understanding where it came from, I can forgive myself; I feel so much compassion for myself." She wept as she shared with the group.

Recognition of the unconscious law allowed her to see her negative behavior and to understand and forgive herself. People hurt other people primarily because they are hurting. We are all, on some level, victims of our unconscious, rigid personal laws that lead to negative acts toward others.

The practice of forgiveness is something we must all undertake if we want to be healthy and able to move from personality-driven lives to soul-guided lives. We start by admitting that we have been wronged, or that we have wronged others. No one is immune from doing things that are shameful and even destructive. The inner critic will lie to us, telling us that we are the only ones who have done hurtful or destructive things. Firing the critic and quieting the voice will be one of the results of self-forgiveness work.

This process will move you from a place of being a victim, as Jennie describes. "As a young child a close friend of my father's molested me. I only began to remember it a few months ago. All my life I have hated myself without knowing why. I also didn't realize that I did hate myself. I dealt with the abuse by developing a harsh core, and I hurt a lot of men by coldly leaving them. When I began to face my behavior, I realized that I had always blamed others for my unhappiness. When my crisis came and I could no longer run from myself, and the memories came flooding through, I found that I really blamed myself for the abuse. Blaming others kept me focused outward, and I never had to look at my pain and the things I had done. Forgiving myself was critical to being able to forgive my abuser. Forgiving myself was difficult and liberating; forgiving him came much more easily."

Recovery from narcissistic altruism, otherwise referred to as codependency, is not a matter of withdrawing from caring or attending to others. Instead we move from self-loathing and overcompensation to self-love, compassion, and forgiveness. Recovery from depression is the same path.

Ruby Falconer, a colleague and friend, came to Venus Rising to heal her narcissistic altruism, and that journey led to her becoming a Soul Whisperer, author, master Shamanic Breathwork facilitator, and lead trainer for Venus Rising workshops and trainings. Ruby exemplifies how diving in to your own darkness can lead to being a guiding light.

When My Soul Began to Listen

Ruby Falconer

My shamanic life began when I was fifty years old. I am a California child of the '60s, a baby boomer, and like many of my generation I had a good many unusual and out-of-the box experiences before I was thirty. I became an astrologer when I was twenty-three, which became my life profession, and I worked at a variety of part-time jobs to support my passion for astrology. I was a teacher of what were then arcane and cutting-edge subjects, including past-life regression and guided meditation, and I offered classes and private sessions in astrology.

I traveled all over the western United States extensively and—oh yes—I became a marijuana addict. I lost about fifteen years to the deepest form of my addiction, meaning that those are the years I really can't remember all that well because most of the time I was stoned. And, as is the wont of addiction, these years became less and less enjoyable as time went on. By the time I was forty-five, I was beginning to come out of my desire to stay perpetually numbed out and was confronting the truth of my situation—that I was in a relationship that was draining me of every bit of life-force energy, living in a house that was crumbling around my ears, and I was desperately unhappy to the point that I really wanted to die. I did not see how I could survive much longer in the state I was in.

I began a circuitous route of searching for something better. I went back to school to study psychology while also working with a wonderful shamanic teacher—Lisa Rafel—and taking transformational workshops at Michael Harner's Foundation for Shamanic Studies. I gradually cleaned up, meaning I stopped using drugs and alcohol, which made the starkness of my situation even more apparent to me. I did not have a clue as to how to get out of the hole I had dug for myself and create a reason to stay alive.

It was then that I met the two authors of this book. I met Star Wolf at my first Shamanic Breathwork experience. I can't say enough about the usefulness of this technique and its pure power to break through the energetic and emotional blocks that keep people stuck in places they do not want to be. Other books have been written by Star Wolf about Shamanic Breathwork so I won't dwell on the topic here, except to say that if you haven't tried it, you should, particularly if you sense that something within you is stuck and needs to move. While I was sober by the time I went to my first Shamanic Breathwork workshop, I was emotionally and energetically clogged to a standstill. I could not hear the voice of my soul on any level, and

I was so unhappy that if something didn't change soon, I was going to die. I simply didn't want to be here anymore, to be embodied. When the will to live dies, the body soon follows, and I was on that path.

Five months after that first workshop, I went to a weeklong workshop with Star Wolf's organization, Venus Rising, where I met Nita Gage. The process of waking up had begun, and, although I did not know it, these two women were speaking to my soul. They nudged it and prodded it into life— and more than anything saw who I was at a soul level under the uptight, frozen, visibly upset, middle-aged woman who sat in front of them. Their craft and art began to help me untangle the knots I had gotten myself into so that I could come alive, perhaps for the first time in my life.

It wasn't an easy process, nor was it quick—although compared to the "lost years," it was very fast indeed. In essence, the unhealed wounds of my childhood had caught up with me. I won't go into the details—it's a story I've told in other places, and although important to me, the specifics aren't really germane to this tale. Suffice it to say, like many people I was raised by wounded souls who did not know how to nurture themselves, and so I grew up wounded too. Drugs and alcohol helped me avoid that fact for a long time—until they didn't.

At that point, I made a choice. I didn't know I was making that choice, or even that there was a choice, but—in essence—I chose life. That's when I scaled back on my drug and alcohol use, gradually stopping entirely, and when I began to go out and search—for something. I didn't know what. The voice of my soul was waking me up, but I was so clouded and emotionally confused that I really didn't know quite what to do or what I was looking for. I just knew that I needed something to change, or I was going to die.

I was ripe for the art of the Soul Whisperer, and I was drawn to Star Wolf and Nita like a moth to a flame. I wanted what these two had—which was indefinable. They were in some way lighter than I was. I don't mean that they were polarized into some sort of light consciousness—they were very down to earth and very funny. But they were also loving and accepting, not just of me but of everyone. They seemed capable of taking people as they were without feeling like they had to change them and without being knocked off their own moorings by other people's stuff. I felt seen by them.

They listened to me, didn't tell me what to do—although they might make suggestions—and they seemed to see in me a potential that I had always hoped was there but didn't really believe.

Ultimately, they saw my soul.

This is what a Soul Whisperer does, and it's also at the core of what was different about what they were doing from other counselors I had experienced. They did not see me as broken. They did not try to give me surface fixes, like a drug, or an affirmation, or a technique. They listened to my pain and, without condescending, acknowledged how hurt I was. They told me their own stories and shared their path of healing. By doing that, they gave me hope that I wasn't irreparably damaged—that I too could become lighter in my being. They created a safe container for me to cathartically release the pain that had been stored up over some fifty years.

That was a gradual process, like warm water slowly dissolving an ice cube. My essence was strangled by years of hurt, by carrying the pain of my family lineage on both sides. It took time to release the fear, grief, and anger that were stored in these cells. It's still releasing, but my primary life-force artery is much clearer now, much less clogged, and I not only have access to my own energy and vitality, but I can also hear the voice of my own soul.

I often tell people that my desire is to have my ego be the servant of my soul. I've never subscribed to the philosophical perspective, which— mercifully—seems to be fading away: that the ego is somehow the enemy and needs to be killed off. I can't quite imagine how one would navigate in this life without an ego taking care of business—making sure the bills are paid, a roof is over my head, and that I stop at red lights.

I've come to understand that the objective of the ego is to keep me here in this body so that I can do the work of my soul. In my years of addiction and emotional pain, my ego had very little desire to live. I had just about given up. I understand now that the reason that happened is that my ego couldn't hear the voice of my soul at all, and without that inner direction there was no real meaning to life. I was totally and completely unhappy. I had none of the things that many people use to fill up their life—no children, no family, I wasn't in love, I didn't even like where I was living, and my work—other than my astrology work—was not rewarding.

I know now that it was a last-ditch effort by my soul to break through my numbness, a sort of soul scream, that sent me on my quest to find . . . something—I didn't know what. But it led me to shamanic practitioners, and, just like cajoling a frightened animal or child, they began to call out my soul. Eventually I morphed into a person who could hear my own soul's voice. I made the changes I needed to make, and now I am able to listen to what has true meaning so that my external life is directed by my soul. It's my ego's job to get daily life done, but my soul determines the bigger picture of where I'm going and why. My soul is in charge.

Now, through my work with Venus Rising as a shamanic minister, teacher, and professional astrologer, I serve as a Soul Whisperer for others. I do my best to emulate my two mentors—listening without judging, offering guidance but not direction, following my clients' lead, and being patient with their process. And letting go of expectations. Knowing that everyone has their own schedule for healing, and some people's process takes longer than others. I can certainly relate to that—my process took almost fifty years to activate. And trusting that under that ego identity, which may be extremely accomplished and competent or may be confused, defensive, and completely messed up, there is a soul longing to be heard and seen.

I learn as much—or more—from those I work with as they do from me. I am continually coming up against some new piece of my wounded past that needs to be acknowledged, accepted, and integrated. It is a joyous process, for with each new "swoop through the loop," as Star Wolf calls it, I hear ever more clearly the voice of my own soul directing me onward through my path of life. Sometimes I go through dark periods, but I know them for what they are—a darkening of my path, like going through a tunnel or a deep forest. And as long as I keep moving, I know I will always come out the other side.

Several years ago, someone gave me a transcript of a speech given in 1996 by holistic health pioneer Dr. Rachel Naomi Remen in which she talks about the difference between "helping, fixing, and serving." She says, "In 40 years of chronic illness I have been helped by many people and fixed by a great many others who did not recognize my wholeness. All that fixing and helping left me wounded in some important and fundamental ways. Only service heals."[1]

    My, oh my, what wisdom there is here—words that I have shared with many of our Venus Rising students. This is at the heart of our frontier—the great shift that is rippling through our culture and into all of our established institutions. We do not need a system where someone else knows what is right for us and tells us how to stop being wrong. We are not wrong, we are not broken, and none of us needs to be fixed. We need to be seen and heard. Someone needs to call to our soul, waking it up, encouraging it to speak loud enough so that we can hear our own soul's longing. When we begin to hear the voice of our soul and find the strength and courage to act upon our soul's deepest desires, then we begin to move out of our dysfunction. We find the tools and the techniques to support our own healing, and we move on to what it is we are here to do. What a gift this process is. I am deeply grateful for it.

8

Shamanic Consciousness
in Everyday Life

What does it mean to live in a state of shamanic consciousness in everyday life? We are hardwired for enlightenment and altered states of consciousness. Every culture in the world outside of modern Western society utilizes altered and expanded consciousness for healing and to generate resilience. Some places use substances to reach these states. It's well known that the substance works by triggering a neurochemical and cellular reaction. That same reaction can be initiated without drugs. Hypnosis, ecstatic dance, meditation, trance—all are examples of altered states of consciousness.

Integrating Ancient Wisdom with
Modern-Day Shamanic Consciousness

Star Wolf explains how she started to use the term *shamanic*.

In the early '90s, I formed my own brand of breathwork training and knew immediately what I wanted to call it—the Shamanic Breathwork process. The word *shamanic* was the only word that felt big enough at that time. It described what I was experiencing on so many levels and what I was beginning to teach others who were showing up in my workshops and private practice. Simultaneously, I was continuing to study and undergo many different kinds of shamanic journeys, ceremonies, initiations, and teachings with numerous Native American teachers,

Mayan shamans, and other indigenous elders. I remained open to the emerging paradigm shifts in the realms of medicine and science. During that time, I began to see the divine connection—the thread that was weaving together what I had sought earlier in my life. It was like a stream on a trail that had disappeared underground. Even when it disappeared from my view, it reemerged again and again with even more force and a clearer view each time in my visions and in my life.

Shamanic Breathwork is an evolution of Integrative Breathwork created by Jacquelyn Small, MS, and Holotropic Breathwork created by Stan Grof, M.D. Shamanic Breathwork integrates indigenous shamanic practices and draws from pranayama yogic breathing techniques. Leonard Orr, the creator of Rebirthing, told Star Wolf that Shamanic Breathwork also has its roots in early spiritual practices and teachings going back to Indian saints such as Babaji.

Shamanic consciousness is a powerful way to live in the world and allows us to see things from many different perspectives all at once without invalidating various points of view. It is this inclusive multidimensional thinking and way of being in the world that is going to help us all break through to other realities. The old-world paradigm that has been running the show for so long is almost extinct. Let's just hope that we don't all become extinct with it.

How does the practice of Soul Whispering fit in to living a life of shamanic consciousness? Employing imaginal experience, Soul Whispering supports people in releasing past trauma, visioning the future self, and connecting with our multidimensional selves. Soul Whisperers utilize energy medicine and shamanic practices, along with neuroplasticity-enhancing techniques, to facilitate transformative experiences. Central to these practices is the importance of expanded states to consciously access collective spiritual states. Additionally, clearing hidden personal blocks that interfere with a connection to the collective is critical to healing wounds and achieving transformation.

To live in shamanic consciousness in everyday life, we must put on another set of eyes and ears. We need to alter all of our senses, to perceive the world differently from how we most often view reality. Changing how you perceive events and situations will change who you are. It may initially cause feelings of separation from those who have not peered into this realm that you are now experiencing. Agreements between self and others about the world and our surroundings are mainly determined by consensual reality. Consensual reality is determined largely by unconscious beliefs learned in early childhood.

The unconscious nature of how we perceive the world is the main reason that people don't change or want to see things differently. How we perceive reality then continues to create our reality. Matter or form follows energetic thoughts and beliefs. We know through quantum physics and science that when you pay attention to matter, the particles of that subject change as a result of being observed. Thus by seeing things differently we shape-shift our reality. Instead of saying, "When I see it, I'll believe it," it really would be more accurate to say, "When I believe it, I will see it." Many people accept their outer circumstances without a lot of reflection or thought about how their reality is created, and you may hear them say or you may have said yourself, "This is just the reality of 'the real world.'" However, the real world is the world we create as we go along with what we believe and see in the moment and interpret it through our unconscious, predetermined set of beliefs.

Consider the situation of a group of people looking at exactly the same situation and each person offering a different interpretation of that situation. Sometimes it's a significantly different recounting of a specific situation. Each person is not only perceiving the situation differently, but they may actually be *experiencing* a specific event differently. They are reacting to a situation in the present through the filter of historical emotions.

SEEING THE WORLD AS AN ALCHEMICAL MAP

The perspective of living shamanic consciousness every day is to develop a unique perspective of seeing things from a sacred point of view. One of the most important ways to see things from a shamanic or sacred point of view is to see the world elementally, as an alchemical map. This consists of using the cycles of change correlated to the actual elements of water, earth, fire, and air with the additional dimension of spirit. When we see everything as a pathway to shamanic consciousness and learn to look for the "bigger archetypal story," we see a spiritual connection in all of the shifts and changes in ourselves and all around us. The influential or governing force that's happening in nature and in the supernatural world creates an alchemical shift in our lives. It also means trusting that there is a natural flow and direction and perhaps even a divine blueprint that's unfolding in every moment.

For many of us, trust is missing in our life. Instead of trusting we are strategizing to create safety or optimize our experiences. Trust involves acknowledging that each moment is unfolding and that we cannot know what is happening next. The illusion of certainty interferes with our ability to trust. The letting go of the illusion of certainty allows the first steps toward trusting. Because certainty is only an illusion, then you are not letting go of certainty, you are releasing an illusory perception.

When we are struggling with transitions in our lives, it may seem very hard to believe that by simply letting go of certainty and opening our minds and hearts we are literally changing our world. When we observe things differently in the world we change our perspective on the things all around us and subsequently see those changes in the outer world. Early in the New Age movement it was not uncommon to hear people using the phrase "You are creating your own reality when confronted with an unpleasant situation." Although there was truth in the phrase, the way it often came across was judgmental and overly simplistic. Even in the more mundane fields of psychology and addiction, especially in family of origin material, we hear talk about taking responsibility for our own patterns and personal growth.

We recognize that old family of origin patterns influence how we see and create our present realities. It is important to dis-identify, or *individuate* (a term from Jungian psychology), from the reality of others if it is not in alignment with our present life. When we let go of the old patterns, we feel better because we are not in a constant state of reaction and regression. We were not even aware of being in those states. Rather, reaction and regressive attitudes were dictating our behavior and how we felt. Just bringing awareness to these states is the first step. Taking action to create new attitudes, feelings, and behaviors is necessary for lasting change. The result is that we are often freed from feelings of depression and anxiety when our family patterns of the past are cleared.

To go even deeper into a shamanic perspective, understand that everyone and everything goes through many cycles of birth, death, and rebirth throughout a lifetime. Through this we all shape-shift our perception of reality on a variety of levels. We are not just talking about the ordinary biological trajectory of life (birth, childhood, adolescence, adult, old age, and eventually death). The change we are talking about refers to every single thing in our lives. If we pay attention to our thoughts (mindfulness) we gain new awareness, insights, and information that will change those thoughts.

The thoughts we are not paying attention to die. Dying thoughts occur because of a process of pruning neurons in our brains so that the thoughts literally are pruned from consciousness. New thoughts and neurons are built through attentive awareness. New thoughts create new patterns of thinking and believing and ultimately new behavior. If we are paying attention we can consciously watch our realities change significantly. We are open to noticing everything around us, which includes the natural world and the laws of synchronicity.

SYNCHRONICITY AS A MARKER ON THE ALCHEMICAL MAP

Synchronicity is the phenomenon that occurs when we have an inner awareness that suddenly opens us to experiences in the outer world. It feels like the universe has conspired to validate our inner awareness. In an earlier chapter, Nita talked about the synchronicity she experienced in her encounter with a tiger. The experience was a series of events that were linked for her because she had created an intentional awareness of the tiger as a significant image. She deepened the experience by bringing awareness to the possible message that the tiger experience had for her, creating meaning and precipitating the spontaneous healing of a trauma. The trauma was her belief that she had caused her mother's death. That belief came from admonitions from her parents. So the synchronicity stimulated healing, because the events were paired with intention and an altered state of consciousness that allowed buried material to surface.

Another example: Perhaps you have a mysterious encounter with a wolf one night in your dreams and then the next day you flip on the History Channel and there is a whole story specifically about the life of wolves. Then you're driving down the road and the car in front of you has a bumper sticker that says, "Raised by Wolves," and later on that day a friend sends you a card with the photo of a wolf on it. Finally, Wolf has your attention, and you question these apparent synchronicities instead of just shrugging them off as coincidences. And you ask yourself, "Could there be a message in the sudden unsolicited appearance of the wolf?" and, "What might its symbolic significance be?"

What might be the reason for the wolf to have shown up repeatedly in the past twenty-four or forty-eight hours of your life? You could say it's just coincidence, which is saying that it really means nothing. Or you could view your wolf encounter through shamanic eyes and say, "Hmm, this feels like a meaningful synchronicity," and, with a sense of curiosity and open-mindedness, wonder at what it all means. Maybe you Google and research the metaphysical or Native American symbolic meaning of the wolf, or order a book about wolves from Amazon. At this point you might suddenly realize that your soul seems to use the wolf as a means to communicate with your conscious outer mind to gain your attention that then signals a powerful transformational time in your life.

Your journey may suddenly change and lead you down a pathway where Wolf reappears from time to time in some form, like a beacon drawing you to new experiences. You find yourself in unusual situations and meet others who are traveling a similar path. Then, one day you know that you have entered a new place within yourself and an entire mythological, archetypal story has come into your life as the wolf. Sometimes big changes occur rapidly. Later on you will always remember this time when the veils parted, for it allowed something to lead you other than your regular ego's agenda. Instead you allowed yourself to follow your soul down a new and unfamiliar path. This becomes a part of your story—a rich cosmology of your own psyche. From a shamanic perspective one might say that Wolf is now a part of your medicine, healing, and a spirit or soul guide. You may even forget about Wolf for a while, and then some years later the wolf comes howling and bounding back in. In remembering the time before when Wolf magically appeared in your life you might ask if this experience is similar to when it showed up the first time. And you might eagerly invite the wolf to be your guide once again to assist you in this new situation.

EVERYTHING IS SACRED

In the shamanic world everything that comes to us is sacred (both in the natural and mystical realms). It all becomes potential messengers for the unseen worlds that live in between the layers of consciousness. Many people live with a more constricted view of reality, where two- or three-dimensional reality rules their minds. Things are divided into black or white. Life is lived as if it were a linear event. Anything that doesn't fit into that linear model of how it should be is seen as being "off." There is something wrong if you step out of the safe, prescribed way of seeing the world. In the spiral world of shamanic consciousness, you can hop energetically from place to place interdimensionally and even realize that you are able to be in several places at once.

Shamanic people are the ultimate multitaskers. They know that today they are feeling disgruntled in one area of their life. However, in another area they are feeling very joyful and creative. In yet another aspect they may be ungrounded. With awareness of several aspects of themselves they can navigate through all of these places throughout the day without feeling that they are losing it or that they are crazy!

They become fluid beings who know that they can change all of these awarenesses throughout the day. Instead of feeling unfocused, they can see themselves as being in multidimensional levels of consciousness. Much like a computer can have several windows open all at once, your essence is the one navigating consciously between the windows of your experience.

When you ask someone how they're doing, the response will be "fine" or "okay" . . . if they are more open emotionally, they might be honest enough to say, "sad" or "happy," for instance. A shamanic person might ask you, "Which aspect of me are you speaking to?" By knowing what the person is asking, a shamanic answer would be one that speaks authentically from a few different perspectives. Also, by knowing what the asker is requesting, the shamanic response will take into account the experience of the asker, not just the experience or the responder. The intersection of realities is the space that a shamanic person loves to occupy. This is the in-between world, the world of the relational, not the reality of "my world" and "your world." Rather, it is "our world."

By knowing where we are energetically we can have a greater influence over changing our reality, and we can truly create our own authentic experiences with ourselves and others. Maybe we can't change everything in the world or anybody else, but perhaps we can change ourselves enough to change the world. A person who is shamanic is familiar not only with the concept and the process of change, but they are also familiar with constant change, such as is found in our constantly changing weather. In the morning it might be misty; by midmorning there is a light mist in the sky with the sun shining through; in the afternoon you might see clear, bright blue sky completely; then suddenly the clouds gather and rain moves through the mountains. Then the sun will shine while it's raining as the rain moves on with the clouds!

Practicing how to live with and through each spin of the spiral with the cycles of change, and holding the consciousness that with change there is a death, whether it is symbolic or real, will create a more realistic and powerful human consciousness. Change always involves letting go of something, letting something die. Perhaps it's the death of an attitude, or the more tangible death of a relationship, or a job, or career, or the actual death of a loved one. Death is at the forefront of change, and hence the human drive to avoid change. Developing shamanic consciousness by definition means accepting the reality of death. This means embracing the reality that death is with us always. Native Americans use the phrase *today is a good day to die* not because it's a lousy day, but rather because it has been a day lived fully and with joy. Living fully and joyfully is the shamanic way, and that happens by accepting the transitory, unpredictable nature of existence and living with curiosity and wonder.

And remember, transformation always happens on a spiral, which has no beginning and no end. The following story from Nita illustrates this key shamanic concept.

Nita's Story
A STORY OF EVERYDAY SHAMANISM

Years after the evening of tigers and redemption, I was working in a soul-deadening job. Again, the energy of shamanic medicine unhinged a false personality piece and opened the way for another soul return.

"You have a dream life and a dream job!" one of my closest friends exclaimed when she dropped by my office on the twenty-seventh floor of a prestigious location in San Francisco. As she spoke these words, I laughed to myself, because, just hours before, I had contemplated leaping off that building. The dream job was actually a nightmare. I would soon discover that many other middle-aged women were trying to survive in this same cult of youth and beauty masquerading as a health care corporation.

One weekend, I spent a day on the beach near my home with friends. Overtaken by despair at the thought of going to work on Monday morning, I fell to my knees asking for guidance and strength to make a change in my life. Following the teaching of Native Americans, I drew a medicine wheel in the sand and began to fashion a healing circle for myself.

In the four directions of the wheel I placed objects from the beach that spoke to me: feathers in the North to represent air; seashells in the East to represent water; bear claws I fashioned out of twigs were placed in the West to represent power, death, and rebirth; and stones were put in the South for wisdom. With all four directions and elements represented, I drew another circle in the center and left it empty to invite in spirit.

As I worked, I felt a presence guiding me—loving me. I became entranced with my creation. My friends, who had walked off in their own contemplation, came back and stood nearby, quietly yet enthusiastically, as I completed my sand painting. It didn't make sense entirely, but I didn't try to understand what I had created. I knew on a deep level that I was externalizing my resistance and offering it up to be transformed into healing. I even found a golf ball on the beach (we were nowhere near a driving range), which I took to represent the corporate world in which I didn't fit (I had long ago realized that I wasn't *one of them,* because I hated golfing). My prayer, as I finished the medicine wheel, was to be released from whatever held me back from pursuing my true purpose. I left the beach feeling a deep shift in the center of my being. I assumed I would have a shift in attitude and be better able to use my job as a path to my true purpose. This was the first of many spontaneous altars—what I call "personal artistic structures" that I created and encourage others to create to call in change when feeling stuck.

On Monday, I went to work as usual. After about an hour of trying to focus on e-mails and phone calls, restlessness began to creep over me. The restlessness grew into urgency. I couldn't handle the responsibilities of my job: e-mails, phone calls, writing, and researching. I felt terribly uncomfortable, like an animal when an earthquake is about to strike.

I paced, tried to sit, and paced some more. I looked around my own office, and my eyes scanned its layout. I could see it was filled with cubicles in the center and offices around the perimeters, all occupied by unhappy women. Cancer, depression, anxiety, disappointment, obesity, and addiction—they were everywhere. The women I saw weren't living from their truth. They defined themselves to be successful, yet they all admitted to being miserable, depressed, and worse.

Soul hunger was everywhere. It was not only my own. It permeated the office, lurking through the corridors and seeping into every cubicle. I felt an urge to jump on top of my desk and start shouting words of spiritual revolution! I thought of Sally Fields in the film *Norma Rae,* whose character was a factory worker who led the fight to unionize. In one evocative scene, she stood on a table and held up a sign that read "Union" and turned circles for all to see—this, despite the knowledge that she would be fired or possibly killed for her defiance in the small, patriarchal town. In that moment, it didn't matter to her.

If I had a sign, it would read "Be yourself," a notion as controversial to maintaining the norm as the union sign had been in the factory. My coworker Sarah worked in a cubicle, which was the corporate equivalent of being from the wrong side of the tracks. On this fateful day, I looked at her and blurted out, "I think I'm losing it. I can't take it another minute, and I can't take the subtle brutality of pretending to be someone I am not!"

"Go home, Nita, before you do something we will all regret," Sarah said without hesitation. Knowing it was worse than I thought, I took her advice. Careful to not be seen by my boss, I crept back to my office, grabbed my bag, and, without even shutting down my computer, tip-toed down the hall to the elevator.

As I walked toward the door, I could feel myself shape-shifting. I knew that if I didn't get out fast enough, I would turn in to a wolf, and my truth would bare its fangs and attack. I hurried out, checking over my shoulder to make sure that my tail wasn't showing, pounced into the elevator, and got down to the lobby, rushing madly to the street.

I ran all the way to the commuter ferry, imagining myself tearing through a forest pursued by predators. I resisted looking back for fear of turning in to a pillar of salt. Once I was across the bay and stepping off the ferry, I regained my senses long enough to call my boss and say, "Hi. So sorry. I felt really ill and had to leave."

"No problem, honey. Take care of yourself," was her response.

Knowing her, this was the last thing she really wanted me to do. No doubt she was actually thinking, *Silly woman. What's the matter? Having a hot flash you can't handle?* I drove home that day feeling like a bird let out of a cage. This feeling soon gave way to the awareness that I had leaped off a cliff and flown, but now I was free falling with no sense of whether I would crash or have a safe landing. For three days I called in sick. On the fourth, I knew I was never going back.

I was the primary source of income for the family. How could I leave my job under those circumstances? I had no savings or other sources of revenue. We lived in a small home with a mortgage payment that had consumed nearly half of my earnings. I had learned early in life that personal happiness did not matter, particularly mine. I believed that I was being responsible and that there was a divine plan for me. This thinking, while helping me cope, was also keeping me trapped. I was attempting to assuage the horrific reality of my life by using New Age practices. I was living in what I came to understand was a state of spiritual bypass.

Spiritual bypass is a mistaken belief that if we pray enough, meditate enough, tithe enough, eat right, and only think positive thoughts, our life will ascend, finally reaching enlightenment. After I left the job (or, rather, ran screaming from it), I struggled for months with feelings of failure based on the belief that I had not been able to withstand the oppression in the workplace.

This sense of failure didn't start with the job; rather, I was in a job that made me feel like a failure because of earlier soul loss. This particular soul loss happened as a young child. At the time of my birth, my mother was busy caring for my physically handicapped sister, so she hired an elderly woman as a nanny for me. This woman adored me and was always with me. When I turned two, my parents decided they no longer needed her, and she left. According to my parents, I was inconsolable, which is hardly a surprise. Thereafter, I was anxious every time my mother left my side.

The loss was intolerable to a vulnerable two-year-old child, and part of me simply left the scene. With that part of me went my desire to succeed. I was left with hopelessness. As I grew, this manifested as a disinterest in expending energy on anything that would make things happen or move things forward for myself. If things did not come easily, I simply let them be difficult. I neither tried to change my situation, nor did I leave it.

Eventually, this soul loss became a diagnosis: depression. My path led me to seek help through transformational methods as opposed to medical ones. I am fortunate that I did not involve myself with the medical world—surely I would have been medicated, and my soul loss would have deepened. Many people experience abuse and complications resulting from further mistreatment in a system that simply isn't designed to work with soul loss. My own inner wisdom led me to shamanic energy medicine, and from there my real healing began.

A component of shamanism and Soul Whispering is a practice called "stalking the mind," and this is something that I learned to do as part of my shamanic training and is something that I actively engage in today. Stalking the mind works to strengthen one's access to a conscious awareness of the soul's purpose. It's a disciplined practice that involves being vigilant about one's thoughts, one's moods, and the quality of one's self-talk. For me, it helps to monitor my occasional feelings of depression, which typically now only last hours—sometimes a day or two. What is pertinent is that my depression is no longer deep, and I have come to see it as a gift—a signal that I am either working too hard or not listening to, or speaking, my truth. I now know how to rectify the situation and how to move on with my life. I have come to embrace the dark times with love and acceptance.

Using the shamanic Soul Whispering tools at my disposal enables me to work through difficult times in whatever way they manifest in my life. My issue happens to be depression, but that may not be yours. Yours may be anxiety, insecurity, or simply flatness—a lack of happiness. Buddhists say that unhappiness is the indication that we are separated from our inner truth and are not following our own spiritual path. Happiness is our best barometer of health and well-being, and the lack of it is the greatest risk factor for illness. Being happy is not a luxury. It is a basic necessity for all of us.

Today, my life exceeds my dreams and rewards me daily. Deepened by experiences (even the darkest ones), I understand that I have been training for and have successfully created a more heart-centered, authentic, and fulfilling life.

ACCESSING THE IMAGINAL PLANE
OF EXISTENCE

Earlier we referenced Einstein's quote "No problem can be solved from the same level of consciousness that created it." In saying this, he was imploring us to leap ahead in consciousness and bring a new vision to the table. We must make peace with letting go of tried-and-true ways and find a new, practical, grounded reality in this space-time continuum. When we do this we are in some ways time traveling. We are reaching into the imaginal future of collective awareness, as a shaman does, and pulling valuable insights and knowledge into the present. When we expand our wings and expand our consciousness in a variety of ways, we really are time traveling into the future. Star Wolf elaborates on this somewhat in this extract from her book *Visionary Shamanism,* coauthored with Anne Dillon.

According to many of the great spiritual traditions—Hinduism, Buddhism, esoteric Christianity, and some indigenous teachings—everything already exists and, in a manner of speaking, has already happened on some imaginal plane of existence; *everything already is* . . . It's not *going* to happen; it's not that it *will happen* someday. However, because of our innate need to focus on times and events sequentially in order to have a "human experience," we are created and designed to see the past, present, and future in a linear space-time continuum. They are reference points that we have collectively created so that we can exist in a spatial reality where our life lessons are learned and synchronistic occurrences congregate to give us clues about the truth of our powerful shamanic natures. . . .

Visionaries like Buckminster Fuller, Henry Ford, and Albert Einstein could easily draw upon this ability. Barbara Marx Hubbard, a well-known teacher of spiritual evolution, refers to this energy as the imaginal cells. She has greatly popularized the notion even though Deepak Chopra has been given credit for coining the phrase, drawing upon scientific findings and research to do so.

The imaginal cells are the very valuable part of us that already have an existence in another realm. In some ways it is as if they have already lived in the future; they are the seeds of the future that are downloading into our human energy fields and into our human levels of consciousness.[1]

Opening ourselves up to the imaginal cells, we allow those cells to download, into our psyche, information about the future, impressions from other dimensions, and codes to reprogram our DNA. Shamanic consciousness is the capacity for transformation or change. Here we are talking about a symbolic death and rebirth, or at least the potential for a rebirth. This is a more user-friendly attitude toward change, in that change is seen as a natural process, as a living process, and the only truly sustainable process for being on this planet. To explore these imaginal realms, you may tune in to the audio track "Contacting Your Future Self" and be open to the transformational journey that it will lead you on.

IMAGINAL AND TRANSPERSONAL PSYCHOLOGY

Imaginal psychology is essentially shamanic psychology; it uses images, journey, art, and music of some sort to communicate with the soul, just as shamans do. The imaginal world is accessed every time one prays, meditates, or dreams. Contemplative prayer and meditation are forms of accessing the imaginal world in that they promote an awareness of nonordinary experiences, such as the phenomena of angels, or the existence of God. Research clearly supports what people of faith already know—that an experience of the imaginal is no different from our embodied knowledge than it is from an experience that is tangible. In other words, if we see and experience angels, or God, we can believe that experience was real and affects us just as any tangible experience would.

Psychology lost its focus on the soul in service of a scientific approach to treatment. The split precipitated a fractured healing in the psychology world in that both therapists and clients were examining only the clients' psychological issues (not their spiritual ones), with the goal being an integrated ego. At the same time, the field of religion and spirituality was fractured, because it taught people to bypass their ego and personal problems and focus only on transcendence.

At the same time that the split between psyche, soma, and soul was being deliberated upon, many thinkers, such as Carl Jung, were simultaneously evolving what were the roots of transpersonal psychology. Freudian students, such as Wilhelm Reich, Otto Rank, and many others along with Jung, were already rejecting Freud's strict separation between mind and soul. Freud himself got most of his ideas for ego psychology from Georg Groddeck, M.D., who in 1923 wrote a book called *The Book of the It.* He had recognized, before Freud had, that his patients' physical complaints all stemmed from unrecognized/unconscious frustrated needs and desires.[2] Carl Jung corroborated this idea when he said, "The separation of psychology from the premises of biology is purely artificial, because the human psyche lives in indissoluble union with the body."[3]

While both psychology and spirituality brought significant gifts, there came a time, in the '90s, when people began to express the need for an integration of the two fields. Medicine also felt this growing consumer demand, and new fields were birthed. Integrative medicine and transpersonal psychology are two of the fields that emerged in response to the evolving consciousness, both individually and collectively.

Another arena where spirituality and healing were integrated was the grassroots Alcoholics Anonymous and all related 12-step programs. Bill W., AA founder, as we stated above, seemed to be influenced by Carl Jung's work on spirit and the shadow. The authors, and many people who are involved with AA and other 12-step programs, agree that the 12-step programs of recovery and *The Big Book* were divinely inspired. Over and over in 12-step meetings you hear that alcoholism is a disease for which there is only a spiritual cure. Over time, the tenets of AA have been adopted for many purposes. And the influence of the concept of spiritual cure has permeated psychology and medicine.

As with all shifts in the paradigm, there are people who are on the leading edge, followed by people who see what they are doing and provide validation. One such leading figure, in addition to Freud and Jung, was renowned American psychologist Abraham Maslow. Maslow diagramed our human needs with a pyramid showing that food and shelter are the foundation of survival and must be met prior to meeting spiritual and transpersonal needs. However, he also taught that without the spiritual and transcendent aspects of ourselves, we will suffer, so it is not a linear ascension from physical needs to spiritual transcendence. Rather, we are living all aspects at once in a spiraling motion of healing, discovery, and transformation.

According to Maslow's hierarchical chart, the first level of need is comprised of the need for safety and survival. The seventh, highest level is our need to connect with the Divine. Interestingly enough, his chart of needs may be likened to the chakra system of the human body, as follows:

Chakra 1: survival—food/shelter
Chakra 2: creativity and sexuality
Chakra 3: personal power/standing in the community
Chakra 4: heart and personal love and connectivity
Chakra 5: voice in the world, truth telling, being recognized
Chakra 6: awareness of inner higher self; knowledge of God
Chakra 7: connectivity to the Divine, God, Higher Power

REACHING BEYOND
THE DICTATES OF THE EGO

The word *psyche* has its roots in the word *soul*. Transpersonal psychology is concerned with waking up the unconscious parts of us to bring our whole being into alignment—mind/body/soul. In this, transpersonal psychology goes beyond ego psychology by recognizing the ontological nature of the soul. Transpersonal psychology goes to the source, working with an exploration of the soul and soul loss, rather than only focusing on ego development and ego structures. Psychological health is dependent on the ability to connect with the soul's purpose, which we may do through the practice of Soul Whispering.

The following are precepts of ego-driven versus soul-driven psychology.

Ego Psychology

Instinctual drives

Human development is linear

Thought dictates emotions and behavior

Frustrated childhood needs shape future

Goal is ego integration

Soul Psychology

Longing for meaning

Development is a spiral journey

Intentionality co-creates with higher self

Soul chooses childhood to learn lessons

Goal is ego transcendence

CHARACTERISTICS OF
THE INNER SHAMAN/SOUL WHISPERER

Soul Whispering, as we have established, is the practice of imaginal shamanic psychology. Following are some of the characteristics associated with it.

- It contacts us through everyday experiences such as bodily symptoms, synchronicities, intuition, and dreams.
- When given the opportunity, through altered states of consciousness such as meditation, contemplative prayer, guided imagery, journeying, and dreaming, it brings forward the imaginal world and shows us what is fragmented and how to bring wholeness back to ourselves.
- It is our inner voice, our intuition, to which we can turn for guidance.
- The inner shaman is nonjudgmental and holds all experiences as sacred: death/birth, joy/grief, success/failure, love/hate.
- It restores balance to our lives by going to any lengths—including painful experiences of loss, illness, or near death—to awaken us to the change that is needed.

- It brings the sense of wholeness and the sense of connection to the oneness, or Divine.

The goal is to awaken each person to an understanding that we are co-creating our lives. We are not victims, and we are not alone. Neither are we in control. Once our reparative work is carried out and we have moved from victim/damaged child to conscious, responsible adult we are at a different place on the spiral journey of spiritual awakening. At this time we can turn our focus, as Maslow has pointed out, to the task of deepening our connection to the Divine. We can then consciously, rather than unconsciously, co-create our lives.

Below is a story from Pam Savory, who, in a program with us, took the leap into shamanic consciousness and in so doing explored an aspect of her hidden shadow that was seeking release and transformation.

The Weavings of a Soul Whisperer

Pam Savory

It is my first shadow Shamanic Healing Initiatory Process (SHIP) five-day, and I have no idea what to expect. We are a committed group of people who have agreed to going through five initiations that last five days each. This is our second week together. I understand that the shadow is something others see in us but that we don't necessarily see in ourselves. The shadow, when unconscious, sabotages self and can hurt others. I trust Star Wolf's words that there is gold to be found in our shadow. What else can I do . . . . I am already here.

And here is a very hard place to be as I have left behind my comfortable world of three children and a loving husband. I don't know if I am more worried about them missing me or me missing them, but I know that I have to be here to do this work.

After a beautiful invocation for our guides and angels to join us, along with some sage to facilitate our clearing and being present, we introduce ourselves. I am fully attentive to the other ten participants, but I don't remember a thing I said!

Soon we are led into a small meditation to have a possible glimpse of the shadow piece that we will be working with over the next several days. Star Wolf has some wonderful music playing and tells us to go to a house, any house. In my mind's eye I approach a house in the woods. When she says to make it something familiar, I immediately see that it is Hansel and Gretel's house. When I put my hand on the railing, it is sticky, so not only does it look like a candy cane, but it is a candy cane. It is fairly dark and sparse inside. I walk by a wall made of chocolate and swipe it with my finger and take a taste (I do love sugar!). I wander around aimlessly, noticing that there isn't much there other than the sweetness of the house.

When Star Wolf tells us to go to the basement door, I open the door and am in my last childhood home. The following is from my journal and recounts my experience.

As I descend the basement stairs, I immediately feel the darkness of our basement seep into me through my shallow breath. Each step has its own unique creaky sound, and without looking, I know I have just stepped onto the fifth step that has a hinged top and that I can fit into. That means six more steps. I glance to the left and see the old upright piano that reminds me of a pumpkin with missing and broken teeth. I have written on the white keys in pencil so that when I sit to play a song I can "read" the music because I have written the corresponding numbers on the notes of the music sheets. Numbers make more sense to me than these black circles with straight lines, flags, and other characters that somehow give the musician a story of rhythm. Today, in the shadows, the piano appears to have a sneering sinister smile as if it knows that there is something disquieting awaiting my presence. I notice the stacks of boxes, papers, and unwanted memorabilia stacked atop the piano and on the ledge above, not quite completely exiled but shunned to the dark corners of memory.

To the right, I see the chest freezer that holds its own terror for me. Being the littlest in the family, I am often the one not doing anything productive, so I am sent to the basement to get something out of the freezer for dinner. The lid is heavy and has no mechanism to keep it up, and each time I have to reach deep inside, I fear falling in, locked away in its dark, icy interior until finally someone notices that I am missing. In front of the deep freezer is the pool table, and as I reach the bottom of the steps, I walk to the 8-ball and *roll it to the farthest hole in hopes to sink it, in my mind saying,* It is bad luck if I miss. I miss. *As I walk around the table to try again, I notice my dad's forbidden upright tool chest. I say "forbidden" because it is the only clean and shiny thing in the basement, actually in the house . . . and no one is allowed to touch it. If there is a tool out of place, he knows it. Below and behind the chest is where the spiders reside, mostly Daddy longlegs. I look to see if they are home today or if they are also on a journey.*

Right at this moment, we are told to approach the shadow. I see a black widow spider that is larger than me, and it covers the entire upright tool chest with its many drawers that seem to hold many more hidden secrets than neatly placed tools. Before I know what is happening, I merge with the widow and become her. There is an instant change in the way I perceive the world. To survive, I have to weave the web and trap and kill my prey. I stay focused and work efficiently as I create the web, eventually settling in the corner, patiently waiting. As the first victim becomes entangled in my sticky web, I watch emotionless as it struggles to free itself and eventually succumbs to its plight of being the smaller one on the food chain. I devour my catch, aware of only a very base survival instinct.

Star Wolf then said to ask for a symbol, and it is obvious to me that it is the black widow spider. As I slowly return to the room, there are words spoken through my third ear, "Where you are going, you will need to know how to spin a web and attract." I am immediately filled with deep shame as I acknowledge this as being a part of me. I am not a predator; I am the victim of a predator! The most shameful thing I could imagine is right here within me.

Only a few people share with the group, and I have no desire to speak about my experience. I just want to go to bed . . . actually, I just want to go home.

Chronic pain and illness over the past several years have created a quest for healing that is a force as strong as my need to be a mother and wife. I know there are answers that only I can find, and on this first of four nights of being away from the family, I feel desperately alone. I doubt my inner voice in being here, yet I have a deeper knowing that this is right. My fears are up and I want the security of what I know and love. But, instead,

I toss and turn in the double bed with my best friend, not even wanting to share with her this shameful part of me. The frustration of another woman in the room who snores like a drunken sailor and regularly has an explosive sound that I can only describe as a train crashing in the snowy quiet of the Swiss Alps makes me long to escape to the riverbank outside our windows and sleep by the calm of the waters. Yet, I know the pressure cooker is turned on, and I am here to find the gold even though it may be in the guise of a black widow spider being buried by this avalanche of sounds in this unfamiliar bedroom.

Let's just say that the next day during the Shamanic Breathwork process it got very real and very interesting. I became the black widow spider and weaved webs, trapped my prey, ate it, and survived. I became a woman dressed in black with an hourglass figure, who held a red muffler on her belly. She was pure sociopath in the way that she had no emotion. This all felt very foreign to me, as I feel everything. I later (as in years) discovered how powerful of an experience this was and how I have allowed myself to find a balance between the out-of-control empath that walked around like an emotional sponge and the stone-cold sociopath. Balance in life is and has been a very powerful teacher of mine.

I have embraced the part of me that needs to leave the emotions checked and realize that things are not personal but always a lesson coaxing me toward my higher truth. It's nice to have deep conversations without tears streaming down my face, and it's nice to be able to do those tears authentically.

The part of the spider medicine that I love the most is the ability to throw out an invisible web to create community. It is a metaphor of gathering the tribe. When facilitating a personal client or a group of people, I can now continue to be heart connected and detached so that I can hold space for them to work at their own pace without my agenda and need for them to do something. My vision is to hold them in wholeness and to see their higher truth.

Getting in touch with the oppositional states of consciousness within me allowed me to find balance. Instead of being the one who was always deemed "the sensitive one," which always felt like a bad label, I have learned to manage my empathy. I can be aware, have compassion, and not feel burdened or responsible. I know also that I have within me a very basic survival instinct and that I continue to throw out the web to gather that which is needed for my good health and desire to live vibrantly. Thank you, black widow spider, for bringing me this powerful medicine!

Over many years, my work became an inner journey of connecting to something bigger than myself, the wounded part of me that knew how to be "out of body," created to escape a difficult childhood. Yet it also was the answer in creating a better life and gave me visions that fed an inner place of belief that this all has a purpose and I was going to find my way through. The shamanic path has been the bridge between fantasy and reality and has allowed me to bring the visions into my body and the world. Once embarking upon the path of discovery and recovery, my consciousness was opened to the mysticism of the universe and all of the Soul Whisperings it has offered me to become my full potential.

Even though I have created many things, I have not yet reached my potential. I am currently working on a book and on a radio program out of Seattle. This is requiring me to let go so that once again I can let in the new. My definition of the shamanic work is to continually be willing to reinvent my self.

It's been a journey full of discovery, recovery, remembering my core essence, and replacing shame with acceptance and surrender to a higher calling. It's been about replacing blame with accountability and patience as I choose to change my programming. It's also been about replacing anger with passion to make a difference in the world and replacing apathy with purpose.

This is a warrior's path (which was also a vision I had during a shamanic journey), but I have put down my sword and armor and replaced it with an inner conviction that is outfitted with only my head, heart, and hands . . . naked to the truth that we all suffer, we all doubt, we all fall down, and we can all rise like the phoenix, fueling our hearts with our pain to make this a better world.

9

The Nature of
How People Change

Awakening is a term that has moved into popular language in the past twenty years. Also known as *enlightenment,* awakening was once the purview of saints and prophets. Waking up and being consciously present is becoming a goal for ordinary people. For many, self-awareness is the point of life, and the events along the way, wonderful or challenging, are stimulants for the awakening. History has shown that very few individuals are considered to have awakened in their lifetime, or to have been born awakened. Christ and Buddha are two. There are others, but they constitute a small handful compared to the vast population of the planet.

Secret initiations existed for seekers of enlightenment or individuals born into a time and place that deemed them a seeker. The Dalai Lama was chosen by a group who believed he was the one meant to be the next holy master of Tibet. As a child, he was taught the initiatory path from a very young age. What would happen if we treated children in the manner in which the Dalai Lama was raised? What are the components of this chosen child's upbringing that result in the becoming of a man like the Dalai Lama? Imagine a world where that was often the norm.

Buddha was not raised with the intention of becoming enlightened. He chose the path for himself. While his upbringing may have been conducive to his making that choice, it was, nonetheless a conscious choice at some point in his life. While most of us do not have the opportunity to be raised to be enlightened, all of us have the opportunity to choose, as Siddhartha did, to transform and awaken.

HOW *DO* PEOPLE ACTUALLY CHANGE?

The nature of how people change is really the illumination of how people become self-aware through a transformative path that we refer to as the path of shamanic consciousness, which opens up the full expression of being human/humane in everyday life. The change is supported through our mindful, embodied awareness of what interferes with this full expression. The field of awareness is both relational, involving others, and intra-subjective—the relationship with oneself. Science, medicine, engineering, and physics are embracing metaphysics as these disciplines evolve into an understanding of the transformation that is happening in consciousness.

AN IMPULSE TOWARD
INTEGRATED SPIRITUALITY

Over the past few decades an increasing impulse toward integrated spirituality as a way of living for everyone has given rise to new careers to assist people to not only heal wounds but also to embrace deeper meaning in life. Awakening can be seen as the process of understanding deep personal motivation, listening to one's inner voice and holy longings, and integrating action with surrender and intention.

Awakening is on its way to becoming a collective human goal, accomplished one person or psyche at a time through relational awareness, uncovering personal emotional wounding, forgiving self and others, releasing stored negative energies, building an enduring optimistic perspective, and developing deep capacity for love of self, others, and all that is. Awakening is often characterized by a deep inner happiness, a sense of presence, compassionate wisdom, and planetary service of some kind.

As a species we are learning, or perhaps remembering, that life is not a linear path that leads to success and happiness. It is a spiral journey that leads us through continual processes of transformation from varying degrees of innocent, naive unconsciousness to a more conscious, compassionate, embodied way of living. Along the path, life provides opportunities that move us out of our comfort zone and into a more vibrant way of living. Moving out of our comfort zone often occurs in a predictable trajectory, and though not linear the phases can be illuminated to create a helpful and more discernible path along the labyrinth of change and transformation.

Star Wolf relays that "through my work I discovered that there are five very distinct cycles that we all go through on the way to making a change. The amount of ease or dis-ease and stress experienced with each cycle is largely determined by how one is able to embody or deal with each stage along the way. Each cycle has a mood or set of identifiable characteristics that distinguishes it from the others. We can enter the cycles from any place on the great wheel of change."

These Five Cycles of Change that Star Wolf mentions above will be detailed in the next chapter. For now, let's examine the concept of change more closely before we look at the specific cycles that she refers to.

CHANGE IS THE ONLY CONSTANT

Change is the only thing in life that is a constant. Today, blogs and articles about change on a personal and planetary level flood our newsfeeds. Still, we live as though the change is random, chaotic, and shocking. We often believe that if we do things in a certain, perfect way, change won't happen. Or we react by becoming rigid and controlling the perceived change.

Fearing and resisting change is considered normal, maybe even desirable. Culturally we support an addiction to the way things are. After all, if we completely embrace change we embrace the transitory reality that flies in the face of a materialistic culture that sells happy-ever-after as long as you have all the right possessions and cling to security. Mindful living includes being fully present and unattached at the same time. Accomplishing that is no longer only the goal of a few Zen monks; civilization is increasingly seeing it as a more balanced way of being.

Our culture, and most of Western civilization, does not teach us a healthy model for moving through change and its difficult responses: grief, anxiety, and loss. Nature, however, does teach us freely if we but know how to pay attention. The leaves are not filing lawsuits or blaming themselves for doing something wrong as they fall off the trees. The birds don't demand subsidies when they have to migrate south or need to explain themselves to others as to why they can't just stay settled in one place. The Earth keeps spinning on its axis, the stars keep birthing, and the never-ending cycles of life keep happening. Imagine a paradigm for living life in an integrated and accepting manner that included dancing with the nature of change through all of its cycles and facets.

A CLOSER LOOK AT CHANGE AGAINST THE BACKDROP OF WAR

The revolution of the 1960s was precisely about letting go of the illusion of a static, secure life that the previous generation had created in response to the chaos and trauma of world wars. Understandably the depression generation came to parenting out of fear, and in an honest mistake they wanted their children to be safe, even if it meant repression of life-force energies and creativity. Western culture was in denial, and many people were suffering from post-traumatic stress disorder (PTSD) brought about by the atrocities of war. At the same time, the war was glorified as it brought the end to Hitler's reign of horror.

Glorifying war made it impossible for most people to see the disturbing effects of the trauma. Men were expected to carry on and simply never talk about it, let alone process what war had done to them. *Shell shock* was the term used to describe the phenomenon, and yet it was only applied to the soldiers who suffered full breakdowns as a result of the war. Families for the most part were supposed to accept the stranger who had returned home and overlook the symptoms of soul loss such as violence, depression, anxiety, and addiction.

Today there is an understanding that PTSD, mild or severe, is experienced by most, if not all veterans. Growing up in the late 1940s and 1950s in Western culture meant that fathers who suffered from PTSD most likely raised you. This is characterized by materialistic indulgence and emotional vacuity based on avoiding pain and fear. There was no room to indulge the emotions, passions, or desires to follow your dreams.

Traumatized people often have lost their ability to imagine. Either they are stuck in a loop of projecting the disturbing event onto a present situation, or they have no response to situations—a blank slate, numbed state of being. Perhaps dissociation, wherein a person goes into what might be described as an intense daydream, metaphorically leaving their body and sometimes not even conscious that they are in a sort of trance, is a substitute for conscious imagination.

Parents, who as a result of trauma are not able to dream or imagine goals, often unwittingly squash the same capacity to imagine in their children. Many people growing up in the 1950s and 1960s often heard their parents say things like "That is not possible" or "Where did you get that ridiculous idea?" or "Your head is full of silly stories." The traumatized fathers of the 1950s and 1960s often were literally incapable of imagining anything. The loss of imagination includes the loss of dreams and/or goals.

Van Der Kolk developed his theories on trauma by working with veterans who were suffering from severe PTSD. In our experience, the effects of trauma are passed on to younger generations, and while the children may not have experienced a severe traumatizing event, they are predisposed to PTSD. *Overly sensitive* was a label lobbed at children of parents who did not understand their offspring's inability to be tough in the face of difficulty.

These collective forces formed the zeitgeist of the middle years of the twentieth century and set the stage for what would follow in the turbulent years of the 1960s.

A HUNGER FOR REAL EMOTION

Growing up in the 1950s and 1960s, young people were hungry for authentic emotional responses that led to deep diving in to altered states of consciousness and a carefree, live-for-today attitude. No wonder the response to life at that time was to revel in its strongest emotional responses through sex, drugs, and rock and roll! Attempting to heal secondhand PTSD symptoms of anxiety, worry, and perfectionism—to name just a few—coming-of-age in the '60s generation opened Pandora's box into another dimension of consciousness. Efforts to close the box have failed over the past four decades.

Pandora was created out of earth and water and in mythology is said to be the first woman on Earth. The gods gifted her with the ability to speak, musical abilities, and curiosity. Zeus, who was mad at Prometheus, gave Pandora in marriage to Prometheus's brother and gifted Pandora with a box that was not to be opened under any circumstances. Prometheus knew by mandating that she not open it, that she would, in fact, open it!

Curiosity motivated her to open the box. Mythology has it that evil escaped and covered the Earth. Another lens through which to see this myth is that Pandora was curious rather than fearful. She was also deeply intuitive and knew that the hidden wish of Zeus was for her to open the box and allow the contents to escape. Pandora held steady as all manner of frightening things escaped from the box. She was determined to see the truth no matter how disturbing. Her efforts were rewarded when the box was nearly empty of its negative contents; the essence of hope was the last thing in the box.

Curiosity is a healthy state of being, one that is necessary for creativity. Curiosity opens the mind and heart and leads to peaceful communication. The deep curiosity and fearlessness of the '60s also did bring out scary and often destructive forces, yet it also rebirthed the essence of hope and brought it fully alive. Hope for meaningful life. Hope for a world of peace and harmony. Hope for a new vision of collective connection and higher consciousness.

Without ritual, ceremony, and a council of elders to guide this generation into the wisdom of experience, revelry was unsustainable and began to die. Like leaves on a tree, one by one, concepts of world peace, free love, personal satisfaction, live for today, blow your mind with drugs, and never grow up withered and fell to the ground. There they provided a rich compost that has fertilized the Earth in giving birth to the new concepts of nonviolent communication, respectful love, being present, expanded states of awareness achieved without drugs, aging consciously, and responsible and relational, compassionate living. New teachers and careers are appearing to support the maturing fruits of seed planted in the 1960s.

Imagine that you are learning to surf. You learn to welcome the waves and know when to ride them and when to let them pass. You don't have to ride every wave, and you don't have to flop around in the ocean being slammed by the waves. Imagine now that you respond to life by accepting change rather than trying to control it. Living in active response to what is unfolding doesn't mean that you will never fall or get hurt. It means that you will have the capacity to make conscious choices. With practice, you will learn to read the waves of your life, and ride them with discernment, determination, and grace.

THE CYCLES OF LIFE

Indigenous cultures have many maps and ceremonies for supporting and enhancing change. Elements of nature are central to understanding and working consciously with change. Teachings of the medicine wheel in certain Native American traditions show that we move around the wheel in stages of life, from birth and childhood to aging and the wisdom it brings.

Most medicine wheels have seven directions, each connected to an element of the natural world: East, South, West, North, Above, Below, and Within. The positions on the wheel correspond to:

- Stages of life: birth, youth, adult (or elder), death
- Seasons of the year: spring, summer, winter, fall
- Aspects of life: spiritual, emotional, intellectual, physical
- Elements of nature: air, fire, water, and earth
- Animals: eagle, bear, wolf, buffalo, and many others
- Ceremonial plants: tobacco, sweetgrass, sage, and cedar (native voices)

Ritual and ceremony are utilized to stimulate and support the transition of the community and the individual through stages of the wheel. Indigenous cultures all over the world use some form of structured concepts and rituals to move through individual, cultural, and planetary change.

Seasons are often spoken of as the metaphor for the cycles of life—birth, maturity, letting go, dying, and rebirth. As a Western culture we are deeply dissociated from nature and, consequently, the natural cycles. Doctors write prescriptions that tell people to get out in nature. The evidence abounds that just walking on the Earth barefoot will improve your health. There is a reawakening in Western culture to the aliveness and transformative qualities of nature itself.

Seasonal rituals and ceremonies have largely been co-opted by materialism in the West and transformative spiritual meanings have been lost. Hunger for meaning and clarity has stimulated an ever-growing interest in indigenous cultures and ceremonies. Seeking guidance from shamans and other medicine elders has created a new market-driven sector of the travel industry to serve those who can afford the trip to South America, Africa, and other exotic lands where there are more authentic experiences of primal connection to a source within—and greater than ourselves—to be had. If you are not personally able to travel geographically to access your inner wisdom, the audio track "Neuroimaginal Journey" may take you there. We invite you to try it.

New discoveries show that humans are hardwired for expanded states of consciousness. Science is revealing evidence that our bodies are capable of accessing astounding states of extraordinary consciousness with relatively simple techniques. Focused breathing and imaginal thoughts will open our hearts to send messages to our own brains that shift us from fear to love. In doing so our higher thinking abilities of creativity and brilliance are turned on in a matter of minutes. Methodology for utilizing these techniques comes from a variety of disciplines, such as Buddhist meditation, heart rate variability studies, and indigenous healing practices. Dr. Lee Lipsenthal and Nita Gage integrated theories and practices and taught shamanic and meditative practices to physicians for many years. Dr. Lipsenthal writes about this in his book *Finding Balance in a Medical Life.*

The primacy of change and the indigenous wisdom of working with change is in the collective unconscious and informs treatment modalities. Motivational interviewing (MI) is a theoretical construct in the field of psychology, particularly utilized in the treatment of addictive disorders. The theory postulates that there are four distinct stages of change: precontemplation, contemplation, action, and maintenance. The model suggests that these stages occur in a linear motion, though one can, and often does, slide back to a previous stage under stress.[1]

Meeting clients exactly where they are in the stages of change is said to be the key to successful outcomes. Important to note in this model is the recognition, for example, that if someone is in the precontemplative state, it is unlikely that your intervention, will have any effect at all on the person. However, if they are in the contemplative stage they are open to intervention, and you may be very effective in supporting them in making healthy choices. The particular stage of change within the model of MI is easily correlated to more primal cycles of life, thus creating communication between the imaginal and the actual.

NATURE'S CYCLES OF TRANSFORMATION

We all have it within us to experience and align with the elemental world of nature as a path of transformation. Having a map of the trajectory of change will give you a way, a metaphor, and framework to wrap your intellect around. And while your intellect is happily engaged with understanding the metaphor, your soul can get on with the business of changing and evolving. By understanding the aspects of change and how we are impacted by nature's elements we are able to alleviate fear and move more fully into surrender with each cycle of transformation.

Imagine that your soul is your dance partner leading you to dance the rhythm of being. We live in times that are both difficult and filled with potential. Each of us is being invited to let go of the outdated belief system of linear thinking and move in to a more holistic worldview. Again, a tool you may employ to help you effect this change is the audio component of this book; the five different tracks will help you awaken the inner shaman/Soul Whisperer within.

From the shamanic perspective, we are multidimensional beings functioning in many realities at once. As we awaken the inner healer/shaman we begin to remember our true selves, and our everyday lives often shift dramatically. As we go through transformational paradigm shifts we may experience both internal and external conflicts. During this time it is very important to live mindfully as we shape-shift our realities, see our world through shamanic eyes, and become aware of the evolving collective consciousness.

Embodying shamanic consciousness means living with an awareness of your individual truth at all times as you walk your unique path in life. By taking time and allowing yourself the space to access the wisdom of your heart and soul, you can bring an enriched understanding of your soul's purpose to your daily life. Each one's experience on the spiral path of constant change is unique. While a seeker may learn some helpful techniques from reading or hearing about the journeys of others, another's path will not take him to his own source of knowledge. Each journey adds to one's personal store of useful information about the other world: its geography, inhabitants, lessons, guides, and teachers.

We are often afraid to see the cycles of nature, however, as we must accept the cycles of our own lives. The fear of death underlies our resistance to embracing change and the natural cycles. Shamans work with the reality of death and practice dying as an act of consciousness. Death is inevitable. Fear of death is a condition that can be overcome.

Transforming the fear of death has everything to do with living mindfully and consciously. As Plato said and Socrates quoted at his trial, "The unexamined life is not worth living." Without consciousness our lives lack vibrancy and meaning, leaving us afraid to die, precisely because we have not lived a worthwhile life.

Living fully will cure the fear of death, and once the fear has abated, living fully is easier. At first it takes practice; letting go of the fear of death is not easy. It is a deep, instinctual fear that stimulates self-care and survival. Overcoming it does not mean losing your drive for survival; rather, it brings that drive to consciousness, stimulating mindful living to support survival. Once one is truly conscious of the fact that death is inevitable, and you are doing your best to live fully, there is much less to fear.

Transitioning from one cycle to another is most often an unconscious process. How we transition and embrace each cycle is driven by patterns of beliefs and behaviors that we have adopted to survive. Many of these transitions from one cycle to another are extremely stressful, even when the external event is a positive one such as marriage. We have programmed ourselves to respond to life as though it is a survival game, when actually it is a journey of awakening.

Healthy and whole people live more harmoniously with the planet and all living things. They are people who are seeking to know themselves and how they move through their lives in a conscious manner. There is a growing awareness that efforts to legislate and force people to treat the planet and her creatures humanely do not work very well. Responsible and compassionate living comes from an inner awakening, resulting in a more integrated being who is capable of aligned intentions of mind, body, and soul.

JUNG'S CONCEPT OF
THE SHADOW FURTHER DEFINED

As mentioned earlier, renowned psychoanalyst Carl Jung coined the term *shadow* to identify those aspects of ourselves that we don't like and are apt to reject. Here we will delve into that concept in a deeper way given that it's germane to our ability to shape-shift our lives through the practice of Soul Whispering. The shadow can be said to be another self, a self that we don't like and therefore have disowned, or a place where our darkest secrets and self-loathing reside.

Much has been written about the shadow and its role in our lives. Each of us carries a shadow that is both our own shadow and the collective shadow of existence. The disowned parts affect not only our own lives but also the lives of others and ultimately the health of the planet. By healing our inner landscape we walk with integrity and compassion in relation to all living creatures and Earth itself.

Understanding the shadow is a key component to consciously working with the five cycles. It will be critical to acknowledge the negative aspects of each cycle to release its energies. If we are trying to be good and not admit when we are angry, for example, the anger may leak out in ways beyond our control, and we will remain stuck in the anger. By acknowledging anger, we are able to make conscious choices about how and when we express that anger.

Jung said that the focus on being good and avoiding evil without healing our wounds is what keeps us locked in our own negative reactions and feelings. Trying to ignore and avoid what we don't like about ourselves, what we believe is unacceptable, unfortunately also hides our passion and sacred purpose. To get to our passion and sacred purpose we must be willing to turn the lights on shadow parts of our lives and ourselves.

The shadow demands our attention, not because we are evil, or even that evil is stronger than good, but because buried underneath that which we loathe and disown is our creativity and soul purpose. The soul wants to give birth to our gifts and sacred purpose. The infant emerges in a mix of blood and mucus; so too the soul's full incarnation emerges from the muck of facing our darkest emotions, thoughts, and fears.

Most often what disturbs us in another person is actually an aspect of our own shadow. Psychology calls this "projection." Or if the shadow contains an unmet desire for accomplishment, the disturbing shadow aspect may show up as envy. In both cases, envy or projection, we are seeing an aspect of ourselves. When we dissociate from our longings we see them as negative or positive aspects of another person. Resentment of another, for example, is the shadow of our own disappointment. By acknowledging resentment, we unearth the sadness. It is the expression of sadness, through tears, that opens our heart. And so it is with all the emotions, thoughts, and desires that we banish to the closet of the shadow. Experiencing our so-called negative emotions and unmet desires is the necessary pathway through healing to transformation.

For some people, joy and happiness are in their shadow. Somewhere they learned that it wasn't safe to be happy. Perhaps they were raised by a depressed parent, and the child's happiness was deemed unwelcome. These people may live as though they are depressed, and doing shadow work will assist in opening the pathways of joy.

Change is a process, not a single act. Change begins almost imperceptibly, and by the time we become conscious of it most of us feel victimized by the events and issues that are forcing change. Perhaps you have heard about some extreme cases where women didn't know that they were pregnant until they went into labor. Thinking they were having an appendicitis attack, they arrived at the hospital to be shocked by the birth of a baby. What is going on that such a dramatic change in one's body, mind, and spirit could be ignored in this way?

Being pregnant for nine months without knowing it is very similar to not seeing the signs that point to a dramatic change in one's life. Being fired, or being left by a spouse, seldom happens without many subtle, and not so subtle, indications. Like the woman who can ignore morning sickness, a growing belly, lack of monthly bleeding, and so on, many people ignore what is happening around them, or the yearning inside of them, until suddenly a birth is happening that was unplanned, unexpected, and shocking.

LIVING MINDFULLY AS A SOUL WHISPERER

Living mindfully means listening to the whispers of your own inner voice—that of your own soul or inner shaman. Perceiving all that is happening in and around you requires that you have the capacity to accept both positive and negative aspects of yourself. Mining deeper truths and forgiving others and ourselves is the nature of working with our shadow. The audio track "Turning the Light on Your Shadow" will take you through an exercise to help you to identify and release your shadow aspects.

This work will unleash creativity and a passion for life. Once the shadow emerges from the dark into the light, it becomes a liberating force and no longer restricts the totality of the individual and his or her expression. In addition to one's responsibility to one's own spiritual health, there exists a collective responsibility to personal healing that involves collective wounds passed down from generation to generation. Today more than ever, people are paying attention to these collective generational wounds and finding ways to release the emotional attachments of the historical energies.

We do this by clearing out our personal negative emotional energies and then relanguaging our stories. Often this requires reliving parts of the traumatizing events to release the energy. Collectively we have been building a grounded field of healing over the past four decades. The paradigm is shifting from simply focusing on healing personal wounds to opening to the profound reality of the unknown. For instance, although it may be predictable that the sun will rise in the East every day, it is also an illusion. The sun doesn't rise; actually the Earth turns. Holding the notion of the sun rising as a concept rather than an absolute truth is a metaphor for holding all of our beliefs lightly and being conscious that we really aren't certain of anything, as everything is emerging every moment.

It is a healthy discipline to stay aware of the emergence rather than stuck in a story of certainty. The connection to being in tune with the truth of the uncertainty ultimately brings happiness. Resisting the truth of uncertainty creates anxiety. This foundational consciousness is opening to emerging transformation. Some say that we are moving from 3D to 5D reality. Neuroscience supports the opening to expanded abilities. Art imitating life is bringing us movies that seem to concretize the possibilities of not only time travel but also interdimensional travel. Messages of humans who channel interstellar beings are pointing to an expanded awareness of our purpose that includes the urge to heal our wounds.

Perhaps it is benevolent interstellar beings who are prompting humans to shift into an awareness of unhealed wounds, or perhaps the urge is an evolutionary phase. Personal growth and healing were once seen as the goal. At one time it was unimaginable that people were even affected by childhood events, let alone that facing them, reliving them, and releasing them would foster physical as well as emotional health. What will the higher octave work of transformation, which is currently unimaginable, create? Is it too much to hope that it may be actualized in the higher octaves of wisdom and love?

Read the story of Soul Whisperer Deb Kotz Irestone and decide for yourself.

Walker between the Worlds

Deb Kotz Irestone

My journey has been one of walking between the worlds. I have long felt an inner calling to reconcile the opposites and find a new, sustainable way of walking on the planet. For me, this has meant learning to bridge the gap between mainstream religious thought and deep mysticism. It has also been a process of appreciating the contributions of Western academic understanding, while honoring my own lived experience. This has been a lifelong undertaking.

I was a sensitive child, born into a family that valued academics. I grew up in a college town, and many of my friends' parents were college professors. My mom was a teacher, and the value of education was instilled in me at a very young age. My love for school and learning has been with me throughout my life.

At the same time, I have always had experiences with beings (spirits and star people) that others around me may not see or believe in. Like many children, once I realized that talking about these experiences was not met with understanding, I began to push the experiences into the shadow. Occasionally in my private moments, I could acknowledge their presence. Most of the time, however, I put up blinders and increasingly shut them out. Spending time in nature or with my pets became the only outlets for the more mystical aspects of my consciousness.

Fortunately, my dad's interactions with the family dogs normalized what I knew about animals. He talked to them as if they understood him and treated them with love and respect. An awareness of the intelligence, consciousness, and intrinsic value of the animal kingdom was taken for granted by my father, and his actions provided a life-affirming role model for me. Love of animals and nature was my first experience of the shamanic world. I read stories about animals and shamans. I rode horses on my grandfather's ranch, often galloping across the South Dakota prairie on Blackie, an old cow horse who responded to my body's signals, without need for saddle or bridle. When social consciousness became too difficult to deal with, I sought refuge in the woods near our home. When my Lutheran pastor once stated that animals didn't have souls, the idea was so ludicrous that I began to question much of what mainstream religion had to teach. Eventually I walked away from both religion and spirituality.

As a young adult, I began working as an engineer for a defense contractor. I had become quite mechanistic in my worldview, cut off from my spiritual connection. In retrospect, although I was alive, I surely wasn't living. A few years into my engineering career, I became pregnant with my first child. This was my first big shamanic initiation, leading me back to my bigger self. The experience of becoming a parent reopened the door to my sensitive side, and Great Mystery flooded back into my awareness. I responded in two ways. My socialized, academic self decided to go back to the church of my youth, albeit in a more palatable form. I joined a local progressive Lutheran church and became involved in a number of church groups. Simultaneously, I began to explore my spirituality through yoga, t'ai chi, qigong, Reiki, and other energy modalities.

I began to look for a way to bring these two sides of myself back together into wholeness. One of the pastors at my church was a closet shaman. She wove teachings of animal wisdom and mystery into her sermons in a *way that truly spoke to me. She talked about the layers of meaning in the Lord's Prayer that could be uncovered when one went back to the original Aramaic, the inclusive language that Jesus spoke. Her teachings gave me hope.*

I decided to take this spiritual journey to the next level, and for me that meant academia. I enrolled in a liberal Catholic university and earned a master's degree in theology and spirituality. I loved the mysticism of the Catholic tradition. All of a sudden I was reading about saints who had had visions and experiences similar to mine. My practicum was in a spiritual direction program in which we discussed at length the fine line between mental breakdown and spiritual awakening. I loved the feeling that the dichotomy between my mind and my spirit was coming together. I was so excited to bring my newfound understanding back to my Lutheran church. I fully expected to be welcomed with open arms. However, the church was in transition.

By the time I finished my training, two of my favorite pastors were no longer leading services. The openness they had embodied and their call to expand beyond our limited understanding was nowhere to be seen. Instead, I was treated to a rude awakening when I met with the newly hired senior pastor to discuss offering spiritual direction in what he now considered "his" church. My ideas of inclusiveness and mysticism were met with harsh words and insulting put-downs. I left the meeting and knew that this church was no longer my spiritual home.

I spent the following years searching for community. I visited churches. I signed up for esoteric groups and shamanic trainings. I talked to friends and scoured the Internet. I became a certified hypnotherapist and offered individual sessions and classes in self-hypnosis and past-life regression. I found that I enjoyed working with altered states and wanted to find more ways to help people use them. I began to study various forms of breathwork, and that's when I came across Venus Rising.

My first Shamanic Healing Initiatory Process (SHIP) workshop was incredible. I was able to revisit some childhood trauma that traditional psychotherapy, as well as all the energy techniques I'd tried, had not been able to release. I spent the entire workshop in a kind of shock but knew that

I was safe and finally getting support in a way in which I never had before. My initial reason for taking SHIP was to learn a new modality to use with clients. I had no idea how profoundly healing it would be for me personally.

Sometime after I completed the first round of SHIP and was well into my apprenticeship in the program, I had a second huge shamanic initiation. I ended up hospitalized, intubated, and in a medically induced coma for what eventually turned out to be a failure of my mitral valve, which required open-heart surgery. I literally experienced a broken heart. During this heart initiation, I was taken to the stars, met with my guides, and signed a new soul contract. At one point, I was given the choice to cross over or go back to my current life. It was so beautiful in this place that at first I didn't want to return to my life on Earth. But then I saw an image of my family and knew that my children still needed a mother. Much like my first initiation, love brought me back from near death.

After I returned, my life was entirely different. Oh, I still had the same husband, children, house, dogs, and cats. But I knew on a deep, visceral level that everything had changed. I now knew without a doubt that we never die. Life continues on, and love is the most important thing.

As I slowly regained my strength, I returned to Venus Rising to continue my training. By now, I realized that I had found my tribe. Star Wolf started talking about authorizing me to teach SHIP back home in Minnesota. I was overwhelmed at first, wondering how I could possibly facilitate such powerful work. But I also knew that I was receiving excellent training from Star Wolf, Brad, and Ruby. Each facilitator was so different, yet each provided excellent support and insight from their own perspective.

Eventually I founded the first Venus Rising congregation, Shaman's Hearth Spiritual Community of Venus Rising, in 2010. Since then, I have facilitated SHIP groups and Shamanic Breathwork in many formats. I have found my spiritual home and opened the doors to other seekers who are also looking for community. It is a joy to support people and create a safe space for them to release their own past trauma and drama. It gives me great hope to witness people as they rediscover their own spiritual connection and soul purpose. I have tremendous gratitude for my teachers and the guides who have supported me in this journey.

Of course, there is always more to learn. After receiving a DM in shamanic psychospiritual studies from Venus Rising University, I decided to go back to school to earn a degree in counseling and psychotherapy. Going back to college at this stage in life has been an interesting experience. I enjoy learning about some of the theories and research that support what we in the shamanic world have known for a long time.

Compared with other modalities, I'm amazed at the depth of transformation that Shamanic Breathwork elicits. I know that the world is hurting and that it is necessary to continue to bring people together through love and respect.

As I continue to integrate the wisdom inherent in both academia and mysticism, I especially resonate with Alfred Adler's concept of gemeinshaftgefuhl. *This can be translated to mean "social interest," or "community feeling." Adler found that those who have high levels of social interest, or a sense of community, experience more positive mental health than those with lower social interest. In the shamanic world, this is often expressed in the Lakota phrase* Aho Mitakue Oyasin, *which translates as "all my relations," acknowledging the connection between all beings. Linda Tucker, the Lion Queen of Timbavati, uses the phrase* love and respect for all beings. *Linda has created an incredible preserve where wild animals can live in that atmosphere of love and respect, with incredible results.*

On a recent trip to Tucker's Global White Lion Protection Trust (GWLPT) in South Africa, I was able to connect with wild animals in a more personal way than I'd ever experienced before. Riding in the back of an open truck, our group encountered and communed with the incredible white lions who live there. We also received messages from many of the other animals who make the GWLPT home. I received messages from a waterbuck, a pair of jackals, and many other creatures. Several of us were profoundly touched by our communication with Helga the hyena.

Helga lives in Kruger National Park and had made her way to the GWLPT while we were visiting. One morning she stopped in front of our vehicle as we were making our twice daily visit to the lions. We were all mesmerized by her exquisite beauty. She connected to us deeply with her beautiful dark eyes, radiating love. She let us know that she was with us and reminded us to call in protection on our travels. This reminder to call in protection came back to us later that day, when faced with a potentially devastating situation.

We were traveling down the highway in the back of an open truck when the left rear tire suddenly came off the vehicle. Immediately before this happened, several of us had remembered to call in protection. The driver expertly guided the truck to the side of the road, avoiding the slope that would surely have caused our vehicle to roll over with disastrous results. What could have been a tragic event ended up as a minor inconvenience.

While the very human, academic, scientific part of me was irritated by what it perceived as poor vehicle maintenance, the shamanic part of me recognized the gift in Helga's loving message. We all felt gratitude toward Helga and spirit for assisting us and our driver from the shamanic realms, allowing us to remain unharmed in spite of the potentially deadly situation. Like much of life, this was a vivid experience of both/and, not either/or.

As I continue to be a walker between the worlds, I appreciate that there is a bridge between academia and lived experience. I know that if you dig deep enough, religion can become a doorway to mysticism. Both are just different ways of looking at our reality as human beings walking on this Earth. Just as we are physical beings living in a body made of earth, air, fire, and water, we are also mystical beings infused with spirit. My purpose at this time is to celebrate both aspects of my humanity and support others in doing the same.

10
The Five Cycles of Change
Star Wolf's Alchemical Shamanic Roadmap

The Five Cycles of Change, an alchemical shamanic map, may be viewed as a never-ending spiral of change for those seekers on the spiritual path. Each time we come around the spiral, we are invited to take another look, though often from a different angle, at the issues with which we are grappling. With each new perspective and transformation we are given the gift of deepening and expanding our capacity for mining the gems of wisdom from the far reaches of our inner knowing as they mirror the universal truths back to us so that we may change and grow from within.

These cycles provide a map of alchemical transformation that clearly illuminate both the positive and the shadow (negative) aspects of our psyches. By gaining a better understanding of the element connected to the cycle that we are currently negotiating, we will be better able to embrace the characteristics of that element and utilize it as a guide during our process. When made conscious, the Five Cycles of Change are a map by which we may live fully, in love and acceptance, and successfully manage fear and anxiety.

Let's now examine the five cycles and their various qualities.

Cycle One

FLOATING/DREAMTIME

The first cycle is related to water or a womblike state of being. It is often associated with a sense of floating and "everything being as it should be." Cycle One may be an authentic stage in which one is simply moved to rest and be free from struggle. In this, it is a powerful place of rest, rejuvenation, and nurturing. In our modern-day, fast-paced, goal-oriented culture, this cycle is often neglected and dishonored, and we do not allow ourselves the time to just be, especially when we are gestating a new vision for our lives. Flowing easily through our lives, feeling connected with people, places, and events, is a pleasant manifestation of Cycle One.

Not everyone enjoys Cycle One, however. For some, it elicits anxiety, because they don't trust going with the flow.

For those who do enjoy it, a danger is in becoming overly attached to it, even addicted. When this occurs, people will do whatever they can to hang on to it even when things are shifting and the cycle is coming to an end.

Maximizing one's experience of this cycle without becoming overly attached will allow one to be full and comfortable and prepared for the next phase of life. Unfortunately Western culture erroneously designates Cycle One as an arbiter of success and moving out of this comfortable, rewarding cycle to be a sign of failure. Nonetheless, as with all of the cycles, it is transient.

Element: Water
Represents: Womb, gestation
Colors: Deep blue, indigo
Positive aspects: Trusting, relaxation, regeneration, meditative, nourishing, a state where all needs are met, floating, playful, becoming, and just being
Negative aspects: Confusion, lethargy, fantasy, sloth, false bliss, dissociative. For example, many addictions are about trying to go back into the womb, back to Cycle One.

Words of Wisdom about Cycle One

The following is what I wrote about the water cycle in my earlier book *Shamanic Breathwork*. We are reprinting it here because it so aptly describes this initial cycle of change.

> Many individuals stuck in a water cycle will have a variety of amazing inspirations and ideas but cannot ever seem to get motivated into action. They procrastinate. There is never a good time to take concrete action or create a serious game plan. They are always in the getting ready or dreaming stage of "one day." They may be obsessive/compulsive in their need to be perfect, making it very difficult to birth things into the real world. These individuals are clearly stuck in the watery womb of the first cycle. They are dreaming their dreams without manifesting them.
>
> In contrast, someone who has been a workaholic and real go-getter may need to enter into the water cycle to temper a fiery nature and avoid burnout. This might include going to a meditation retreat, taking time by the ocean, or sitting by the fire reading a good book.
>
> People who have had a negative womb experience tend to feel that it is not safe to be born—to make changes and move forward—and experience an ongoing syndrome of being "out there" and disembodied in their lives. It can feel like helplessness.[1]

These people may be unable to enjoy life, because it requires presence in the moment. Practicing presence may be enhanced by working imaginably or actually with the element of water. Many people fear water, however, and nearly everyone has an innate fear of deep water and the unknown that it represents. Swimming or being immersed in a Jacuzzi or deep hot bath done mindfully can help to quell this fear and create a water experience that will inform and transform you.

Cycle Two

CHOP WOOD, CARRY WATER

Cycle Two is one of the most difficult cycles of transformation for the majority of people facing change. Each cycle has stumbling blocks and gifts, but because of the feelings of helplessness and hopelessness that can be inherent in this cycle, one risks the danger of becoming depressed and/or giving up during this phase. We see many people becoming stuck here and rushing to the doctor for a quick fix—many times, a prescription.

At this point in the process, there is a growing restlessness that eventually turns into extreme discomfort if one is resistant to change or otherwise in denial. Even for a willing soul, this stage will still cause some discomfort, as the old familiar crutches fail to work. In addition, there is a distinct feeling that there is no place to escape or hide from one's current situation.

A common paradox experienced as the earth cycle begins is as follows: "I can't stay in this situation, but I don't see any way out of it either." When I hear a comment similar to this, I can immediately recognize the calling card of the earth cycle, for it arises from having outgrown the present situation or circumstance and feeling the squeeze to move on, even if unwillingly.

For most, Cycle Two also brings up the issues of limits and boundaries. After bathing in the comfort, security, and even bliss of Cycle One, we begin to outgrow the present course in life. This may be experienced, for example, in a work situation or a relationship. In some cases, major perspective changes occur, and our entire worldview may shift.

In this cycle, it is vital for one to set limits and boundaries with other people and situations. If this is an unfamiliar experience, it will be difficult, and one may tend to resist setting boundaries and instead begin to feel resentful when no boundaries exist. Setting boundaries with other people means understanding what you need from someone in a given situation. You may love someone and still need to be clear with them about the extent of what you are willing to do for and with them, even if that seems to hurt their feelings.

In the long run, telling your truth will increase closeness, because you will honestly be saying "yes" rather than feeling "no" and then saying "yes" and being resentful as a result. For example, a sister repeatedly shows up at your house without calling, and your attempts to imply that this is not convenient for you have not worked. You will need to say, "Do not come over without calling; it does not work for me." If she responds with hurt feelings, you can say, "I am really sorry it hurts you. I love you, but I really need my privacy, and it will make things so much better when we are together." Even if she continues to feel hurt, that is not your responsibility. In fact, the kindest thing that you can do is be honest and allow her to have her feelings.

Element: Earth

Represents: Struggle, perseverance

Colors: Brown, black

Positive aspects: Preparing for change, coming out of denial, admitting one needs help, embracing uncomfortable feelings, holding creative tension, paying attention to details, being grounded, exploring limits and boundaries, taking practical action one step at a time, having faith, teachability, seeking answers

Negative aspects: Uncomfortable, indecisive, fearful, stuck, anxious, irritable, depressed, panicky, body aches, fatigue, impatient, critical, judgmental, victimization, addictions, perfectionism, martyrdom, codependency, crises

Words of Wisdom about Cycle Two

Cycle Two is often accompanied by an external crisis as the soul struggles to right itself. Crisis happens in our lives as a wake-up call. If the call is ignored, something will happen to create crisis—a demand from the soul or the inner voice to be heard.

Crisis is not failure. Most people will not experience transformation without the introduction of some sort of significant disruption. The Chinese word for *crisis* is made up of two characters: one is "danger";

the other is "opportunity." Crises and other disruptions in our lives—an unfulfilling job perhaps, or an abusive or failing marriage—serve to open our eyes to underlying yet significant unhappiness and discontent. We cling to these unhealthy situations out of an illusion of security.

Why do we tolerate these lives instead of changing them? Because we are not consciously aware that we are tolerating anything, as we simply accept the life we have been handed. The fog of comfort and security seduces us, yet with open eyes we may see that what once fulfilled us no longer does, and we may become willing to let go. If we can see the crisis as a wake-up call and an opportunity, we may surrender and re-create ourselves rather than languish and shrivel.

In the early stages of a loss or crisis, we often view our lost lifestyle with wonderful nostalgia. In time, however, most confess to having had experienced long-lived unhappiness before the crisis struck. We might, despite a refusal to acknowledge it, feel unfulfilled at work for years before being suddenly fired. While engaged in a seemingly happy, stable relationship, one partner may abruptly abandon the relationship, delivering a shock to the other. Following a chance to reflect and assimilate the experience, those who have come through such crises have described their state of being leading up to the event as one of mild discontent. Others report having been deeply depressed or even suicidal for significant periods of time.

There also exists a significant risk during the second cycle to succumb to alcohol or drugs to self-medicate and remain in denial. Similarly, there is temptation to bury oneself in a career to experience "success" as we have come to understand it—never quite feeling the satisfaction we expected or believed others felt. *Anything* may be used as a device to stifle the inner voice that beckons change. Maintaining a sense of security and staying in the fog of our comfort zone is the goal even when we are miserable.

Our memories may betray us as well, becoming an enemy. Elephants in circuses are trained from a young age using a simple method: One leg is tied to a post, tethering the young animal in place. As the elephant matures and its strength grows, it never attempts to free itself, despite possessing the overwhelming ability to do so. Similarly, our memories and old "tapes" of being told what we are supposed to do—where we are supposed to stay—become our posts in the ground. We remain obedient and unquestioning.

We may do things differently from that which our parents demanded and even believe that we have taken an entirely different direction in life, yet the ties that bind are unconscious. Even when we think we have broken out, we are, in fact, tethered to beliefs and limitations that shape our lives. To truly be free, we must *remember.* At times, we must be retaught and shown that the rope holding us in place is a tiny one. Not only that, it is breakable, and we can move freely. What would it take to realize that you're being held in place by a tiny rope?

Crisis is only partially the result of a disruptive event in our lives. Our reaction to the event can exacerbate the situation and lead to a crisis rather than an event to be responded to. Perhaps this is part of something that's unfolding in your life, not necessarily a full-blown disaster. Over our lifetimes, each of us evolves. Some of us go through dramatic, shocking metamorphoses. Imagine if the caterpillar were resistant to the change at any (or every) stage. Who could blame her if she doesn't surrender to the cocoon that's developing and encasing her, which must feel like being buried alive? Who wouldn't support her as she screams and thrashes inside the cocoon and, literally, begins to dissolve? If she makes it through that, there would be no shortage of people who would help by cutting open the cocoon and setting her free before the cocoon has time to open naturally. However, we know that the caterpillar must remain entombed and patient. Prematurely emerging with malformed wings would spell certain death for her, for being unable to fly, she would simply fall to the ground and die.

Modern methods of health and healing, particularly mental and emotional treatments, have proved similar to opening the cocoon to save the caterpillar. Suffering is a natural psychospiritual modality of transformation, and to interfere with productive suffering kills the process. The caterpillar has *imaginal cells,* which contain the blueprint for the butterfly that it will become. Is it possible that we have imaginal cells that contain *our* creative blueprint? Could it be that, like the caterpillar, what seems like the end of our lives is in fact a rebirth? Can we trust our imaginal cells and be patient with others and ourselves as we wait for the transformation to begin?

The elephant, thwarted at an early age, is a victim of circumstance. On the other hand, consider the caterpillar, not thinking about her destiny but simply emerging. These are lessons of passivity and surrender.

During Cycle Two we may experience periods of profound grief as well as the experiences/emotions listed above. To understand grief, we must recognize the differences and relationships between *grief, sadness,* and *depression*—three distinct states of being. Grief is not an emotion, but rather a state of being that comes about as the result of loss. Not to be confused with grief, sadness is one of the ways that we process the grieving phenomenon. Sadness emanating from grief should not be confused with depression, which is the dysfunctional result of unprocessed grief and unexpressed sadness. Many times during a transformational experience, friends and family as well as healing professionals may mistake the process of grief for depression.

> *Give sorrow words; the grief that does not speak whispers*
> *the o'er-fraught heart and bids it break.*
>
> WILLIAM SHAKESPEARE, *MACBETH*

Grief is never too much or felt for too long. Yet Western culture dictates that grief be experienced for a few days openly and then, if you must continue grieving, it should be done quietly and privately. Most jobs allow three days for funeral leave. Beyond that, the employee is expected to return to work, endure the condolences and awkward expressions of sympathy for a few more days, and then continue with business as usual.

The media glorifies the repressed and stoic demeanor of a grieving widow, who holds her head up high and doesn't shed a tear except at the appropriate moment. Why not show the face of grief that is passionate, raw, and authentic? A Native American friend once playfully remarked to me, "Geez! White people don't know how to grieve. At a funeral for my grandmother, everyone ran up and threw themselves on the casket and wept and wailed—that's how you grieve!"

Many times grief is only considered acceptable when there is an obvious and dramatic loss such as death of a loved one. Even divorce is not seen, generally, as a reason to grieve. It's a reason to be angry or to feel pity for another but not to grieve. In reality, grief is the natural reaction to loss of any kind.

Loss is not always perceptible to others and sometimes not even to ourselves. When no obvious event has triggered our grieving, the soul is pushing through—grief is signaling a transformational, healing opportunity to examine the effects of our loss. This situation is commonly mistaken for unexplained depression, and feelings of shame rush in as we attempt to repress our "unjustified" grief. Repressing grief is debilitating. Without the physical releases of crying and expressing anger, grief produces stress hormones that not only affect emotional well-being but compromise our immune systems as well. Unprocessed grief comes to the surface every time we experience a loss—even from traumas unrelated to the current ones. Years of unprocessed grief from past losses will suddenly overtake us when a seemingly small loss occurs in the present. This has a compounding effect as our feelings of shame grow exponentially.

Too often this synergistic effect triggers the aforementioned repression response, and we lose another opportunity to process our grief. This unprocessed, unspoken grief simmers impatiently in our bodies, waiting for an outlet. We then, mistakenly, project this unresolved grief into the future as we imagine the next opportunity for grief—the next loss—and we experience anticipatory anxiety, imagining the woes that lie ahead. Fully experiencing and releasing unresolved grief is the only way to avoid such dreadful anticipation. Further, managing anxiety as it arises yields the peace of mind in knowing that, if our fears come to fruition, we will manage the grief with grace and not only survive but also thrive. We may live peacefully in the moment rather than fearfully in the future.

Cycle Two can be a glorious opportunity to understand who we actually are at our core. Limitations tell us who we are not, and with curiosity leading the way, we can take an honest look into the unfamiliar terrain of our inner landscape and allow our true desires from our heart and soul to emerge. Without judging or needing to change anything, in Cycle Two the task is to be with ourselves and with compassion be open to the question, What is birthing through me?

Cycle Three
CHAOS, URGENCY, AND TURMOIL

When people are experiencing anxiety, anger, or impatience, they are often somewhere in the third cycle of the transformational journey, the fire cycle. Rather than trying to alleviate these symptoms, it's important to find a way to express emotions in a safe space, which often frees up the stored energy so that it can be used in a more productive and creative manner. This release into creative action is what facilitates our birth into the world and the generation of new energies.

Many people are afraid of the power of this cycle and the anger or energy within themselves. When this power is disowned there is a tendency to revert to the earth cycle and become temporarily stuck in the process, or to strike out and project anger or rage onto another.

In the third cycle a person's life may be in complete chaos, turmoil, and confusion. This is the negative aspect of the fire cycle. To have what we really desire, we have to release certain aspects of what we have. While we may not tear down the entire house, we may have to make a complete mess while remodeling. If we can remember this and remain conscious during the shift, we can have the patience to know that things will eventually come back together at a higher octave in an elevated way.

The third cycle is one of chaos and creative destruction related to the element of fire. A place that is full of powerful transformative energies, it brings with it an inherent urgency to create change with feelings of "it's now or never" or that it's time to "get off the fence." When someone comes to me for healing, for Soul Whispering, I listen to what people say and notice their body language, which tells me volumes about a person and where they are energetically. If a person comes into my presence fidgety, anxious, talking fast, and expressing anger or impatience, I can make a pretty good guess that they are somewhere in the third cycle of change. Rather than trying to be rid of these symptoms, I would encourage a deep, full, inward examination and expression of emotions in a safe space. This often frees up the energy to be used in a more productive manner.

Anger is simply built-up energy that needs to be released into creative action. It is what gets us born into life (or anything new, for that matter), yet most are afraid of the power of this cycle and of its destructive energy. When disowned, we can fall back to stage two and get stuck in the process—at least temporarily.

Element: Fire

Represents: Breakthrough, creative chaos, and opening

Colors: Fiery orange, red

Positive aspects: New energy, taking action, creative chaos, passion, exhilaration, breakthrough, courage, strength, sense of urgency, power, hopefulness, appropriate expression of anger, momentum, right use of will, kundalini awakening

Negative aspects: Mania, addiction to drama, impulsiveness, thoughtlessness, unrealistic expectations, unpredictable behavior, ungrounded, rage, burnout, arrogant, unteachable, risky and unhealthy behaviors, adrenaline addiction, willfulness

Words of Wisdom about Cycle Three

Cycle Three is about untethered energy. It is the energy of breaking through. We feel as though we are free and beyond ordinary laws of gravity, structure, or form. It is a fearless time—one of sureness in which we must destroy what is no longer working and manifest our dreams. It is a passionate and exhilarating time; however, its shadow side may lead to an addiction to the excitement and upheaval. Some feel a manic high, discarding all that feels constrictive and repressive, destroying relationships and careers.

During a fire transformation, all that has been accepted as truth will be called into question. Our personalities are disorganized montages of conflicting beliefs, desires, and unexamined assumptions. If we are open to the possibility that we are so much more than our personalities, we will find the core integrity of our essence—our soul.

Deconstructing the personality and rebuilding it from a conscious, self-loving foundation is the work of Cycle Three. This cycle is necessary, because we have all been wounded and have developed habitually negative behavior and ways of being to protect ourselves from further hurt. These were, at some point, functional ways of coping with threatening situations in our childhood—beliefs and behaviors that we think keep us safe but that now limit our capacity for happiness, creativity, and serenity. What we perceive as our personality—who we are in the world—is the work of our false self. The inner critic, the voice of the false self, keeps hidden that which we need to transform to become happy, encouraging us to grasp aspects of the personality that we, in reality, wish to shed. The false self, whose job was to keep us safe, has now become a prison. Our true essence is locked away in storage, longing to see the light of day. We can, however, open to change and live from our vibrant truths. We may abruptly wake up from numbing our desires and heed the call to transformation, realizing that the imagined safety isn't worth the price of denying the soul's longing.

With the wake-up often comes a righteous anger.

Many people, particularly women, have great difficulty expressing their anger regularly and appropriately. Repressing anger leads to bitterness and bouts of explosive rage. Some experience anger as sadness and depression. For others, it is likely that the unexpressed anger will cause physical illness.

Expressing the raw anger is not the ultimate goal. Learning to know when you are angry—feeling it and knowing when your boundaries are being violated is the point. Healthy people feel angry when they are betrayed, violated, dismissed, or judged. Many of us, however, learn from childhood to accept these transgressions and to not stand up for ourselves. Repressing anger was a tactic for survival, as expressing it was viewed as unacceptable, and we would risk a loss of love and security as a result. In abusive upbringings, showing anger is not only emotionally risky but threatens physical safety as well. To be safe and loved, we learn to hide the anger and, in the process, forget what even made us angry.

Healing the damage caused to our bodies, minds, and souls from unexpressed anger is often a very difficult step to take. Whether a person has frequent rage or represses and turns anger inward, learning to own the anger and admit difficulty in expressing it can be very challenging.

Rage is not a healthy expression of anger. Rage is the result of repressed and denied feelings of anger, as the feelings are held down like steam under a pressure cooker and eventually, if not released, explode. These episodes happen in a dissociated state, and memories of the incident will often be vague. One might remember being upset, or a bit angry, or take a defensive stance over the right to be angry.

Many believe that even authentic anger is unacceptable, and recognizing rage especially produces deep shame. This originates from the deeper unconscious experience of having one's boundaries violated and the conscious experience of not feeling entitled to the anger resulting from this betrayal. Passively allowing others to hurt or take advantage is another form of unexpressed anger.

Anger is natural and is not dangerous, but holding down our anger and the denial or unconscious awareness of it, again, leads to stress. Stress increases blood pressure and releases hormones that increase one's risk of developing heart disease, diabetes, depression, and other illnesses. Knowing how and when to express anger keeps us safe. Beginning the transformational process of expressing a lifetime's worth of repressed anger can be challenging and requires a supportive environment with appropriate people and a safe setting. When we uncover and allow the toxic, buried emotions to come forth, we then face the remedial task of learning how to express anger and set boundaries in a healthy and effective manner in the future.

Creative destruction—energetic release and breakthrough—is the theme of Cycle Three. While all cycles have a shadow component, Cycle Three is intended to call forth and go into the shadow. Chaos has been given a negative meaning as we have forgotten that order is born of chaos. Without it, nothing happens. There is a time for nothing, and there is a time for explosion. Moving through the cycle of chaos means letting go of what no longer serves one's life. It can be very frightening when one has worked to create a life that is predictable and contained. Learning to experience the energy and rhythm of chaos will unlock the creativity needed for transformation.

Cycle Four
ENERGIES OF LOVE

If you are a person who usually lives in a high-energy, frenetic, or manic manner, you could mistakenly confuse Cycle Four with feeling depressed. However, if you consciously reflect on how you feel, you will notice that you are not experiencing sadness so much as an unusual quietude or solitude. This cycle occurs when we can surrender ourselves completely without attachment to outcomes around any given situation and have faith in the process and ourselves; it is when we know that we have done our part to co-create change in our life, and it is no longer up to us alone. In AA, it is referred to as turning your life and will over to a Higher Power to do for you what you cannot do alone. This is an act of surrender to something greater than the human ego and requires letting go without conditions.

In Cycle Three there is the need to push, but in Cycle Four there is a need to stop pushing and to fall into the heart of ourselves and just be with the truth until we are somehow miraculously moved to the other side of the situation. This is not to be confused with passivity or even with Cycle One. And this is not a space of nothing happening. It is the active use of will, and it is hard work to let go and trust that everything will all work out in the end.

The following is what I wrote about Cycle Four in *Shamanic Breathwork*.

The fourth cycle of spirit actually brings water, earth, and fire; emotions, physical body, and mind into the highest transformational energy field of being and heart. This is the place of the supernatural—that which transcends time and space. This is a cocreated place between human and the spirit, where the soul finds embodiment. In this place and time we open ourselves and fully surrender to the archetypes and to God/Goddess. We surrender ourselves to the Divine, where magic, synchronicity, miracles, and transformations occur. It is the place of high alchemy and change.[2]

When we are fully in this cycle, one minute we are standing in the chasm and in the fire pushing ourselves forward, and then, suddenly, we are free-falling into a whole new way of being. We see the light at the end of the tunnel and may not be able to immediately reach it, but we move toward it anyway. What once seemed impossible now begins to form our new reality.

Element: Spirit, love

Represents: Conscious surrender into our hearts

Colors: Green (any color associated with surrender to the journeyer)

Positive aspects: Love, surrender, forgiveness, ease, grace, gratitude, humility, acceptance, serenity, connection to the sacred, letting go of attachments, being supported by the universe, high alchemy, acceptance, inner peace, living in the now

Negative aspects: Blind faith, giving your power away, feeling empty, lack of motivation, inaction, giving up (different from surrendering), inertia, misinterpretation of (God's) will, fundamentalism, irresponsible behavior

Words of Wisdom about Cycle Four

Surrender is the invitation, finally, for grace to come into our lives. The spirit cycle is about dropping down to the base of our existence. Unlike Cycle Two, we are not stuck on the Earth, but we are held by Mother Earth and the love of the universe as we let go of all struggle and all longing. Surrendering into co-creation is the beginning of conscious completion of the five cycles, leading to rebirth and transformation.

> *In Defeat, we are forced to lay down our sword; in active surrender, we consciously choose to lay it down.*
> Marion Woodman, *Coming Home to Myself*

Changes will occur in life that, while painful, are ultimately for the higher good. By consciously working the cycles we surrender to the bigger story—the understanding that only in letting go do we experience the grace of something much bigger than the ego. Having the humility to reach out for help will open your heart. An open heart leads to trust, and trust leads to the wisdom of co-creation with your soul/spirit.

Whenever we surrender the ego to spirit, what we are really surrendering is our will. Despite having no attachment to the outcome, there is a knowingness that we are not alone. It is, however, a solitary place. A deep peace, unrelated to what may be going on in our immediate surroundings, washes over us as we step out of the chaos of Cycle Three into a new cycle of peace, serenity, and nonattachment. Like being in the eye of a hurricane, we observe the chaos from our chamber of inner calmness. It is here that we know that we have done everything there is to do—now, we must simply let go. Grace is co-creator, and something larger than our ego is now in the driver's seat, moving the process of transformation forward. We let go even of letting go. We allow rather than do.

Cycle Five
TRANSFORMATION/REBIRTH

As expressed in *Shamanic Breathwork:*

> Air allows us to take a deep breath and incorporate the elements of our whole experience. It is a place of becoming the teacher and being willing to share our experience as a teacher, writer, counselor, leader of some kind, and mentor. From this place of embodiment we have a

much bigger picture, and the journey, along with the lessons learned along the way, begins to become much clearer. We can see like the winged ones. All the chakras are opened, allowing breath into the lower part of the body.[3]

At last, in the air cycle, we have room to breathe! Everything makes sense, and the struggle is over. Gratitude, vision, and clarity are three characteristics of Cycle Five, and we want to share with others what we have learned or gained from our journey. Where there once was a wall of doubt, confusion, and pain, there is now an opening. Even though there may be excitement and relief during the air cycle, there is also a period of adjusting to this new reality—this rebirth.

One of the images that comes to mind is the butterfly that has emerged from the closed chrysalis state in all of its beauty and glory. It takes some time, however, for it to dry its beautiful wings to fly. We may also imagine the powerful phoenix, rising up into the sky from the flames and ashes below.

When we enter this cycle there is a visceral knowing that change has occurred, and there are often dramatic changes in our outer reality as well. It is important to take note of all that was necessary to deliver us to this incredible place of renewal and change. These memories will assist us in the future as we embark upon the next spiral of change, which is surely just around the bend.

Cycle Five is a portal to living in an awakened, shamanic consciousness in everyday life. We have touched on a relationship with our inner truth and spiritual guidance. Maintaining that relationship, like maintaining any relationship, requires intention, practice, attention, and action. Intention says that we are willing—simple willingness ignites the process of awakening. The practice of listening to our inner truth can be done daily and may also require taking time away from daily routines for retreat and to kick-start the process.

Daily practice develops the ability to pay attention to what is true right now. Action follows naturally when we set intention and practice paying attention, living in the present despite any turmoil or commotion that may surround us at the moment. Setting intention that we are willing to face to discover our deepest truth is a commitment that should not be taken lightly. When we make this commitment, we give permission to our soul—our higher self—to take charge and move us along the path of awakening. It's not a path that someone else has smoothed out for us. Much of it will be bushwhacking as we embark on a new adventure into the unknown of our psyche.

Element: Air
Represents: Embodying shamanic consciousness
Colors: Shades of blue, purple, white
Positive aspects: Rebirth, embodiment of spirit, celebration, freedom, energetic, grateful, deep release, connected to the bigger picture, timeless myths and archetypal stories, completion, new beginnings, expansive, focused, attractive and magnetic, leadership, clarity, vision and wisdom from experience, discovery of sacred purpose and authentic self
Negative aspects: Religious fanaticism, disassociation, spiritual bypass, guru status, superiority, elitism, ungrounded, irrelevant, spacey, lack of empathy, linear thinking . . . ta-da thinking.

Words of Wisdom about Cycle Five

Cycle Five is the place of the North on the medicine wheel—the place of wisdom. We do not have to stay stuck or bumble through life blind and clueless. We can learn from those who have gone before us. While their experience can only be a guide, it is invaluable to find a mentor. Elders, coaches, therapists, counselors, and teachers all have their places in our lives. Most important, however, is our inner teacher— our soul's voice. It is always there, whispering to us if we can stop long enough to tune in and listen. Developing it can begin with intention. Often, we have a deep, unconscious inner message, and being in nature may stimulate that message, bringing it into consciousness. We may be in the process of a divorce or career change, feeling uncomfortable and not knowing what to do next. Walking down the street with curiosity and the intention of receiving a message, we may see a leaf fall from a tree and have the simple recognition that it's time to let go. With practice, listening for messages in nature will deepen into expanded awareness of not only the Earth but the stars and beyond as well.

As you read the accounts of Soul Whisperer Carley Mattimore and her husband, John, below, bear witness to the many seasons of change that they have cycled through in their lives. Also keep in mind how the world of nature reached out and touched Carley, calling her to the sacred work that she is doing today with the white lions of South Africa.

Healing Journey

Carley Mattimore

I have been on a shamanic journey all of my life, but not consciously aware of it. My soul was guiding me, but I wasn't awake yet. It was like I was in a fog, following my path but not consciously. I now understand that this was akin to my birth process. My mother gave birth to me under anesthesia (ether). This was my first imprint as I entered the world, to move through my life as if in a fog.

Another imprint: I was breastfed (for which I am thankful), but it was on a schedule of every four hours. I had to suppress my own body's need for nourishment to conform to an outside source. So I learned to detach from my own "hunger" and let others guide me. This letting others guide me was further molded in me given that I was the oldest of six children, wherein I learned to be the mature, responsible, and good child taking care of my younger siblings. My hunger for life was suppressed, but it was still very active in my cellular makeup.

During my teen life, my passions were activated as I moved away from my family dynamics and began to explore life. Being a responsible child in a family that was very overwhelmed gave me new freedom. My thirst awakened for peace, social justice, and equality among all beings and for making a difference in the world. I marched for the end of the war and worked within and outside the system. I gave speeches on racism, mental illness, and making a difference.

I took healthy risks, pushing back the constraints of childhood upbringing and the early imprints. I woke up and came alive.

I met my first husband, Russell, during this period of coming alive. He was different, and a nonconformer who had had so many experiences, many of which I didn't believe at first. He broke through perceived obstacles both in what he accomplished and what he didn't. Our time together was filled with adventure. From him I learned that life is to be lived, and nothing can stop that except death.

However, in our first year of marriage, my parents separated and then my father and sister were killed in a car accident on their way to visit my husband and me. Three other siblings were in the car, and two were critically injured. Our family of origin fell apart. Then nine years later, in 1985, my husband also died in a car accident, leaving me to raise our two daughters, ages one and four, alone.

Grief activated my early programming, and I reverted to hyper-responsible behavior. I had to finish my degree and protect my daughters from the effects of losing a father. My grief was suppressed as I stepped up to the plate of being competent. I went deep into the fog and moved through my life with a big persona attached to my ego.

In 1988, I married again, to my current husband, John. Together we blended our families—his two daughters and my two daughters—and we had one daughter together. He was a perfect match for me, a man whose father had died when he was three years old. He was also detached and shut down from his own grief. Yet, he was a man with whom I fell in love and who shared a similar commitment to family, social justice, and nature.

As our children grew, I became exhausted with the demands of raising five daughters in a blended family, holding a lot of responsibility for making it work as I modeled a competent woman, mother, and wife. Things began leaking out sideways; I just couldn't juggle it all. As our daughters grew and moved away from home, there was some relief as the demands were less. I had more room to explore me again.

My first awakening experience was in a guided visualization during a workshop in 2005 with a dear friend and colleague; she took us through our chakras, asking each chakra for a message. When we got to my third eye, I burst into tears as I received the message *"You are a healer."* I had no idea what this meant and asked my friend. She said, *"Well, you are a psychotherapist and thus a healer."* I knew that it was deeper than this.

In 2005, my husband attended a Priest Process workshop in Kansas City. Although it was a stretch for him to attend, he joined my dear friend's husband. A man named Brad Collins, cofounder of Venus Rising Association, was leading the workshop. John came back from it full of enthusiasm about something called Shamanic Breathwork. This experience had opened a pathway for him to heal from the death of his father at age three. John said, *"Carley, I can see the two of us doing this work together."* He saw us bringing it to other folks so that they too could heal. He wanted it available on *"every street corner."*

My first Shamanic Breathwork session came several months later at Venus Rising's Wise Wolf Council. In the breathwork, I was given the message to do healing work with my hands. It led me to my first Reiki session, in which I encountered a child, a son of mine from a previous lifetime who died at age nine. This opened profound grief with many tears for that lost son. I am responsible and contain my feelings, yet this could not be contained. It was in me. I wasn't even sure that I believed in reincarnation. How did all this work? The deeper I explored, the more connections appeared.

The dots were beginning to show me a much bigger and richer life than I could imagine; a shamanic life. In March 2011, I showed up at Venus Rising to attend the first monthlong Shamanic Healing Initiatory Process (SHIP). I must say, there was a lot of resistance as these early imprints were very much in my field. In a guided visualization on the first day, my body became a snake shedding its skin, and I found myself on a spiral path moving through my life with another imprint of *"I don't want to go through this."* I didn't want to experience the deaths of my father, sister, or husband. I didn't want to tell my daughter that her father had been cremated . . . I didn't want to be here at Venus Rising. Yet here I was.

In this monthlong time frame, I went into a cave and retrieved my dragon, the energy that it was taking to suppress the grief over the loss of my father. The old, stagnant energy was released from my body, and the kundalini began to flow. When I shared this grief in my processing group outdoors, a large water snake came up out of the pond and crossed my path, affirming that early vision of shedding my skin. For me this was a breakthrough.

The magic of the shamanic world was opening to me, and I was awakening. The last day of our monthlong process happened to be on the thirty-fifth anniversary of my father's and sister's death on April 16. During the closing ritual, I reenacted going into the cave and retrieving the dragon as I sang my favorite song, "Puff the Magic Dragon." I learned that the dragon hoardes the gold to protect us until we are ready to bring the dragon back and receive the gold. At this point the dragon becomes our ally. Interestingly enough, a year later, I would be in the Drakensburg Mountains (known as the Dragon Mountains) in South Africa on the anniversary of my father's death as someone sang "Puff the Magic Dragon" in the backseat of our vehicle.

With this newfound energy, passion, and perspective on life, I returned home to Springfield, Illinois, from the monthlong retreat and told my husband that we were going to start a congregation of Venus Rising. He jumped on board as this was affirming his own vision. We searched for a name to call our new congregation and settled on aahara, which is a Sanskrit word meaning "to breathe." How fitting for me, given that this is what this work has done for me! It has helped me to breathe my truth, passion, and purpose without having to hold my breath or be in a fog of ether.

Part of the shamanic perspective tells us that we are on a spiral path of change from the moment we are born. We move through a process very similar to our birth as we move through change. We experience gestation (water), moving down the birth canal (earth), the opening of the cervix (fire), and then surrender (spirit) as we birth (air). In my work at Venus Rising, I had come through the birth canal and been reborn into the air cycle, where I had a new understanding of my life, a new perspective to share with the world—with others who needed help and transformation as I had.

After being certified as a Shamanic Breathwork facilitator you can become a master practitioner if you go through SHIP again. In my second time around, I opened to a bigger experience that aligned me with a larger sacred purpose. I was awakened in a Shamanic Breathwork by the white lions and Maria Khosa, a lion shaman, and was called to South Africa. It had been predicted by the indigenous people of South Africa that the white lions of Timbavati would return to Earth, foreshadowing great evolutionary change on the planet as they usher in a new age.

I have traveled to the white lions four times since 2012 and led my own tour of seventeen people there, together with Linda Star Wolf and my husband, John, in March 2016. I have a formalized relationship with the Global White Lion Protection Trust as an advocate for the lions in association with their U.S. office. John and I will be attending the GWLPT's White Lion Leadership Academy as advanced practitioners at the invitation of Linda Tucker and bringing some of this training back to Aahara and Venus Rising. Venus Rising and the trust are formalizing their connection as well as we unite the wolf and the lion.

Aahara is in its fifth year of offering Shamanic Breathwork workshops, advanced trainings, the Shamanic Healing Initiatory Process (SHIP), shamanic 12-step, and many other workshops. We delight in bringing in guest speakers, musicians, and facilitators from around the world. In addition, the shamanic work of the lion, in particular the white lion teachings, continue to be large part of our work.

Our community here in the Midwest has been enriched by the work that we do as those who show up and share themselves in this sacred work have also enriched us. Many others are opening to their shamanic path and stepping forward in their sacred purpose and enriching our community with their work.

At this juncture, I am reclaiming and embodying another level of my spiritual warrior self so that I may be of service to the world with sensitivity, compassion, and courage at a critical time in the evolution of humanity.

There's No One Else I Want to Be

John Malan

My wife, Carley, has been a part of my journey from the very beginning and is now my partner in the work that I do. When I came home from my first breathwork I told her how big the experience was for me, and then I said something that may have surprised me more than it did her, "I can see us doing this work together someday."

She was a psychotherapist with more than twenty years' experience at the time, and I was an emotionally shutdown computer programmer and middle manager, so this was quite an unexpected statement, not least because she had no idea what breathwork was when I uttered those fateful words.

She experienced a breathwork herself a short time later, as she describes earlier, but what I want to add is this: it may be possible to do deep transformative work dredging up trauma and grief from thirty, forty, or fifty years prior without going to pieces repeatedly, but that's not how I did it. Carley stayed by me when I was a raging, weeping, whiny pool of misery and self-pity on the floor and has done her own work to heal and grow as well.

In all my previous relationships, codependency was the foundation and dysfunction was the rule. I really never thought I would have a conscious, challenging, and loving relationship with a woman who would not only stay with me as I changed but change herself at the same time. Our relationship is taking us places I never thought I would go, both physically and spiritually, and the potential for growth, deepening, and intimacy is greater all the time.

This is not the life that I thought I was going to have; it is infinitely better, warts and all. This would not have happened if I had not gone to that first breathwork in Kansas City.

When I am facilitating workshops now, I often refer to my own problems. Sometimes people who don't know me are surprised by this. It's common to expect the workshop leaders to present themselves as people who have done their work and who don't have the problems of ordinary people anymore. But what I have learned is that the shaman is the wounded healer. It's precisely our wounds that give us the experience, compassion, and insight that we need to be of service to others. One of the ways that I measure my own progress is by the extent to which I can talk about my wounds without feeling or sounding like a victim. These wounds are gifts; they have made me who I am, and there's no one else I want to be.

11

The Magical Power
of Archetypes

Mythological Keys to Transformation

Do the archetypes change under a cosmic plan of some sort? Or are *we* changing, and so we change our archetypes? Just as the sun keeps us alive the archetypes are keeping us alive through the planetary influences of interstellar multidimensional beings. Jung said that there are psychic forces within the human psyche. Perhaps these forces are downloading into the human psyche at this time.

The big, mythological, archetypal stories really help to save our human hides. It's through the understanding of these energetic patterns that we are swept up in at times of great transformation that we begin to understand how we human beings are really linked very intimately and intricately with the gods themselves. It seems like the deities, or gods, are a psychic blueprint of the universe somehow. They come down through us as energetic patterns. The archetypes are the structures that underpin our psychic awareness and shape our personal and collective soul stories.

The collective psychic energies, or what are called "gods and goddesses of mythology," have lived these stories in another dimension, shaping these stories through different times and cultures, replaying them in many ways. Some stories have been written down, others are more of an oral tradition. Many of the same stories are reworked and rewritten as the evolution of our planet continues. Themes run throughout, from the earliest myths to fairy tales to modern-day movie themes.

The famous mythologist Joseph Campbell said that all myths are true—so at the biggest level of consciousness these stories are the actual lifeblood of our lives. "Mythology is not a lie, mythology is poetry, it is metaphorical. It has been well said that mythology is the penultimate truth—penultimate because the ultimate cannot be put into words. It is beyond words, beyond images, beyond that bounding rim of the Buddhist Wheel of Becoming. Mythology pitches the mind beyond that rim, to what can be known but not told."[1] As soon as we have an awareness that the myth or the story we are living out has its roots archetypally in a much bigger story, we understand that we ourselves are in a much bigger story. We are all, at times, a big, fat, hot mess, but we are a hot mess with meaning! We are in an alchemical process wherein we're hot and it's for a reason. If we're cooking, it's for a reason.

Knowing that the gods and goddesses themselves survived these stories is inspiration for us to keep going at our darkest hour. Not only have they survived them, but they've made them alive and kept them in the Akashic Records, the sacred archives, for us to access when we are at the end of our rope. We are only a vibration away from the archetypes themselves. We are just at a different frequency. And as they're feeding us those stories, we are digesting them and reworking them and reloading them to the Akashic Records for others to download when they need them. Through the archetypal stories we each get to see ourselves in one another. And many would say the gods see themselves in us.

The cosmic dance is going on all the time. The archetypes are our dance partners. Throughout our lives we might dance with many different partners for a moment. We interact with that energy, and it touches us. That archetype helps us move somewhere through our lives, much as we might move across the dance floor. Sometimes the music stops, and we let go of the archetypal partner. And some archetypes become our partners for many years, or our entire lives, or across lifetimes. You might be drawn to look at the archetypes in your life, the larger themes that you may not have recognized. One way of doing this is to familiarize yourself with timeless myths. This is a path of self-awareness that can bring understanding and comfort to what feels like meaningless events.

INANNA
The Oldest Sumerian Myth, a Feminine Tale

The story of Inanna is one of the oldest myths on Earth, originating, it is believed, from Sumeria. Inanna was the queen of heaven who decided to go to see her dark sister, Ereshkigal, the queen of the underworld. In an audio track accessible through a link provided at the end of this book, Star Wolf tells the story of Inanna set to rhythmic drumming to take you on a journey with Inanna. The highlights of her story are below.

This tale is an allegory for what we must go through on the path to wholeness. Inanna heard the call that beckoned her to leave her secure and comfortable life as queen. She let go of her prized possessions, leaving them in a place where she believed she could come back to retrieve them. She encountered a crisis and had to clear her heart and soul of everything she took to be true. With the help of friends and strangers, she emerged into clarity with compassion. She integrated disowned parts of herself to co-create her future.

When Inanna arrived at the gates of the underworld she sent a message to her sister, Ereshkigal, that she was there to visit. Ereshkigal was not at all pleased. She resented that Inanna's light and glory had been, to some extent, achieved at Ereshkigal's expense, and she was enraged. Ereshkigal punished and tortured Inanna and left her for dead.

The only one who came to help Inanna was her uncle. Enki had compassion for his niece. Not only did he value the journey Inanna had undertaken, but also he did not forget that her existence was vital to humankind.

When Ereshkigal agreed to release Inanna she did so, in part, because she had projected her pain into Inanna, and to release Inanna was to release herself. But the rules of the underworld had to be maintained, so a deal was made with Inanna before she could be released. In essence, Inanna could not be allowed to again forget her neglected, abandoned "sister"—that part of herself that was Ereshkigal. A passageway had been created from the conscious to the unconscious, and it would now be kept open.

Some mythologists interpret the outcome of the story to mean that Inanna herself must return over and over to the underworld. Others say that it is about Inanna having to appease the gods of the underworld. The authors of this book believe that Inanna is being told that she must speak about her journey and send others to the underworld, not to torture them or to appease the underworld gods; rather, having found her freedom through facing her darkness, Inanna now has the compassion to know that sending others through the darkness will set them free.

The Inanna myth comes alive in many women and men when the desire to leave the comfort of their lives outweighs the fear of the unknown. The journey of Inanna is a journey to find and explore our darkest repressed urges, beliefs, and tendencies. Unexplored, these urges drive us to act and believe and feel in ways that deaden us and disconnect us from our spirit-guided wisdom. They separate us from our soul and its constructive whisperings to us. The German existential philosopher Heidegger suggested that the problem with life is that we are trapped in what he referred to as the tranquilized obviousness of daily life.[2] We do indeed live lives of quiet desperation. Numbed by routine and distractions we don't notice that we are incomplete and unfulfilled until a crisis strikes and wakes us up.

OTHER DEITIES AND GODS
OF THE ANCIENT PANTHEON

In addition to the story of Inanna, we would like to detail other age-old gods and the myths that surround them. These are the archetypal guides and principles that lead us through our shamanic journey to awaken the power of our hearts. In this section you will find what we will refer to as the more recent and popular interpretation of these powerful archetypal forces as well as Star Wolf's own phenomenological direct experience with them in the form of messages received during shamanic visioning. She wrote about all of this in her earlier book, coauthored with Nicki Scully, *Shamanic Mysteries of Egypt*. We all have the capacity to have direct experiences and messages from the archetypes. Below are the Egyptian archetypes from which Star Wolf received spontaneous messages while traveling in Egypt with Nicki.

The Dove
Initiate/Innocence/Trust

The dove represents the archetypal principle of the initiate who is innocent and trusting. The dove is also the one who hears the call to enter into the shamanic Egyptian mysteries and to trust his own heart as he encounters challenges on the path of direct experience of the Great Mystery. Following his heart off the cliff into the swirling void, the initiate carries an olive branch as an offering of peace and to honor the powerful transformative forces that will be encountered along the way. The little white dove is the bridge between the present world of humanity and the ancient past. For most people the dove will automatically evoke some kind of spiritual connection, similar to the olive branch that evokes peace and reverence.

Nekhbet Mother Mut
Alchemist/Wisdomkeeper/Grand Mother

Nekbet Mother Mut is the grand old dame of ancient Egypt who would be considered the crone or the elder of the pantheon of Neteru. She is most wise, direct, precise, and must be approached with respect if one wishes to gain permission into these sacred mysteries. She does not mess around and is a disciplined taskmaster to assist the initiate in making the decision to enter fully into the process of alchemy and change. Once the decision has been made to move forward, Nekhbet Mother Mut's loving, watchful eye is always upon the initiate to ensure safe passage through the portals of shamanic initiation.

Nepthys
High Priestess/Intuition/Great Mystery

Nepthys is the hidden or veiled one who serves as a medium between worlds. She comes to us in dreams, flashes of intuition, and visions. Nepthys is an aspect of the triple goddesses, which includes Isis,

Nekhbet, and Mother Mut. She relies upon spirit to direct her in all things, and she holds the Mystery teachings of life, death, and rebirth deep within her essence. As an inspiritrix she whispers her secrets in the wind as she dances exotically under the moonlit, starry sky with her magnificent serpents winding around her beautiful bronze arms.

Isis
Holy Queen/Mother of Us All/Embodied Manifestation of Higher Love and Wisdom

Isis is the pure, clear essence of spirit embodied in matter. She is always with us as a loving, supportive force through every transformation we undergo. Isis remembers us as we die the shaman's death and makes us whole again as she urges us forth into a new incarnation and way of being at a higher octave of consciousness. She is the queen of both heaven and earth and unfolds her brilliant rainbow wings to connect the rainbow bridge of love between the world of form and formlessness.

Khnum
Master Craftsman/Creator of Form and Grounding Energy/ Organizing Principle

Khnum is the highly skilled master craftsman who creates the never-ending evolving varieties of form upon his potter's wheel. He holds the universal secrets of the organizing principles of DNA and life itself. Khnum lovingly and carefully re-creates the new body, or form, that will house our renewed heart at an even more expanded level than before.

Sphinx
Divine Messenger/Cosmic Library/ Earth Altar

The sphinx is a divine messenger and repository of cosmic Akashic wisdom. As an earth altar and cosmic library, this mysterious one holds the stellar messages from our ancient ancestors who have been simply waiting our opening and readiness to receive their sacred downloads and transmissions.

Sobek and Horus
Reconciliation/Forgiveness/Understanding

These two very powerful opposing psychic forces reside in all human beings. They represent both the old and the new parts of each of us. The old part is the reptilian brain, which holds all of the old teachings and evolutionary patterns from which we have evolved and is that which has kept us protected, alive, and growing forward. The new part of our brain brings in more complex functions and the higher charkas. Ultimately these two are adversarial allies who must find a harmonious union of sorts within our psyches to create balance in our lives.

Sekhmet
Transformation/Fierce Compassion/Shape-Shifter

Sekhmet is a compelling fiery Neteru who comes to us whenever we are in the midst of the alchemical fires of transformation. She shows us her fierce compassion as she assists us in healing the dual natures within and helps us to shape-shift into our future selves, which we are struggling to become. She opens and purifies the heart space while creating fertile ground to receive the visionary seeds of who we are at our next level of consciousness.

Ma'at
Truth/Radiance/Balance and Acceptance

Ma'at is the powerful balancer and adjuster who is able to help us to accept and love the truth about ourselves: "The light the dark no difference." Her brilliant radiance reflects our own radiance back to us so that we may truly see who we really are and where our work is as we move toward greater wholeness. She is the great and regal mistress who reigns over the hall of mirrors. She sees beyond right and wrong and creates divine justice in our affairs.

Thoth
Illumination/Architect of Wisdom/Enlightened Communication

This sacred holy scribe and wisdomkeeper urges us ever upward toward higher learning so that we are able to make deeper meaning from our life lessons and experiences. When we have embodied the truth of our lives we are able to articulate and share the wisdom authentically from an enlightened place. This form of communication has its basis in the soul's fountain of wisdom.

Kephera
Cycles of Change/Planetary Guardian/Spiral Dancer

The mighty scarab Kephera serves the planet Earth as a loyal guardian and spinner of cycles that brings forth the necessary changes for Creation to continue to move forward. S(he) is a spiral dancer who faithfully filters and transmits the powerful stellar and cosmic energies that are being radiated to all Earth's creatures. Kephera knows how to spin the energies and hold the balance of time and the turning of the ages in his/her mighty feet.

Bast
Holy Longing/Desire/Instinct and Sensuality

The sensual cat goddess named Bast creates the compelling, strong desire to be born into form. Her instinctual holy longing is irresistible in its urgency to create new life. She shows us that birth is sacred and that being born into form is a blessing, not a curse. She is our guardian through the birthing chambers each time we are ready to renew our form. Without her allurement and promise of new delights we would never have the impetus or courage to reenter the cosmic birth canal and be born over and over again. With each birth we celebrate the joy and magic of our precious incarnation here on Earth.

Anubis
Surrender/Shaman Within/Enlightened Heart

Anubis is the enlightened-heart shaman who is the opener of the way, meaning that he has gone before us, as one of us, to pave the way for us to follow in his footsteps. Anubis knows how to surrender his heart and his truth to ever-expanding cycles of death and rebirth so as to step more fully into his divine humanity here on Earth: "On earth as it is in heaven." He is the original wolf spirit from the Dog Star, Sirius, who is our ever faithful companion. He assists us in our ego deaths and a renewal of our soul's true purpose. He is a walker between worlds and knows how to sniff out the path that comes and goes from form to formlessness. He cares deeply about us and guides us if we will only call upon him during our own shamanic journeys between the worlds.

Osiris
Regeneration/Transmutation/Beauty

Although Osiris has long been associated with death and is called the lord of the underworld, truthfully it is more appropriate to acknowledge him as the archetypal regenerative principle that transmutes the outworn deteriorating form into its renewed, shining manifestation of beauty. Osiris invites us to let go and rest deeply upon his earthy green chest as he wraps his supportive arms around our bodies and turns us into that which we are in the process of becoming.

Hathor
Magic/Medicine Woman/Integration

Hathor is the beautiful Neteru and medicine woman who has integrated the light and dark into a magical blend of higher love and wisdom in her golden/silver cauldron of healing. This resolution of inner conflict results in a sacred marriage within that brings forth the possibility of unconditional love for oneself and others. The outcome is a peaceful empowerment and the ability to co-create one's outer world. All of Earth's creatures feel blessed and safe in her presence and long to be close to her heart.

Set
Shadow/Sacred Adversarial Ally/Trickster

Set is the embodiment of the darker aspects of our natures and is often projected out onto others. He is the scapegoat who carries the sins of the world upon his back and tricks us into meeting our fate in the outer world so that we may evolve forward to higher levels of consciousness.

He is in truth both an adversary and an ally, hence his more dignified name is the "adversarial ally." If we refuse to meet and own this part of ourselves in a conscious manner, our actions can turn in to the evil we have no wish to be.

Wadjet
Kundalini Life-Force Energy/Purification/Divine Awakener

The great kundalini cobra serpent spirals her way into our lives, opening our chakras and becoming the divine awakener who purifies our motives and gives us the gift of humility. We can learn from wisdom or learn from woe, but Wadjet insures us that we will learn her lessons and take greater responsibility for our thoughts and actions in the world. She reminds us that it is not now or never, but now or later!

Sothis
Star Consciousness/Bodhisattva/Generosity

Sothis is a pure channel for divine love and wisdom. She rises into the night sky and pours forth her spiritual essence, stellar energies, and compassionate wisdom upon all beings. Through her willingness to offer us these precious gifts and guidance we are elevated to a greater understanding of our own soul's purpose and why we are here on Earth at this time. She is the star of humanity calling forth the best in each of us and inspiring us to step into our greater selves and offer our own unique gifts back to the world.

Khonsu
Moon Energies/Divine Timing/
Communion and Blood Mysteries

Khonsu brings spiritual nourishment to our bodies and souls. He knows the exact timing in which we are ready to receive communion and "eat the flesh of the gods" so that we may become as "one of them." Khonsu works on our behalf to fertilize our minds and hearts with the seeds of our own divinity. He engages the power of the moon to bring forth the healing rains that cleanse our old belief systems and renew our DNA at a cellular level. He governs the tides of the oceans and human emotions. This keeper of the lunar mysteries restores our souls to their very core.

Amun Ra
Solar Energies/Transfiguration/Royalty

Amun Ra ushers spiritualized matter, dignity, and royalty into one's true nature. The powerful light from the solar mysteries shines upon us and transfigures our consciousness. We turn ourselves toward the shining light of the sun and become spiritually mature beings that seek to embody shamanic consciousness in everyday life. Amun Ra helps us to realize that we have everything we need to heal ourselves and our world within our reach.

Ptah
The New Aeon/Imagination/Visionary Prophet

The powers of imagining a new world and opening the mouth of Creation to issue it forth belong to the great creator god Ptah. He is a prophet and a seer of the future eons. He holds the potential of a golden age in his mind's eye, which we can tap in to to harness his powers of sound and speak things into being.

Geb and Nut
Union/Creation of Sacred Purpose/ Divine Parents

Geb and Nut are the personification of the dreaming universe. Unified with passionate intent they are in a sacred union of wholeness and co-creation. They are our divine parents who help to initiate and birth us into our sacred purpose as we spiral around the great wheel of life/death and rebirth on the heart/mind path of embodying shamanic consciousness. We are meant to awaken and remember our connection to the Divine so that we can become adult children of the gods and assume more responsibility for caring for the Earth and all of life upon this sacred planet. We also inherit the sacred powers of the ancient ones as we grow in their likeness.

THE MYTH OF OSIRIS AND ISIS REDUX
Star Wolf and Brad's Archetypal Love Story

Star Wolf and her late husband, Brad, embodied the archetypes of Isis and Osiris as you will read below. When living these archetypal stories many people report a sense of looking back on the story and exclaiming, "Wow!—that wasn't just two people, or an event, or an accident, or something meaningless—it was chock full of meaning!" When we pay attention to our meaning we become closer to godliness. That is, we have an expanded capacity to understand that the story is relevant to the human experience. It is easier to see the meaning and the message after the experience settles, as opposed to when you're in the middle of it. But it is in the middle that we have the choice to wake up—not at the beginning—but in the middle.

If we wake up to it, we can make that journey so much more conscious and even go to the great depths to begin to have an ecstatic energy of the experience, rather than only an ordinary one. We know that we are not alone and that many others have gone through similar mythological archetypal journeys and that there is a pathway through. Each time one of us goes through it and lives to tell the tale and see the bigger picture, we clear that story out for humanity a little more, maybe even for the gods themselves.

Star Wolf's Story

CONSCIOUS EMBODIMENT OF AN ARCHETYPAL STORY

As I look back over my entire life from higher ground, every twist and turn has had a sacred purpose and meaning no matter how low or high it has felt at the time. It is in hindsight that the true meaning and purpose become crystal clear, and yet even though the story has ended, another sequel begins and hopefully from a higher and wiser perspective.

I have been able to do this kind of reconciliation between my heart, soul, spirit, and body with every heartbreak in my life, and the archetypes have been potent and multitudinous throughout the course of my life. I seem to carry a portal around in my field for them to come through, and it is through this lens that I have healed myself a number of times and have also helped others with their own transformation and healing.

However, the latest shamanic journey and turn around the great wheel of life has been the most profound challenge in my life, and it has taken everything that I have learned on my journey in my life prior to this initiation for me to survive the depths that I have experienced over the course of the past two and a half years.

It really begins with the story of Isis and Osiris, one of the greatest love stories ever told, and it became my story and really our story, Brad's and mine. I share it with you here in hopes that it will somehow touch your own bigger story as you walk through the dark night and eventual rebirth of your own soul's journey.

Brad and I were newly in love and excited to finally be living out our dreams together in our ultracool, split-level home in the redwoods of sunny Fairfax, California. We were both trained breathwork facilitators and in fact had magically met at a breathwork weeklong training called Embracing Your Inner Beloved several years before we actually came together as lovers and partners.

We both used breathwork in our daily spiritual practice and engaged ourselves in longer sessions during times when we were seeking a deeper meaning, message, or direction in our lives together. About six months after moving in to our dream home, Brad met with a breathwork friend who held space for him to enter into a breathwork journey session that ended up having a profound effect upon him at that time and eventually on the course that both of our lives would take over the next twelve years.

Sometimes breathwork sessions are truly previews of coming attractions, and this was certainly the case in this situation. During Brad's session he had an amazing archetypal journey where met the great goddess Isis, whom he merged with and realized that she was his inner feminine figure that represented his true beloved. He shared this with me, explaining that in his session he had once again met with and had brief encounters with every significant woman in his life from throughout the years. He kept asking them if they were his beloved, and each would simply shake their head no. Then finally he met Isis and asked her the same question. Her response to him was that all of his external beloveds were a reflection of his inner beloved, including her, and he could only find the true feminine spirit of his beloved within himself. At that point she entered him, and he merged with her spirit and felt a deep and abiding presence of love for himself and forgiveness for things in the past that he had done that were unloving both to him and to others, including all the women he had loved.

He understood that in some way, every woman he had ever loved was an emanation of the goddess Isis for him. He realized in his session that she lived inside his own psyche as the embodiment of undying love and would never leave him through each death and rebirth of change in his life, because she was inseparable as his inner beloved.

Because of many synchronistic events that occurred right after Brad's "Isis" breathwork, we were drawn, out of curiosity, to read to one another the beautiful and mysterious shamanic love story of death and rebirth between the great Egyptian goddess Isis and her beloved husband, Osiris. Even though neither of us were very familiar at the time with Egyptian mythology and their archetypes, except in a very general way, we both felt mysteriously connected to their love story and journey together and somehow saw some connections to our own love story . . . little did we know how prophetic that would be and ring true in the years to come.

Shortly after sharing his shamanic journey with me, a variety of synchronistic events happened in mythic ways that caused us to pack up and rather suddenly move across country to the South. The Blue Ridge Mountains of western North Carolina called us to them, and we purchased a large plot of acreage called Iris Cove Lane, and soon after we arrived we decided to rename Iris to Isis Cove. We felt a bigger mystery and story calling us both, which resulted in the co-creation of an incredible dream come true. Together with the support of dear friends, we birthed the Isis Cove Community and Retreat Center, named after the Great Goddess herself.

The Isis Cove Residential Community grew into a community that consists mainly of individuals who are progressive spiritual teachers, authors, and shamanic pyschospiritual facilitators committed to planetary service. The Isis Cove Loveland Retreats have served thousands of people seeking shamanic consciousness, wholeness, personal healing, and professional training over the past dozen years.

From the first day we walked into Isis Cove, Brad made the observation that he felt like he was walking into a sacred womb (the womb of Isis). This is a place where one could completely leave the outside world behind and immerse themselves in nature and nurture and into the shamanic Mystery schools hidden within our psyches as well as the mysterious smoky Blue Ridge Mountains, which are enclosed in the safety of the cove, like a womb. We both felt that it was a safe haven for us and for all those who entered so that they could just drop into a deep place of inner healing and transformation.

Shortly after moving into and renovating the old mountain house at Isis Cove, I was hit with the inspiration that we needed to make a journey to Egypt with our group and ask another dear shamanic soul sister Nicki Scully to guide us. Nicki had been leading hundreds of people to Egypt for magical journeys for decades, and I knew that there was no one else that I would rather go with than her. On the spot I picked up the phone and called Nicki, and we started to collaborate on a trip to Egypt. When Brad heard that we were going, he immediately said, "Not without me!" He felt such a deep connection to Isis and there was no way he wasn't going, so about a year later we made the trip of a lifetime to that ancient land with a large group of soul friends and kindred spirits.

It turned out to be a magical trip indeed for everyone involved and truly the most incredible trip I have ever taken before or since. It also turned out to be very challenging for me personally on many levels, which I have written about in my other books. However, the challenges were met and in the end resulted in the writing of two books, coauthored with Nicki Scully (*Shamanic Mysteries of Egypt* followed by *The Anubis Oracle*) and then another one written with my wonderful friend and colleague Ruby Falconer (*Shamanic Egyptian Astrology*).

Of course, Isis and her husband, Osiris, played a significant role in all of these archetypal writings as well as many other shamanic Egyptian deities. The aftereffects of that incredible journey became an even more foundational energy piece in my life and in Brad's.

A well-known psychic teacher who came to Isis Cove once said that he sensed how strongly the essence of Isis and Osiris energetically lived at Isis Cove, not only through the spirits of the land but also through the energetic force field and soul mate relationship between Brad and myself. It was embedded in our great love for one another and our joint dedication to serve the world with our love at both the personal and transpersonal levels.

Over time, Brad and I became increasingly aware of the depth of these shamanic mysteries that were associated with Isis and Osiris and the energies of symbolic death and rebirth that were inherent within all the changes in the cycles of life that everyone must go through each time a significant change is made in their lives. We always acknowledged and honored these powerful archetypal forces and helped to facilitate and guide the many students and seekers who came our way through these powerful initiations on the spiral wheel of change.

Even though we both knew the climactic end of the traditional, powerful, and seemingly tragic love story between Queen Isis and her beloved husband, Osiris, neither one of us ever imagined how deeply the archetypes were moving through our own lives and the eventuality of that story and ours entwining so deeply.

This next phase of our journey together began one day in 2012 when Brad returned home from a doctor's appointment. Entering the house, he calmly walked over to me, saying, "Well, I have cancer." I said, "What does this mean?" He said, "I have fourth-stage throat cancer." When he said those words, I think my heart stopped beating. Everything entered a slow-motion effect. We held each other in silence.

It was like I could see our whole life passing before my eyes in a matter of seconds to that very moment. I couldn't imagine where we were going to go with this in that moment. All I did know was how precious this man in my arms was, and no matter what the future was going to bring or what Brad was going to go through, I knew that I would be with him every step of the way.

The next year and a half, Brad would undergo sixty-three radiation treatments, twelve chemo treatments, four surgeries, and myriad holistic and alternative treatments and remedies. He would learn to eat through a tummy tube, breathe with an oxygen tank, and together we learned to deal with all kinds of horrendous side effects from the treatments. Over that time the cancer would take away his ability to eat, drink, swallow, and eventually most of his voice. It would take away his physical strength, fifty pounds' worth, and he only weighed a hundred and fifty-five pounds to begin with, but it never took away from the beautiful essence of his spirit.

Brad seldom complained, and up until a few hours before he passed away he was still laughing. The morning before he passed away, he got up before me, and he had gotten a little white board to write as his communication. As I went into the kitchen to make his shake, he had written on it, *Good morning darling, I love you.*

I remember one night putting my arms around him like they were the great wings of the mother goddess Isis, and we both let go as we miraculously fell asleep for a few hours before he had to get in his chair where he was more comfortable to sleep because of difficulty breathing. That next day they admitted him into the hospital for the last time.

Neither one of us slept that night even though we were both exhausted on every level. It was clear that Brad's precious body was beginning to give out, even though he was still able to move about and was on very little pain medication because he insisted on being conscious. We planned to go home later on that day after his procedure in the afternoon.

On the day Brad passed away I was home for a few moments before I went back to the hospital, and on that day there must have been a huge birthing of black butterflies because there were hundreds of them that I hadn't seen before. When I saw this, it reminded me of the vision I had of Brad's soul turning into a huge black butterfly.

Shortly before I arrived back at the hospital there had been a fifteen-minute downpour of rain and thunder, which had created a soft glow of twilight surrounding Brad in his room.

As I walked toward my beloved, he was looking very intently toward the ceiling at an angle. He didn't seem to notice when I came into the room, which was very unlike him. Wind Raven, a friend and nurse, was sitting at the end of the bed, rubbing his feet. Brad was in a reclined position on the bed, breathing deeply like he was on his archetypal journey. Every few breaths he would reach his hand in the air as if reaching for something in the distance.

I felt a strange centeredness and peace come over me as I gently lay down beside him and began whispering in his ear. I slowly placed one hand under his back and the other tenderly on his heart as I lay beside him. I told him how much I loved him and how much I wanted him to get well and come home. And then I remembered the rest of the conversation we'd had the night before when I told him of the butterfly and said I could see who he was in the suffering but couldn't see who I was; I felt lost. He pointed at the white board and said he could see who I was becoming. He wrote down "Isis."

I quickly said, "I can't be her because she had to give up her beloved, and I could never willingly do that."

Incredibly, with my heart pounding and my hand on his heart, I felt myself embodying the spirit of Isis, wrapping myself around him in a protective manner and beginning to repeat to him, "I love you so much, but please don't stay here for me any longer. If you see that light, breathe into it, and go toward it. Thank you for all we have done and been. We will always be together. I release your body, I release your spirit."

He then started breathing deeper and faster, and I continued to encourage him just as if we were breathwork partners. I encouraged him to breathe deeply and let go. I watched his eyes get brighter and wider and a soft glow began to emanate from him. I said to him, "Isis is here with you, Brad, she's here with you and will take you anywhere you need to go, and I will always love you." And as Isis, I gently lifted my husband forward as he peered into the otherworld with my encouragement to surrender and let go into the otherworld. He leaned up slightly, coughed three times, and then gracefully stopped breathing, and I knew he was free. I knew in that moment that we had completed a powerful shamanic, mythological, archetypal, human drama of two great lovers who had played their parts perfectly to the very end.

I spent the next two hours whispering through tears as I lay with him, stroking his face and hair. I washed his face with my tears, combed his hair, and dressed him in his Peruvian pants and favorite tie-dye T-shirt. Last, I placed a favored hawk feather into his hands and some of his flowers, from his garden, onto his chest. When they came to finally take his body away, I knew that he was no longer there. I followed them down to the car, and kissed his forehead as they took him to the crematorium.

At a little past 9:00 p.m. as my friend and I drove silently home, I felt a rush of cold air pour into my chest and fear come over me as I thought, *How will I ever be able to live without him?* It was at this exact moment that I heard his voice say to me, clear as a bell, "Turn the radio on, baby, this song is for you."

At first I thought I was just imagining Brad's voice, but then I heard him again. And even though I didn't want to turn on the radio, I felt compelled to do so. As soon as I pushed the button, the very first notes of our wedding song, "Woodstock," were just beginning to play. I quickly turned off the highway into a strip mall parking lot. I threw the car into park, turned the radio on full blast, and jumped out of the car, reaching my hands toward the moon that had just come out from behind the clouds, and one bright star.

And I joyfully spoke these words, "Thank you, my beloved. I love you, Brad. I'm so grateful you are letting me know how much you love me and that you are reaching out to touch me again with your big, deep love for me, letting me know that you have made it safely to the other side, and making it easier for me on this side of the veils."

My friend and I danced in the parking lot, singing "Woodstock" at the top of our lungs, celebrating Brad's rebirth to the other side. I said to her, "Can you believe that Brad managed to move heaven and earth to play this song to me? So that I would know that death cannot separate us, nor destroy our bond of love?"

She simply smiled and said, "Yes, he loves you that much. There are no lengths that Brad will not go to, to let you know that he is all right and reaching back out to you." She went on to say, "Having been an emergency nurse and worked in ICU for several decades, I have never witnessed such an incredible passing and magical connection between two people."

From the very beginning of our relationship, until the end of Brad's life on Earth, we had always been lovers larger than life.

12

Holy Shit!

Compost for the Soul

What we run from, what we want to hide from in ourselves and the world, what stinks, is often the richest fertilizer for our growth. Recycling our own habitual and no longer useful thoughts, beliefs, and values is more valuable than either hanging on to them or discarding them entirely. It is vital to recognize that there is a time for our thoughts and beliefs and even everything we hold dear to fall away and rot. Transformation requires getting up close and personal with our own shit and watering it and turning it until it composts into the sweet ground for our souls to rise up and take the lead in our lives.

THE HIGHER VIBRATION
OF A NEW CONSCIOUSNESS EMERGING

What used to be considered spiritual teachings or concepts are coming at us from all directions: science, art, religion, medicine, engineering, and even government, to name a few. These truths seem to fall into a few categories, and depending on the discipline that is espousing them, the descriptions can vary, yet the essence is the same. We live in a time when the recognition of what we don't know may be the most important sign of what we do know. The unknown, or the Great Mystery, is the name Native Americans and other indigenous people have for the notion of what some religions call "God."

Increasingly the Native American nomenclature, Great Mystery, is the most fitting to describe the increasing awareness of what we don't know. Medical science tells us almost weekly that new biological discoveries are shifting how we should eat, move, think, and breathe. Cholesterol no longer is the culprit. Animal fats are suddenly good for us. What you feel and think are one thing this week—the cause of physical health or illness—and next week, the result of our physicality. Nutrition is trumped by nurturing, and then back again. What you eat causes what you feel, which dictates what you eat. Endless cascades of information flood our newsfeeds and admonish us to be, feel, think, or act in a certain way as though our lives depended on it—only to be contradicted by the next news cycle.

Chaos and information overload make us feel as if we are living under the reign of the insane Queen of Hearts in *Alice in Wonderland*. Or, we find ourselves at the Mad Hatter's tea party where he doles out chaotic and contracting edicts about how to behave. The Caterpillar is smoking hallucinogens and representing himself as the Sage while he espouses utter nonsense to an already confused Alice. And like Alice, we are left to figure things out on our own as the advice being handed to us often makes no sense and is from sources that we can no longer trust as sane.

Reality and collective perception is shifting. Some describe it as moving from three-dimensional reality to multidimensional reality. Others describe it as moving from the individual to the collective, and still others describe it as higher vibration. The consensus is that a new consciousness is emerging, and trying to understand it in the usual cognitive manner will not work. An open heart is more important now than an open mind.

SHIFTING THE PARADIGM FROM TRAUMA/HEALING TO INITIATION/TRANSFORMATION

Development of consciousness, in Jung's terms, is a process of initial healing and then expanding into something bigger than oneself. The

concept of healing involves foremost releasing the traumatic initiated belief of personal unworthiness. The belief that we are unworthy, or worthless, leads to justification for many dysfunctional and
self-destructive behaviors. For example, if you are worthless you are
likely to abuse your body rather than treat it as a temple of treasures.
Worthlessness is underlying overeating, undereating, substance abuse,
sex addiction, depression, anxiety, and ultimately doing harm to others.
As children we conclude that we are unworthy when we are abused,
neglected, or invalidated. As we have stated elsewhere, two people can
experience the same trauma and have different responses because they
develop very different beliefs about the experience.

The so-called X factor, (no, not the TV show!) was coined in the
1970s by psychologists trying to explain why some children in horrific,
abusive situations seem to thrive despite their personal history. Today
we know it has everything to do with the emotional responses that
become stored in the amygdala region of our brain. These stored emotional responses, often preverbal, get translated as beliefs by the limbic
system and solidified into personality structures. Despite this, because
of something called neuroplasticity, this does not have to be fixed and
unchangeable. Let's look at why this is so.

SCIENCE AND
SPIRITUALITY ARE MERGING

Neuroplasticity is a recent term coined to describe the functions in the
brain that change, re-create, and open new pathways as we shift from
emotional reactions to spirit-guided responses. Ultimately shifting emotional responses will change our beliefs and our behaviors. Cognitive
behavioral theory and therapy holds that changing beliefs first will alter
our behavior. While this is sometimes true, somatic emotional shifting
exercises are far more effective in reprogramming the brain.

We *repeat what we have repressed,* and the way out of the repressed-
repetition cycle is that we must embrace and dive in to our repressed,
rejected, and frightening personal underworld to be free.

MAKING THE DARKNESS CONSCIOUS

The shamanic energy medicine practice of Soul Whispering is a method of bringing unconditional love to ourselves through embracing both the parts we perceive as loveable and those we perceive as unlovable. Mother Teresa says that loving the unlovable brings healing. She also credits her selfless compassionate work with being a result of her understanding that within her is a little Hitler. Mother Teresa understood that the darkness within is real and cannot be ignored. Instead, it can and should be reenergized and mitigated by bringing it to light and consciously choosing to overwhelm oneself and others with goodness and love. The same concept can be applied to the parts of ourselves that we unconsciously repress and reject.

Making the darkness conscious to become enlightened may seem counterintuitive to some. Many religions teach that the way is to focus on the light, on the goodness, and to push away what are considered darker thoughts and emotions. The misunderstanding of positive psychology is that a balance of self-exploration and coming through the darker, painful experiences, followed by a practice of using positive thoughts and emotions, is necessary for healing. You cannot skip the step of facing your darker and more painful memories if you want to be whole.

The job of making the darkness conscious is ongoing, yet it need not continue to be our focus in raising consciousness. Once we learn methods of seeing, understanding, and accepting our flaws and pain, we arrive at self-compassion. Self-compassion is the act of accepting our flaws and loving ourselves anyway. Loving ourselves is a prerequisite to loving others.

R. D. Laing once told Nita that the Ten Commandments were originally written as descriptions of states of enlightenment, not admonishments for how to behave. It would be more like this: when one is in the light and of the light, one will love and have compassion for oneself and therefore be able to extend that love and compassion to all people.

Getting to self-love and compassion is everyone's responsibility.

Admitting that we have been hurt and as a result carry resentment and vindictiveness is the first step. Imaginally reexperiencing that hurt in a safe environment with a Soul Whisperer at your side might be your next step. Taking responsibility to release the energy of the hurt means admitting, owning, and finally letting go of resentment and vindictiveness. Doing so leads to living fully in the moment with compassion and humility. Living fully is wonderful, yet not the end game.

The development of consciousness and transcending the personality and ego to become connected and living from our embodied soul center is the goal. We are connected to everything. Separation is an illusion. What happens to one of us is happening to all of us. What we do to a tree, person, or even an inanimate object reverberates through everything. We have to help as many people as possible experience this shift in consciousness and have the realization that we are all interconnected.

Time may run out; action is needed now. Ecologically it doesn't look good. The problem with this ideology is that it can backfire and inspire apathy. If the end is near, why do anything? Let's party and numb out! In fact, the end is always near; tomorrow is always an illusion. Death is with us personally at every minute, so the end of the planet is just as immediate.

We confuse living in the present with a post-hippie philosophy of "la, la, la, live for today . . ." meaning live as though your personal enjoyment is all there is. Living in the present, consciously, is a capacity for riding the energies of birth and death that are present with us all the time. In those luminous moments of near-death experiences, people always describe having a connection to oneness, of loving everyone and everything.

Compassion, right action, and right motive are natural in a state of presence and luminosity. Love is all that matters. Again the flower children were correct, yet they knew not what love really is. Love is the energy of being present and connected, a state we are hardwired to experience. Hormones and pheromones will produce it temporarily. Accessing the state of connection simultaneously with the luminosity of being fully conscious and present is just as obtainable, yet so few tap in to it.

Spiritual by-pass and being possessed by the light interfere with embodied awareness and consciousness. Spirituality in the twenty-first century emphasizes personal spiritual practice and a move away from gurus, priests, and experts. We are evolving away from looking outside ourselves for divinity to finding divinity within ourselves—a divinity made up of connection to self and others and everything. People are finding a deep connection to their own soul, to a shared divinity and an embodied spiritual self.

However, there is fallout from the popularization of personal spiritual practices. Many doctors, therapists, and even corporate supervisors tell people to meditate as though it is the equivalent of climbing on an exercise bike. Meditation is a powerful and deeply impactful practice. For most people it is an empowering process that leads to better health and expanded consciousness. Yet for some, without guidance and in-depth training around the process, it can lock them into light polarization, a condition that too quickly strips their ego and leaves nothing with which to structure the impending abyss that occurs with ego disintegration.

As the saying goes, "Before enlightenment, chop wood and carry water. After enlightenment, chop wood and carry water." The saying is a metaphor for the importance of a mature personal structure that will allow you to be in the world and simultaneously be detached from it and live from a connection to soul and expanded awareness.

Shamans are adept at this and walk between worlds with grace and skill. Without the deep grounding that comes from the personal awareness of our unconscious beliefs that are of a more negative nature, focusing only on emptying the mind though meditation can be useless and at worse dangerous and dissociative.

Personal healing work must go hand in hand with enlightenment work, including meditation. What form that takes depends on the individual. At a minimum some exploration of childhood events and subsequent belief systems is advised. Once a person understands that their personality is structured primarily by decisions made from the wounds of a one- or two-year-old, one is then ready to reprogram the deeply held and dysfunctional reactions to life.

Experiencing a dark night of the soul is for everyone, not just saints. Some form of facing darkness and healing must precede the attainment of higher consciousness. This dark night of the soul may come as personal crisis or we can walk into the darkness consciously through structured and intentionally altered states of consciousness experiences. Healing our emotional and physical bodies is integral to transformation. For some, transformation means a literal, physical death. For others it is a symbolic emotional or ego death.

Meditating and thinking positive thoughts without also mining our darker side and uncovering our flaws and shame will also leave us vulnerable to collapse. This is similar to bandaging a deep wound without cleaning it out or allowing healing light to reach it. The wound will heal on the surface but continue to fester underneath and eventually erupt internally or externally in a toxic surge.

WHEN THE SOUL CALLS

When the soul calls, a life that once seemed so important and fulfilling seems irrelevant. We feel constricted by what used to feel expansive, and we wonder what is wrong with us. When the soul call emerges, it can be confusing and disturbing. Most often it is a nagging sense of unrest. If you know anything at all, you only know what you don't want to do. It is the time of letting go, not knowing what your life will be, but only knowing it is no longer true for you. From somewhere deep inside of you a powerful voice or a feeling is pushing you—this is the whispering of your soul.

Native American women of the Hopi tribe in northeastern Arizona have an ancient practice of leaving home when the children are grown, literally disappearing and not letting anyone know where they are for as long as needed. When they return to the tribe, they have become the crone. The vision quest requires letting go of their home base and is the initiatory process required to become the wisewoman. After this time of being alone, the woman joins a council of elders where she is not alone but instead serves the collective.

In parts of India, men are expected to live their lives in thirds. For the first third they are students, the second they are householders, and for the final third they are seekers of spiritual experiences. On this final leg the men leave home, often taking up the begging bowl as an act of trust that they will be cared for on their journey.

In modern Western culture we are being called by a similar urge. You might call this a longing for creative expression, or recognize the call is to a path of higher consciousness and transformation. The doorway to this path is an initiatory process that requires us to let go or sacrifice what had provided security and to follow what calls us from our bones. What is being called forth is a trust in the self to follow one's own deeper wisdom.

Seeking spiritual experiences takes many forms. Investing time and energy to heal wounds and name our truth is, for many of us, an important step on a spiritual path. The path is nondenominational and is one that embraces an embodied human experience of our spiritual being. Aboriginal Australians go on a walkabout, a rite of passage done alone in the desert.

Western seekers go on pilgrimages. Pilgrimages are journeys that are taken to religious or spiritual sites. But in recent years we have also been going on self-designed walkabouts and pilgrimages of many forms, although all are aimed at putting us more deeply in touch with our own truths. Pilgrimages are an honored and respected component of many spiritual traditions. They are a time to drop out of routine life and tune in to the inner voice. The definition of a pilgrimage is taking time and space to connect with your inner truth. Individuals on pilgrimage can contemplate what the next right step is and let go of the past.

This spiritual experience may not look like much to an outsider, yet each person who is determined and brave enough to do the work necessary to live consciously also contributes to the overall spiritual health of the collective. Personal healing creates healing for the generations who have gone before and those to come forming new structures and pathways for the healing of trauma and allowing authentic expression to come through.

Personal healing is the beginning. With personal healing comes collective healing, and with collective health we open ourselves to evolution and transformation. The new paradigm of transformation is grounded in collaboration and support that gives permission to others to follow their truth.

This path follows some of the traditional steps of a spiritual awakening, including:

- A period of discontent
- Taking time out to seek without knowing what you are seeking
- A dark night of the soul
- Surrender
- Finally, redemption and rebirth

NURTURING YOUR TRANSFORMATION

The first stage of change is like the germinated seed of a plant that is unformed but pushing up through the soil. Listening to stories of how people transformed their lives, one hears that they often knew that something was pushing up into their consciousness as if it wanted to burst forth. Some ignored it or pushed it back underground. Others listened and took action. When our deeper voice, our soul, speaks to us, it is often in the form of an impulse or desire to do something different. And when a different impulse rises, we fear there is something wrong with us, and we try to ignore it or fix ourselves.

Believing that our desires are not important leads us to ignoring the call of the soul. Or, we fear that following our desires will jeopardize our security, cheat our children, disappoint society, and bring some kind of retribution. For many, having a successful career becomes the driving force in our lives. Despite reaching the pinnacles of a career there often comes a time of despair as one no longer feels nourished by the success.

Today we have neuroscience to understand how our beliefs are formed from our emotional reaction to adverse childhood events. We also have neuroscience to understand the impact of spiritual practices. How wonderful to be in a time when the duality of science and spirituality is dissolving into a collective understanding that we are human, we are bodies, we are consciousness, and we are energy. What we call the soul is the collective of this holy trinity. The body carries emotions stored and used in the limbic brain with messages from our hearts. Consciousness has not definitively been found in the body. It is more likely that consciousness is multilocalized within and without our body. The energetic field is within and without and encompasses space beyond our body's physical limits.

Shamanism operates, and has for centuries, from the understanding of this sacred trinity, and finally science is catching on. Shamanic energy medicine uses the reality of the personal and collective trinity in healing and transformation. Clearing belief systems and dysfunctional emotional reactions from adverse childhood events shows up in shamanic energy medicine as soul return work. Blowing the returned soul parts into the body, shamanic energy medicine is acknowledging and affirming the integration of emotions, mind, and body. Rituals and practices of purification further mirror the importance of what modern science calls "clearing negative beliefs."

Stop, breathe, drop into your heart, and be present now. Allow your pain, loss, betrayals, perpetration, and victimization to become compost for soul growth. *Become conscious!* Let this mantra be the new version of the Delphic oracle's command to "Know thyself." The leading edge of human evolution has spent the past few centuries working on knowing thyself. From Socrates to Freud to every practice of human growth and development, the focus has been on deep personal knowing. Healing childhood wounds, understanding our unconscious beliefs and motivations, reprogramming our brain activity, and managing and befriending our stress hormones have become household practices. We are evolving at a personal and planetary level into beings of expanded consciousness. Enough with the healing, and on to transforming!

The following is Joe Doherty's account of his own transformation. In it, he tells the story of how, following a traditional education in psychology as a precursor to becoming a professional therapist and counselor, he became a shamanic practitioner. As such, he utilized the fine art of Soul Whispering, and healed himself in the process.

Dancing with Jaguars

Joe Doherty, Ph.D.

My maternal grandmother, Nora, was a seer! As a child she would tell me how the Blessed Virgin would appear to her and leave her roses. She would also tell me about the man who committed suicide, who she would see hanging from the hook on the back of her bedroom door. She wondered what he was trying to tell her. When she would babysit the six of us kids, she would watch Alfred Hitchcock later in the evenings, and of all my siblings, I was the only one she wanted to do this with. She was afraid to watch, but also fascinated (as was I at nine years old!).

She would also tell my fortune by "reading" the deck of playing cards. We called her "Momma Nonie" given that she had seven children and fifty-two grandchildren. When she died, she had more than one hundred statues of saints in her house, enough for each of us to get two! I of course picked the pink church with the glow-in-the-dark figurines of Jesus/Mary/ Joseph, which also had an image of the Blessed Mother in the middle. When you genuflected in front of her, she closed her eyes and brought her hands into prayer position (what we yogis call "Namaste hands"—who knew back then that I would one day become a yoga instructor!). I also picked St. Martin de Porres, the only black saint she had a statue of and the patron saint of the poor (who knew back then that I would become a social worker!).

I remember once at that age going to the rides and arcades at Revere Beach with my family. There was a stuffed gypsy in a glass booth, and if you put in your coin she would push out a capsule with your fortune; it would be dispensed down a chute to you. I begged my parents to let me try it. I even had my own coin, but they said no, that was the devil's work, and we were devout Catholics, after all. I was an altar boy and a choirboy at the Catholic parish where I attended school and was admonished,

"What would Father Sullivan and the sisters (of St. Joseph, coincidentally) think"?! So I internalized that message into my young brain, repressing for many years the gift of walking between the realms that had been gifted to me by my Irish heritage and by my grandmother.

Fast-forward: At the age of twenty-one I witnessed my eighteen-year-old brother's murder while my parents and family were out of town. He was shot to death by our neighbor's son, who was an expert marksman (and psychotically paranoid). The gun had exploding bullets in it. We lived at the end of a dead-end street, and as I stood in shock waiting for the police/ambulance to arrive (they kept missing the street) I heard my younger brother moan in pain as he lay in the neighbor's driveway.

I remember a strange sensation of something clawlike at the back of my left shoulder, as if it were preventing me from going to him. During the second murder trial that I had to testify at (the first was declared a mistrial after the neighbor was convicted of murder) I was asked to identify my brother's bloody clothes while being asked by the district attorney, "Why didn't you go over to him?"

As I sat in the witness box stunned and frozen in guilt and shame I stuttered, "I don't know," tears rolling down my twenty-two-year-old face.

At my words, the state's attorney turned and faced the jury and stated, "Because you would have been shot and killed as well!"

I knew he was right, but I had had no conscious awareness of that when the murder had occurred. It was only many years later during my Shamanic Healing Initiatory Process (SHIP) initiation that I journeyed with the jaguar whose claw had pierced my left shoulder and held me back.

At age forty-nine, when I first met Linda Star Wolf, she came over to me as I was on my side lying on the floor of my yoga studio where I was participating in my first Shamanic Breathwork. She sat behind me and put both her hands over the exact same spot on my shoulder (that the claw had connected with). I felt that I experienced a healing in that touch, not only of the jaguar's wound but also of the survivor's guilt that I had not died in that neighbor's driveway instead of my younger brother . . .

Star Wolf had asked to rent my studio for the event and had said to me, "We can pay you, or you can attend the workshop in exchange . . ."

I didn't know what this workshop was even about, but I said "Breathwork . . . yoga . . . sounds compatible; I'll come." And my path of becoming a shamanic psychotherapist unfolded before me.

Being a gay man, I had long identified with the berdache, the two-spirited medicine men/women/nonbinary members of indigenous cultures. I had experienced how painful at times it was to walk between the worlds of heteronormative and LGBTQQ cultures. I got pretty good at it . . . and it was this ability to walk between worlds that I believe was also a preceptorship in assisting others to achieve this on so many more levels than those merely pertaining to sexual and gender identity. It was no surprise that in deciding to move to Oregon I came across Tom Spanbauer's book The Man Who Fell in Love with the Moon *and discovered the character of Shed, the berdache in the book, who leaves home to find his true self as a healer. I too left "home" in my journey of the lone wolf (as Star Wolf describes in her book* Spirit of the Wolf*) . . . I left family and friends. I left social and professional networks of thirty-seven years behind, to move to a place where I knew no one. Yet inside I knew that this sacred pilgrimage was leading me toward my true path.*

I had been traditionally trained as a Freudian analytic psychotherapist at the Harvard University psychiatric training hospital and received my master's degree from Smith College, an Ivy League institution with the most traditional psychodynamic clinical MSW program in the country. I had been working in the field of psychology since age twenty-two, with severely mentally ill patients, much like the man who murdered my brother. I was unaware of the concept of the wounded healer and just intellectualized that I was trying to understand what made someone's mind unravel to the point that they would do such terrible things.

I do remember my first dalliance from my traditional therapist path when I was managing four psychiatric programs, including a twenty-four-hour crisis team, and feeling quite burned out and filled with "compassion fatigue." I needed to do something that didn't involve my left brain and was nonanalytical. I saw a class for learning to read the tarot, which I had been fascinated with from the days of my grandmother reading the playing cards to me. The class was down the street from my apartment, so I signed up, and what started as a ten-week hobby class ended up as a yearlong study of the Jungian symbolism in the Crowley Deck (which is often misunderstood as a deck of the devil's work, much like my childhood desire to get my fortune told). It turned out that the tarot is the tool of divination that speaks the most strongly to me; I do now use it in sessions with patients.

After my first experience with Shamanic Breathwork, I had drunk the Kool-Aid! It was as if the last number in the tumbler lock of my psyche had fallen in place, and my awareness of other ways of knowing just fully sprang open . . . That was quite mind shattering for this jaded psychoanalytic cynic of anything spiritual. I was scheduled to travel to India that December to celebrate turning fifty. Instead I canceled the trip and signed up for the Shamanic Healing Initiatory Process (SHIP) on the Oregon coast. I wanted more of this knowing! Unbeknown to me, spirit had another twist in place, and the training was canceled alongside my trip. But true to form, the right experience appeared, and I was offered the opportunity to travel to Isis Cove, the new *Venus Rising* in North Carolina, and to begin my shamanic initiation.

When I arrived at the Cove that next February, I still had major doubts (the diehard skeptic), but on that first evening when I walked into the sanctuary on the side of that mountain I had no doubt that I was "home"!

After completing SHIP, I was drawn to experience more. I was no longer satisfied with just knowing what would be helpful to my patients with my left hemisphere; I was tapping more and more into feeling their needs. As an apprentice in several eight-day trainings I witnessed stories and transformations of those with significant wounds/traumas who had done years of traditional psychotherapy, like I had (eons really!). These amazing souls would discuss how the Shamanic Breathwork journey would act like an accelerant to move them far beyond the healing that traditional therapy had offered them. I had experienced this myself, time and time again, as I had gotten deeper and deeper into the work. This being so, how could I in any good conscience not explore this in my professional world as well? As Star Wolf so often would remind us, "The training is the healing, and the healing is the training."

I knew that my own healing had brought me to a place that was limited *in traditional talk therapy. I also knew that what I had never recognized and honored as a psychotherapist was that the theories I had mastered were only a framework for the success that patients experienced in our work together. What I had ignored was that in my work I had always used the power of my intuition, which had resulted in my work being a deeper and fuller experience for my patients. As my mother had often said, "He was a sensitive child, with big feelings."*

I came to understand through my trainings in Shamanic Breathwork that this was more than my own big feelings. I was attuned to and in tune with the feelings of others. My shamanic training opened the portal that allowed me to dial in to a realm of knowing that was not about me, but rather was transmitted through me.

I was honored to be asked to be among the first class of graduates from Venus Rising University to receive my doctorate in shamanic psychospiritual studies. For me this was passing through the portal to step fully into my sacred purpose from a traditional psychotherapist to a shamanic psychotherapist. In writing my dissertation, "The Non-Duality of Shamanic Psychotherapy," I was affirming the belief and experience of the integration of my traditional therapy "roots" with the "trunk and branches" of shamanic healing. I have chosen to share this writing in some of the most traditional therapy training programs in the country with the intent of training other psychotherapists to move beyond the routine lens of change into a more expansive and balanced method of mind/spirit transformation.

When I contacted the dean of my very traditional psychodynamic master's degree program at Smith College School for Social Work and shared my dissertation with her, I was pleased to read her response, which is as follows: "You are right, of course. We should include shamanism as a spiritual means of transformation in our coursework for our advanced certificate in spiritual psychotherapy. I will put your dissertation before our curriculum committee. . . ." This degree allows me the street cred, so to speak, to present myself as an expert in shamanic psychotherapy and to open doors so that I may train new and seasoned therapists in this dynamic, integrated model.

Today I am honored to be recognized by my sacred soul family as

Jaguar Falcon Wolf, a shamanic minister/certified Shamanic Breathwork facilitator, and shamanic psychotherapist . . . , but most lovingly of all, as a member of the Wolf Clan of the Venus Rising Association for Transformation.

A SPIRAL, NOT LINEAR, PATH

As Joe so eloquently says above, the spiritual healing path is not linear; we can and must do our spiritual practice along with our ego reparation work. Utilizing the imaginal world through practices that help us access what we are unconscious of will make it possible to work with the ego and the soul simultaneously.

By finding our place in the shamanic world we live in, we know that we are among our elders, the animals, trees, plants, and minerals. Shamanic consciousness is what will allow us to collectively rebirth ourselves into a new level of consciousness on this planet, which will sustain us because it will help us find the balance of the old with the new. It will also help us find the way through our present struggles and dilemmas, which threaten to create mass extinction with many species and potentially even humankind.

Harnessing this innate shamanic energy medicine imbues people with an enhanced and mature sense of self. Spiritually evolved people walking on the path of their soul purpose are not living in states of stress, depression, or anxiety. Instead, like Joe, they are living in the present, responding from love not fear, and embracing life with gratitude and joy.

13

The Gravity of Love

Integrative medicine propagates the concept that love heals. This kind of love, unconditional love, is one that embraces all aspects of humanity, its cultures, and the planet at large. When treating a patient, the integrative physician is as focused on the soul's health as he or she is on the patient's physical, social, emotional, and mental well-being. The ideal holistic physician is fully accepting (loving) of the person and allows the patient to experience this unconditional love, perhaps for the first time. The Healing Power of Love, the second tenet in the list of principles for a holistic medical practice, directs holistic physicians to relate to patients with grace, kindness, and acceptance.

Living with shamanic consciousness and walking the path of a Soul Whisperer is to live from curiosity, openheartedness, and, most importantly, love—the gravity that keeps us connected to our essence and the essence of others. Soul Whispering reaches and affects us when we are open to receiving love from another and can give it freely and unconditionally in return.

In the verse that follows, Star Wolf shares the nature of the gravity of love in her story of how her shamanic nature allowed her to transform heartbreaking loss into heart-opening consciousness.

The Gravity of Love
I feel it growing stronger now, with each waking
*   moment.*
I know I am being stalked, as it pulls the cords of my
*   solar plexus*

my aching heart, and my pulsating sex.
It turns me upside down, sideways, and rocks my world
    to and fro,
shaking me up and creating chaos
where once there was order in my so-called life.
This kind of love doesn't care if it rains or shines
or if the strong winds blow me wildly
along the shoreline and knock me to my knees.
Giant tidal waves of my longing engulf me
rendering my will helpless in their wake.
Reluctantly
my surrendering body lets go of the struggle against
    gravity
and my rising spirit becomes silent
and as vast as the seemingly endless battering waves
that pull my broken will along the sandy bottom,
and at last I let go and drift out to sea
where now the gravity of love quite effortlessly carries
what is left of me downward into the watery arms of
    the deep
bottomless ocean where even the fish no longer have eyes
    to see.

As fast as I run, as well as I hide, love somehow always manages to find me with its awesome energy and colossal power. Why would I (or anyone) run from such a love? Only that which we love with such dedication, passion, and reckless abandon has the power to bring us to our knees and tear our worlds apart.

The beloved can show up as a human being, an animal, the trees, the oceans, the mountains, or even an idea. The airwaves are full of soul-stirring love songs and stories of all kinds. Love inspires us—love for the two-legged or four-legged, the winged or finned, our enemies or our kin, for nature, or for a cause that stirs passion within—love is that insistent longing, inexplicable to the rational mind, which refuses to be ignored. Perhaps love calls us to a return, attempting to reclaim some lost parts of ourselves: passion, power, gentleness of spirit, tenderness, vulnerability, or innocence. Love rouses our essence back into consciousness. Below Star Wolf shares what love means to her.

Star Wolf's Story
LOVE IS FINDING ME

Whenever I have lost my way and feel most alone, I find myself called back to nature. It is here—often looking out over the lush woods of the majestic mountains that I call home, during one of our biblical sunsets—that I fall to my knees and my heart bursts open in love. The sunlight saturates me in rapture and awe, and I am with God and his physical presence imbued in the natural world surrounding me.

In the 2014 movie *Interstellar* the gravity of love finally created the link to an interdimensional pathway between a father and his daughter, opening a portal that transcended space-time and preventing humanity's extinction on a dying Earth. I watched this movie three times, in part to better comprehend the science, which was beyond my understanding. At a much deeper level, I knew that there was something for me in this story. Having lost my husband a few months prior to watching it for the first time, I had been experiencing a feeling of his physical presence, as if he were attempting to connect with me in dreams, in breathwork experiences, and in other random ways during the routine of my daily life.

There were many of these experiences, coincidences—perhaps I was even experiencing mild psychosis. Nevertheless, I chose to pay attention to these encounters with him—encounters such as the one recounted earlier wherein I heard his voice as clear as day on the way home from the hospital after his passing. He instructed me to turn on the radio just as our wedding song—the song to which we walked down the aisle— began to play. It seemed that he was choosing to come to me through our love of music, given that every morning for the next several days I would awaken to a call or message on social media from a friend or loved one with a special message for me. They would be passing on to me a song, they said, that Brad had told them to deliver to me, which they had received during a dream or a vision. Time and time again, it would prove to be a favorite song of ours.

I paid attention as well to electrical phenomena. For weeks, the fire alarms would suddenly sound for no reason, the lights would uncharacteristically flicker, and circuit breakers would trip under normal conditions. Songs would suddenly begin to play on my computer, and photos of Brad and messages from his social media accounts would appear on my monitor. The septic system began malfunctioning, and odd shadows and images appeared on my living room ceiling in broad daylight—occurrences that were seen by others in my presence and that have not been repeated since.

I called electricians, plumbers, and friends to help repair or at least figure out what was going on, as other synchronicities continued. One of the most shocking of these was a conversation with a gifted psychic, who echoed back to me the precise messages that I had received from Brad when he appeared to me during a breathwork session just hours before.

In yet another undeniably synchronistic experience, I playfully asked Brad to please find another way to connect with me without disrupting the electric and plumbing, because it was costing me a small fortune to repair everything. The next morning, I found a small chipmunk lying dead on my kitchen floor, still warm and in perfect form. It was the first chipmunk that I had ever encountered in my home, and I took his little body outside, reverently placing it under a flowering bush that Brad had planted in our backyard.

I returned inside to read my messages and begin my day, and my attention went immediately to the subject line of an e-mail. It read, "Dream about chipmunks." A friend of Brad's, from whom we hadn't heard in some time, had messaged to share his dream from the previous night in which he and Brad chased a chipmunk through our backyard. Oh, yes—and the chipmunk sang opera as well. I was taken aback and called my friend and business manager, Ruby, who shared that the day before, a chipmunk had run across her feet as she sat at her computer.

At that point, I gasped (perhaps audibly), unable to deny the evidence of Brad's influence on recent events.

Later that day, during a break from working, I casually searched the Internet using the key word *chipmunk* to perhaps learn more of its spiritual meaning or what the appearance of these three separate chipmunk sightings might have represented from a shamanic/animal medicine/spirit guide perspective. I discovered a shamanic totem site with the following words from the author, Presley Love.

> The symbolic meaning of Chipmunk teaches the blessing that there are always spirit guides around you, ready to help; but you must invite the assistance of the spirits, and the instant you do you will feel the essence and energy of their presence and can begin communicating your requests. Again, this is the perfect time for you to ask your guides for signs. Chipmunk spirit animal is a symbol that something good is on its ways to you, something wonderful that delights your heart, something that makes you smile and laugh. Chipmunk totem energy is also a sign that you will have an important conversation with someone close to you very soon, pay attention to the details! Chipmunk always pops up out of nowhere, and just as quickly it vanishes into another world, the world of the Chipmunk. It has hidden pathways and secret tunnels hidden in plain sight all around you. Chipmunk the magic of: intuition, wishes granted. Whenever you see a Chipmunk totem you can be sure that magic is afoot, synchronicities are in the air; pay attention, you may even glimpse a fairy. Fairies most assuredly are in the midst. Chipmunk and fairies appear, encouraging you to believe in magic just like you did as a child.[1]

When I saw the words "The symbolic meaning of Chipmunk teaches the blessing that there are always spirit guides around you, ready to help," I gasped (audibly, for sure), and I think I may have even let out a little scream. Even though I consider myself tuned in and, for the most part, used to these kinds of magical occurrences in my life, this series of events that grew stronger day by day destroyed any remaining doubt about Brad's supernatural presence and reinforced my need to continue to pay attention to the events that demonstrated his transcendent presence.

I didn't want to miss the message—the help that I believed was being offered to me by Brad, who I felt was doing his best to assure me that he was all right and watching over me from the other side and would continue to do so. Indeed, over the course of the next few months, I felt his promise deeply in my day-to-day life.

He assisted me with beginning to reconnect to the Earth. When he died, a part of me had gone with him. I disconnected from my own body and the things around me. This response was unconscious. Then my heart started to react in physical ways. It was broken—off-track. It beat irregularly and then raced, making me feel faint, flushed, and dizzy. My doctor told me that I had a broken heart, which is, as it turns out, a serious form of heart disease that can ultimately lead to heart attack.

I was physically in danger and realized that, if I was going to stay on Earth, I must allow the gravity of my love for the Earth—for this plane—to draw me back and retrieve me from my grief. I was going to need to fall into love and surrender to the pain and suffering of Brad's death, feeling it as it ran through my body. I opened to the love that remained here for me in this life.

It took awhile, but eventually my heart began to open. I allowed my love to flow (albeit a trickle, at first), until one day I detected happiness entering my felt body senses again. Then, while in an altered state during a breathwork journey, Brad appeared and reiterated his promise of love and support as a spirit guide from the other side but said that it was time for me to, in a way, let him go. Brad loved me enough to remain at a lower vibration for a long time. I realized, however, as long as I insisted that he stay connected to me as my loving husband—just as if he were still here in his physical form—that our relationship would not be able to evolve or advance into its next octave.

His willingness to be in this heavy love brought tears to my eyes and opened my heart even wider. I finally began to accept the high-frequency spiritual being into which he was now transforming. I really wanted that for him. After so much suffering for so long, I wanted him to be totally free and without care. I would not have believed that letting him go in this way would also release my heart, which opened even wider and deeper and brought my life into a new experience.

On February 14, 2015, I knew that I was ready for this release, and my heart began its journey back.

Since that time, there have been so many events clearly influenced by Brad. His spirit remains with me, his children, his beloved students, and even with folks who never met him on this Earth plane. He continues to make it abundantly clear that he is still here in some way and that, despite his abandoning of his physical form and regardless of his distance (or perceived distance) in time and space, the gravity of his boundless love persists and, in fact, continues to grow stronger.

Gravity is defined in several ways: As a noun, it means being grave, earnest, or very serious. In physics, gravity is the natural force that pulls objects toward sources of mass. One who possesses the quality of gravity acts with a deliberate seriousness. Linguistically, its origins can be traced to Old French; it is borrowed from the Latin *gravis,* "heavy," and *gravitas,* "weight/seriousness." Personally, I connect most with the term as it applies to our physical world. Gravity draws objects toward each other, and this force is greater as the weight—the mass—of an object increases.

At times, with genuine sincerity, and being the shamanic Soul Whisperer that I am, I reflect and search the depths of my soul for an answer to a question: What could make it possible for Brad to be able to reach out to me in such unmistakable and powerful ways? The only answer that comes to me is gravity—the gravity of Brad's big, overwhelming, awesome love, massive enough, in fact, to tear through the veils of space-time and formlessness, opening a portal for the most powerful force in the universe to flow to me and into the world around me.

Time spent with those I love on a very personal level, my family and closest friends, reminds me to count my blessings: how fortunate we are to have each other. My grandchildren bring me a special kind of love that makes me recommit daily to showing up on this planet. Of course, my four-leggeds always have my back. In addition, I am so blessed to have consciously walked the shamanic path for almost three decades, which has allowed me to offer my sacred work and purpose to countless kindred spirits around the world, and yes, I do fall in love with everyone who crosses my path! How could I not, when they show up with such open hearts and share the deepest parts of themselves with me? No matter what may be going on in my life on my personal journey, having the privilege of sharing and working with others always transforms my own challenges into blessings and gifts.

Grandmother "Gram" Twylah Nitsch, my adopted Wolf Clan grandmother, used to say that to fully be here on the Earth, we need to stay connected to our clan, our tribe, or our pack. It is up to each of us to be fully present while we are here, sharing the best of we have with all those we love and hold dear. Love's gravity kept her alive and sharing with others into her nineties despite suffering several major heartbreaks, including severe illnesses and the death of her husband and her adult son.

I remember two of Gram's famous quotes that always bring me back home to my own heart: "We all need each other. We are not supposed to do it alone. If Creator thought that, then there would only be one of us!" and "Remember these teachings, and share them with others so that the teachings may live."

There is a type of loyalty within us that will risk everything to be true to what we love most in our lives. In some cases, we would put our lives on the line and even die for those we cherish. Certainly, love can lift us upward, but it can also pull us firmly to the Earth when we risk losing a loved one. We become dedicated to protecting what we love: Julia Butterfly sat in the redwood tree named Luna for more than a year, defying those who would cut her down; members of Greenpeace put their well-being at risk to deter whaling efforts; a visitor at the zoo jumped into the lion's den to protect her small son who had fallen in.

Love that is both divine and embodied carries a gravitational pull that we eagerly welcome. Without it, we feel emptiness and lifelessness, void of passion or purpose. Without its weight, we fail to thrive, and perhaps this is the plight of so many who feel plagued with depression and anxiety and why addiction runs rampant in our society and in the world.

Finding right relationship and creating love with everyone in our lives, friend or foe, is our blessed task. As the sacred saying reminds us, "We are all related." Sometimes we must love others with a loving detachment and release them for a time or perhaps forever on this plane. As we have learned, love is not limited to this dimension but can reach across great gulfs of distance and death.

Over my many years as a shamanic Soul Whisperer, I have learned and relearned a lesson: The greatest gift that I have to give to others, as I walk my own path of teaching and sharing, is myself—my open heart. It shows up during breathwork or other shamanic energy medicine tools when, rather than setting out to heal someone, my purpose is to be fully present, listen deeply, care greatly, and share what I am called to share via a heart connection. When I open myself to the field of plenty, which Grandmother Twylah taught, I realize that I have endless love to give. I know I feel it—a massive, archetypal love, filling the aural field around us—and others have shared the love they felt during our time together as well. The gravitational pull to one another allows us to open and trust. As the biblical Christ said, "Where two or more are gathered, there will you find me also."

WHAT THE WORLD NEEDS NOW IS LOVE

At the end of the day, when all else fails, love itself is the greatest shamanic energy medicine. It brings us back to what we have temporarily lost and makes life worth living once again. We, the author's, know that our paths have required us to open our hearts and consciousness and drop our judgments a multitude of times. When beginning anew, we must trust the void until love's gravity pulls us home again to what we love the most and to what loves us. This is how we know where to go, whom to be with, and what we must co-create in our world.

On earth as it is in heaven describes the balance we have found that we need on our paths to be true walkers between worlds—with the energy of an infinitely expansive love that resides in our hearts.

Glossary

addiction: Any self-defeating behavior that is obsessive and compulsive, where one experiences dysfunction and an ensuing loss of power.

Akashic Records: The records of the soul's incarnation from lifetime to lifetime, including the soul's original intent and purpose; sometimes called the *Book of Life*.

altar: A sacred space created for the purpose of performing rituals and meditations for personal or group healing; can be dedicated to specific deities or spiritual forces.

altered state: A nonordinary state of consciousness that supports access to one's higher self and other worlds; can provide insight into shadow or unowned parts of the self, as well as a deeper understanding of aspects of external reality.

amends: Taking responsible action to apologize for your part in any past hurtful and dysfunctional interactions with others. This may include writing a letter, making a phone call, meeting with someone in person, or performing a forgiveness ritual on your own or with a co-journeyer as a witness.

archetype: The psychic blueprint that lives in the realm of the soul and makes itself known to us in times of great change. Archetypes are also symbols that exist across cultural boundaries. Examples include the trickster, inner child, lover, and crone.

ceremony: The process of creating ritual space in order to connect to the Divine, either in celebration or as an area for transformation. An example of ceremony is the Shamanic Breathwork process.

codependency: An inauthentic, reflected expression of self; any relationship in which we give away our power to any person, process, or thing.

consciousness: Our everyday waking state. The spiritual warrior seeks to continually bring insight and awareness into conscious reality.

cycles of change: The alchemical map of shamanic consciousness that describes movement through the five elemental pathways of death and rebirth.

death/rebirth: Symbolic sequences of shamanic experience that lead from one level of consciousness to the next.

ego: The part of a human being that has, for survival purposes, adapted to cultural norms and to a projected ideal of who we should be and how we should behave. The ego is formed in early childhood as a result of interaction with one's family of origin and other significant caretakers.

elements: The four nature elements—water, earth, fire, and air—as well as the fifth super-nature, or supernatural, element of spirit.

grounding: The process of incorporating altered states, otherworldly experiences, or spiritual experiences into our physical reality.

Higher Power: The Divine as each individual understands it: God, Goddess, and/or Great Mystery.

Holotropic Breathwork: A form of breathwork created by Stanislav Grof, M.D. One of the first techniques to use breath, music, and art to create an altered state for healing.

Integrative Breathwork: A form of breathwork created by Jacquelyn Small, which includes many Holotropic Breathwork techniques and the integrative aspects of 12-step recovery, with an emphasis on group process.

Jung, Carl: Famous Swiss psychoanalyst and protégé of Sigmund Freud, sometimes called the grandfather of transpersonal psychology. He coined such phrases as *archetype, shadow, sacred marriage,* and *collective unconscious.*

Kali: The Hindu goddess of creative destruction. Revered in parts of India as the Great Mother.

linear path: This fading, patriarchal model states that life travels in a straight line; it has been dominant for the past three to four thousand years. The imbalanced yang path consists of symbolic archetypal images.

medicine: As referred to by Native American people or other Indigenous cultures, whatever is uniquely helpful or healing to each individual. For example, essential oils, breathwork, Reiki, nature walks, or gemstones may be considered medicine.

persona: The ego's small self as projected to the outer world, masking the shadow from others. The persona houses the ego's agenda and is often motivated by fear.

rebirthing: The original form of breathwork. Leonard Orr discovered and developed the practice, which he told Star Wolf was inspired by his studies of the Hindu saint Mahavatar Babaji. Rebirthing was also taught and popularized by Sondra Ray, an internationally recognized spiritual teacher.

recovery: The ongoing process of transforming addictive, compulsive behavior into a healthy, conscious lifestyle.

ritual: A sacred act that involves spiritual intent and provides assistance for creation, healing, and change.

shadow: The repressed, unconsciousness, disowned part of the psyche. The shadow must be uncovered and integrated to reach wholeness.

shaman: In various cultures, a priest, priestess, healer, or medicine man/woman is referred to as a shaman. The shaman is the "wounded healer," one who has experienced and survived many ordeals, or "deaths," and returns to the community to share acquired healing wisdom with others.

Shamanic Breathwork: A form of breathwork founded by Linda Star Wolf that synthesizes ancient shamanic practices with current breathwork modalities and relies heavily upon group process techniques.

shamanic consciousness: Having the eyes to see and the ears to hear beyond the mundane outer appearance of any situation and move into higher levels of love and wisdom. A state of consciousness within which one moves continually through processes of death and rebirth.

soul: The vehicle for our essential self as it travels from one state of consciousness to another. The soul is the mediator between our spiritual and human self and carries qualities of both.

soul purpose: The original, encoded spiritual imprint or mission of the present lifetime.

soul return: The process of reclaiming lost soul parts, which are various aspects of self that have been lost through misuse, abuse, or trauma.

Soul Whisperer: An individual who has learned how to truly listen to the murmurings of their soul as opposed to the voice of their ego. This individual may be a professional counselor, a shamanic healer, a medical intuitive, or the person next door. In accessing the higher wisdom of the soul, patterns of dysfunction are eliminated, various levels of victimhood are released, and spiritual transformation is attained.

Soul Whispering: The method of communicating directly to the soul, Soul Whispering may be performed by individuals known by the moniker of Soul Whisperer. It may also occur as an inner Soul Whispering, bestowing higher wisdom and guidance to the spiritual seeker.

spiral path: A philosophical model symbolizing the orbiting evolution of our lives through our soul patterns to learn lessons resulting in spiritual growth;

an ancient symbol representing the emerging synthesis of linear and circular paths.

spirit: The pure essential self that lives in a unified field of consciousness beyond time and space.

spirit guides: Energetic beings that can take many forms, such as ancestors, angels, totems, or historical figures. They may appear to us either in our imagination or in external reality to support our path on Earth.

stalking: The process of the sacred witness seeking out those aspects of consciousness that need to be transmuted to higher levels of awareness. The stalking aspect of the psyche is sometimes called "the double" or "the spiritual warrior." Its role is to seek out undeveloped, shadowy, and ill-formed aspects of personality for ensuing transformation.

surrender: The process of letting go of attachment to outcome, resulting in a sense of inner peace and well-being. Trusting the process.

symbols: The hieroglyphs of the soul. The creative images that emerge both spontaneously and intentionally during meditation or shamanic journeys.

synchronicity: A Jungian term for the noncausal connection between two or more various phenomena. Remarkable and/or meaningful coincidence.

synthesis: The energetic blending of various aspects of healing that results in the sum being greater than the parts; an example is the synthesis represented by the term *shamanic-psychospiritual.*

transformation: Moving from one level of consciousness to another through the process of death and rebirth. Comprehensive change.

trauma: Outer events that deeply affect the psyche and leave a cellular impression of wounding that blocks the experience of wholeness. Trauma creates energetic blocks that must be broken through and released.

unconscious: Everything not known by the ego mind; 85 to 90 percent of our psyche. The purpose of the shamanic process is to make the unconscious conscious.

Notes

CHAPTER 1. SEEKING WHOLENESS

1. Herder, *Outlines of a Philosophy.*
2. Lipsenthal, *Enjoy Every Sandwich,* 194.
3. Ibid., 125–26.

CHAPTER 2. SURVIVING PSYCHIATRY

1. American Psychological Association, "Trauma."
2. Hall, "Letter to the Mother of a 'Schizophrenic.'"
3. Lewis, *Ecstatic Religion,* 165.
4. Laing, *Politics of Experience,* 48.

CHAPTER 4. STEPS IN THE JOURNEY OF BECOMING A SOUL WHISPERER

1. Lipsenthal, *Finding Balanace in a Medical Life,* 87–96
2. Laing, *Divided Self,* 205.
3. Schwartz-Salant, "Mystery of Human Relationship," 58.

CHAPTER 5. AVOIDING THE VOID

1. Mate, *In the Realm of the Hungry Ghost.*
2. Miller, *Breaking Down the Wall of Silence,* 154.
3. Schoen, *The War of the Gods in Addiction,* 56.

CHAPTER 6. SHAMANISM'S INCONVENIENT TRUTH

1. Capra, *Systems View of Life,* 14–15.
2. Star Wolf, *Shamanic Mysteries of Egypt,* 65–72.

CHAPTER 7. EMOTIONAL CANCER

1. Remen, "In the Service of Life."

CHAPTER 8. SHAMANIC CONSCIOUSNESS
IN EVERYDAY LIFE

1. Star Wolf, *Visionary Shamanism,* 8–9.
2. Groddeck, *The Book of the It* and *The Meaning of Illness.*
3. Jung, *Factors Determining Human Behavior.* Quoted in Daintith, *Biographical Encyclopedia,* 396.

CHAPTER 9. THE NATURE OF HOW PEOPLE CHANGE

1. Miller, *Motivational Interviewing.*

CHAPTER 10. THE FIVE CYCLES OF CHANGE

1. Star Wolf, *Shamanic Breathwork,* 84.
2. Ibid., 89.
3. Ibid., 90.

CHAPTER 11. THE MAGICAL POWER OF ARCHETYPES

1. Campbell, *Power of Myth,* 206.
2. Heidegger, *Being and Time,* 399.

CHAPTER 13. THE GRAVITY OF LOVE

1. Love, "Symbolic Meaning of Chipmunk," *Universe of Symbolism,* www .universeofsymbolism.com/symbolic-meaning-of-chipmunk.html.

Bibliography

American Psychological Association. "Trauma." www.apa.org/topics/trauma (accessed December 20, 2016).

Campbell, Joseph, with Bill Moyers. *The Power of Myth.* New York: Anchor Books, 1991.

Capra, Fritjof, and Pier Luigi Luisi. *The Systems View of Life: A Unifying Vision.* Cambridge, UK: Cambridge University Press, 2014.

Childre, Doc, and Howard Martin, with Donna Beech. *The Heartmath Solution.* San Francisco: Harper, 1999.

Cowan, Tom. *Fire in the Head: Shamanism and the Celtic Spirit.* New York: HarperCollins, 1993.

Daintith, John, ed. *Biographical Encyclopedia of Scientists, Third Edition.* Boca Raton, Fla.: Taylor & Francis, 2009.

Damasio, Antonio. *Looking for Spinoza: Joy, Sorrow, and the Feeling Brain.* Boston: Houghton Mifflin Harcourt, 2003.

Eliade, Mircea. *Shamanism: Archaic Techniques of Ecstasy.* New York: Pantheon, 1964.

Elliot, T. S. *The Four Quartets.* New York: Houghton Mifflin Harcourt, 1971.

Freedman, Milton. *Prime Time: How Baby Boomers Will Revolutionize Retirement and Transform America.* New York: PublicAffairs, 2002.

Freud, Sigmund, James Strachey, et al. *The Standard Edition of the Complete Psychological Works of Sigmund Freud.* London: Hogarth Press, 1953–1974.

Friedson, Steven. *Dancing Prophets: Musical Experience in Tumbuka Healing.* Chicago: University of Chicago Press, 1996.

Gage, Nita. *The Women in Storage Club: How to Reimagine Your Life.* New York: Dog Ear, 2012.

Graham, H. "Animism rather than Shamanism: New Approaches to What

Shamans Do (for Other Animists)." In Betina. A. Schmidt, *Spirit Possession and Trance: New Interdisciplinary Perspectives. Continuum Advances in Religious Studies (7),* 14–34. London: Continuum, 2010.

Groddeck, Georg. *The Book of the It.* New York: International Universities Press, 1976. Originally published in 1923.

———. *The Meaning of Illness.* London: Hogarth Press and the Institute of Psychoanalysis, 1977.

Grof, Stanislav. *Healing Our Deepest Wounds: The Holotropic Paradigm Shift.* Newcastle, Wash.: Stream of Experience Productions, 2012.

Guignon, Charles. *The Cambridge Companion to Heidegger.* Cambridge, UK, Cambridge University Press, 1993

Hall, Will. "Letter to the Mother of a 'Schizophrenic': We Must Do Better Than Forced Treatment." *Psychology Tomorrow* 18 (October 2, 2015). Available at http://psychologytomorrowmagazine.com/letter-to-the-mother-of-a -schizophrenic-we-must-do-better-than-forced-treatment.

Hamayon, Roberte N. "Are 'Trance,' 'Ecstasy' and Similar Concepts Appropriate in the Study of Shamanism?" *Shaman* 1, nos. 1–2 (Spring/Autumn 1993).

Heidegger, Martin. *Being and Time.* New York: HarperCollins, 1975.

Herder, Johann Gottfried von (1803). *Outlines of a Philosophy of the History of Man.* Translated by T. Churchill. New York: Bergman Publishers, 1966. Originally published 1800.

Huxley, Francis, and Jeremy Narby. *Shamans Through Time: 500 Years on the Path to Knowledge.* London: Thames and Hudson, 2004.

Jung, C. G. *Memories, Dreams and Reflections.* New York: Vintage Books, 1969.

———. *The Red Book (Liber Novus): A Reader's Edition.* Edited by Sonu Shamdasani. New York: W. W. Norton and Co., 2009.

Kcane, Webb. "The Evidence of the Senses and the Materiality of Religion." *Journal of the Royal Anthropological Institute* 14 (2008): S110–S127.

Keating, AnaLouise. "Speculative Realism, Visionary Pragmatism, and Poet-Shamanic Aesthetics in Gloria Anzaldúa—and Beyond." *WSQ: Women's Studies Quarterly* 40 (Fall/Winter 2012): 51–69.

Ketcham, Katherine, and Ernest Kurtz. *Spirituality of Imperfection: Storytelling and the Search for Meaning.* New York: Bantam, 2002.

Laing, Ronald David. *The Divided Self.* London: Penguin, 1965.

———. *Politics of Experience and the Bird of Paradise.* New York: Pantheon Books, 1967.

———. *Politics of the Family.* London: Penguin, 1972.

Lambek, Michael. "From Disease to Discourse: Remarks on the Concepualization of Trance and Spirit Possession." In C. A. Ward, *Altered States of Consciousness and Mental Health: A Cross-cultural Perspective,* 36–61. Thousand Oaks, Calif.: Sage Publications, 1989.

Lewis, Ioan. *Ecstatic Religion: A Study in Shamanism and Spirit Possesion.* New York: Routledge, Taylor, and Francis Group, 2003.

Lipsenthal, Lee. *Enjoy Every Sandwich: Living Each Day as if It Were Your Last.* New York: Random House, 2011.

———. *Finding Balance in a Medical Life.* San Anselmo, Calif.: Finding Balance, 2007.

Love, Presley. *Universe of Symbolism: Signs, Symbols & Totems by Presley Love.* www.universeofsymbolism.com.

Lown, Bernard. *The Lost Art of Healing.* New York: Ballantine Books, 1999.

MacKinnon, Christa. *Shamanism and Spirituality in Therapeutic Practice: An Introduction.* London: Singing Dragon, 2012.

Mate, Gabor. *In the Realm of the Hungry Ghost.* Berkeley, Calif.: North Atlantic Books, 2007.

McCraty, Rollin, Mike Atkinson, Dana Tomasino, and Trevor Bradley. *The Coherent Heart: Heart–Brain Interactions, Psychophysiological Coherence, and the Emergence of System-wide Order.* Boulder Creek, Calif.: HeartMath, 2006.

Milkman, Harvey B. "Natural Highs: A Positive Approach to Mood Alteration." *Huffington Post.* July 18, 2012. www.huffingtonpost.com (accessed November 15, 2015).

Miller, Alice. *Breaking Down the Wall of Silence: Liberating Experience of Facing Painful Truth.* New York: Basic Books, 2009.

———. *Drama of the Gifted Child.* New York: Basic Books, 2007.

———. *Thou Shalt Not Be Aware: Society's Betrayal of the Child.* New York: Farrar, Strauss, and Giroux, 1981.

Miller, William, and Stephen Rollnick. *Motivational Interviewing: Helping People Change,* vol. 3. New York: Guildford Press, 2013.

Mindell, Arnold. *The Shaman's Body: A New Shamanism for Transforming Health, Relationships, and the Community.* New York: HarperCollins, 1993.

National Library of Medicine. *Native Voices.* "Medicine Ways: Traditional

Healers and Healing." www.nlm.nih.gov/nativevoices/exhibition/healing -ways/medicine-ways/medicine-wheel.html (accessed July 15, 2015).

Peck, Scott. *The Road Less Traveled*. New York: Random House, 2003.

Porath, Nathan. "Freud among the Orang Sakai. The Father Archetype, the Talking Cure, and the Transference in a Sumatran Shamanic Healing Complex." *Anthropos* 108, no. 1 (2013): 1–17.

Remen, Rachel Naomi. "In the Service of Life." *Noetic Sciences Review* (Spring 1996). Edited from a speech given by Dr. Remen at the 1996 Temple Awards.

Schoen, David. *The War of the Gods in Addiction*. New Orleans, La.: Spring Journal, 2009.

Siegel, Bernie. *Love, Medicine and Miracles*. New York: Harper and Row, 1986.

Star Wolf, Linda. *Shamanic Breathwork: Journeying beyond the Limits of the Self*. Rochester, Vt.: Bear & Company, 2009.

Star Wolf, Linda, and Anne Dillon. *Visionary Shamanism: Activating the Imaginal Cells of the Human Energy Field*. Rochester, Vt.: Bear & Company, 2011.

Star Wolf, Linda, and Nicki Scully. *Shamanic Mysteries of Egypt: Awakening the Healing Power of the Heart*. Rochester, Vt.: Bear & Company, 2007.

Schwartz-Salant, Nathan. *The Mystery of Human Relationship: Alchemy and the Transformation of the Self*. London: Routledge, 1998.

Taylor-Bolte, Jill. *My Stroke of Insight*. London: Hodder and Stoughten, 2009.

Tobert, N. *Mad in America* (featured blog). January 14, 2015. www.madinamerica .com (accessed October 10, 2015).

van der Kolk, Bessel. *The Body Keeps Score: Brain, Mind, and Body in the Healing of Trauma*. New York: Viking Penguin, 2014.

Ward, C. A. "From Disease to Discourse: Remarks on the Conceptualisation of Trance and Spirit Possession." In C. A. Ward, *Altered States of Consciousness and Mental Health: A Cross-Cultural Perspective*, 36–61. New York: Columbia University Press, 1989.

Webb, Hillary. "Expanding Western Definitions of Shamanism: A Conversation with Stephan Beyer, Stanley Krippner and Hillary S. Webb." *Anthropology of Consciousness* 24 (May 2013): 57–75.

Woodman, Marion, and Jill Mellick. *Coming Home to Myself: Daily Reflections for a Woman's Body and Soul*. Newburyport, Mass.: Conari Press, 1998.

Index

How to Use the Soul Whispering Audio Tracks

The audio tracks that accompany this book are designed to be used as an enhancement to the book. Download at

audio.innertraditions.com/souwhi

They are guided meditations and journeys that are generally focused on getting you out of your cognitive mind and into your intuitive mind.

Prepare for each experience by creating time and space for yourself. Be sure that you are in a comfortable place, either sitting or lying down, and be sure that there are no distractions in your immediate environment. The narrative on the audio tracks will guide you into each experience with spoken words and accompanying music designed to activate and enhance your experience. They are not intended for easy listening or to be used while driving or handling machinery.

After the experience, it is suggested that you further integrate your journey by writing in your journal, creating a piece of artwork, listening to relaxing music, or taking a walk or a bath. Stay hydrated and well rested as you return to your regular schedule and your outer world.

1. **Neuroimaginal Journey (16:10):** Nita Gage takes you on a guided visualization of a shamanic journey. This guided experience, replete with drumming and chanting, will bring you into contact with a guide and assist you in receiving messages from your own inner wisdom. This experience is like a virtual vision quest—guiding you to imagine that you are in nature, allowing you to see yourself near

a mountain, and calling on spiritual creatures and guides.

2. **Creature Teacher Medicine Journey (21:52):** Star Wolf guides the listener through an in-depth journey around the sacred shamanic medicine wheel while also instructing you how to call in your individualized creature teacher for each direction on the wheel. The shamanic guided journey is supported by the beautiful, award-winning music of Michael Brant DeMaria.

3. **Turning the Light on Your Shadow (13:48):** This guided experience will assist you in accessing your shadow. As we have learned in the book, the famous Swiss psychoanalyst Carl Jung coined this phrase to denote aspects of ourselves that we reject because our ego does not want to identify with them. However, the shadow is where much of our potential resides. When we examine our shadow we are able to bring its fruits to manifestation and, in so doing, have greater awareness of and compassion for the shadow aspects of others as well as others' suffering. This meditative track is narrated by Nita Gage.

4. **Contacting Your Future Self (9:18):** We limit ourselves by believing that who we are is real, when actually most of who we take ourselves to be is a hologram of the past. This meditative exercise will give you an experience of your own higher wisdom, that which you have not yet lived into but can if you open to your own imaginal cells and your own true possibilities. As such, this experience can serve as an antidote to the limiting beliefs of the past by putting you in contact with your own deeper truth. Nita Gage guides you through this exercise.

5. **Inanna: A Feminine Tale (1:07:43):** The story of Inanna is one of the oldest myths on Earth, originating, it is believed, in Sumeria. Star Wolf has created her own version of this myth, one that speaks to the modern experiences of the sacred journey of the feminine in both men and women. We often see ourselves only as little beings—little ants running around the Earth—doing things and keeping busy. We don't remember that there is a psychic blueprint behind whatever it is we are experiencing. Without the understanding of a bigger story, for some life becomes a soulless and desperate grab for connection. It

feels dark, alone, pointless, and meaningless. When we understand that the difficult as well as joyous stories of our lives reverberate throughout humanity, as well as in multidimensional realities, our story can take on more meaning, no matter how painful it may be. Star Wolf narrates her version of the story of Inanna; the full text of this audio track is in the book.

CREDITS FOR SOUL WHISPERING AUDIO TRACKS